The Happiest Days:

Schooldays are the happiest days,
The happiest days of your life
. . . .

(Old song)

The Happiest Days?
How Pupils Cope with School

Peter Woods

 The Falmer Press

(A member of the Taylor & Francis Group)
London • New York • Philadelphia

UK The Falmer Press, Rankine Road, Basingstoke, Hants RG24 0PR

USA The Falmer Press, Taylor & Francis Inc., 1900 Frost Road, Suite 101, Bristol, PA 19007

First published 1990

British Library Cataloguing in Publication Data
Woods, Peter *1934-*
    The happiest days?: how pupils cope with schools.
    1. Learning by school students
    I. Title
    370.1523

    ISBN 1-85000-730-6
    ISBN 1-85000-731-4 pbk

Library of Congress Cataloging-in-Publication Data is available on request

Typeset in 12/14 Bembo by
Chapterhouse, The Cloisters, Formby L37 3PX

Printed in Great Britain by Burgess Science Press, Basingstoke on paper which has a specified pH value on final paper manufacture of not less than 7.5 and is therefore 'acid free'.

Contents

Acknowledgments

The material in this book has benefited from discussions I have had with many colleagues over the years. I would particularly like to thank, for comments they have made on parts of this work at some time or other, and for general influence on the development of the ideas within it, Andrew Pollard, Colin Lacey, David Hargreaves, Andy Hargreaves, Martyn Hammersley, Lynda Measor, Martyn Denscombe, Rosemary Deem, Ali Rattansi, Brian Davies and Stephen Ball. As a teacher, I found that pupils, while they might get me down occasionally, could always be relied upon to pick me up again. This was especially noticeable after a bad day. Equally, as a researcher I have found them a great source of inspiration. It is difficult to pick any out for particular mention, but perhaps an exception might be made for Caroline, James and Rebecca, three excellent key informants. Special thanks go to Kath for expert advice, research input and general support; and to Sheila Gilks for defying all my attempts to mystify her with much-corrected, labyrinthine drafts.

Earlier versions of parts of chapters 1–3, and chapter 5 were published in *Sociology and the School* (1983) Routledge and Kegan Paul; part of chapter 4 was previously published in 'Pupil Perspectives and Cultures', unit 12 of Course E208, *Exploring Educational Issues*, The Open University; chapter 6 combines two papers, previously published as 'Relating to Schoolwork', *Educational Review*, Vol. 30, No. 2, 1978, and 'Negotiating the Demands of Schoolwork', *Journal of Curriculum Studies*, Vol. 10, No. 4, 1978; chapter 7 combines and updates papers previously published as 'What's Red and Screams?' *New Society*, March, 1983; 'Coping at School through Humour', *British Journal of Sociology of Education*, Vol, 4. No. 2, 1983; and 'Having a Laugh', chapter 5 of *The Divided School* (1979), Routledge and Kegan Paul. My thanks to the editors and publishers for permission to reproduce this material here.

Introduction

Schools are happy places. A visitor to a school might witness the *joie de vivre* of youthful high spirits, the merry camaraderie of the staffroom, the affectionate banter in teacher-pupil relationships, laughter ringing along corridors and around playgrounds, the sheer fun of pupils associating together. Many pupils, whatever they have achieved, claim to have had a 'good time' at school, and say they will miss the teachers. Some cry on departure, so sorry are they to leave.

Schools are also miserable places. The same visitor selecting another route or day through the same school might witness bitter inter-pupil rivalry, incredible staffroom pettiness, teacher-pupil confrontation, the heavy pall of boredom, teachers under stress. The literature abounds with portraits of schools as grim places from Dickens, Lawrence, Maugham, Spender and others to the 'deschoolers' (*see*, for example, Lister, 1974). Pupils have likened school to 'prison', 'concentration camp', 'a battleground'. They experience demands and pressures that they perceive as running counter to their interests. Leaving school is like escaping from constrained and hostile surroundings into the free and real world, and beginning life in earnest.

Schools, thus, are places of struggle, where teachers and pupils do their best to cope with the problems set up where social constraint collides with personal intention. The results of this struggle can lead to happiness or misery, or a combination of the two. For some pupils the struggle is the essence, calling for undivided attention and all their abilities, and success in it can be profoundly satisfying. Other pupils engage in less extreme 'coping strategies', requiring skill and creativity no less, but which are more accommodatory, less confrontational. They are coping with school demands, teachers, their fellow-pupils, work, new knowledge, transitions between educational stages, their own developing self, and the assaults of others on it and attempts to change or fashion it. In this activity they draw on their own considerable resources, both collectively from background, and school-generated cultures, and individually, exercising personal choices differentially according to interests.

Schools are also places of learning. Pupils do, at times, acquire skills and knowledge in line with official intentions. Much depends on the opportunities that are given teachers to teach, and to pupils to learn. This 'opportunities to teach and learn' model has been expounded in Woods (1990a), which also deals with the first, teaching, part of the model. This present book is addressed to the learning aspects. Opportunities to learn are not just about conducive circumstances, like a reasonable teacher-pupil ratio, decent buildings and accommodation, adequate resources, and supportive school ethos, though those are important. They also include good teaching (*see* chapter 1 for how this is defined) and good relationships (*see* chapter 6). Essential to this is a degree of cultural attunement to pupils by teachers and effective 'matching' along a range of dimensions and in various areas. This includes cognitive and curriculum matching, as discussed by Bennett *et al.* (1984). This involves, for example, setting pupils appropriate tasks for their abilities. Such opportunities also include a range of social factors which do not stand apart from cognitive factors, but influence the way pupils think, how they behave, how they are motivated, how they assign value, how they perceive themselves. Though a teacher and a class within a classroom constitute one teaching situation, there are, in effect, a number of teaching-learning situations, since each pupil, or groups of pupils within the class may subscribe to different cultural influences. The more obvious ones are those based on social class, gender and 'race'. Pupils come to the classroom via different avenues and equipped with different ways of seeing, thinking and talking, and with different degrees and varieties of 'cultural capital' (Bourdieu and Passeron, 1977). Some groups can constitute 'cultural islands' if sharply differentiated from other groups and from the teacher. If the teacher subscribes to a dominant culture, regarding all other kinds as inferior, defective, and in need of reform; and/or if the school differentiates systematically among its pupils by, for example, streaming, banding or setting (chapter 2) so that some groups are consistently disadvantaged, pupils from alternative cultures may be forced into struggle or coping or 'resistance'. Some pupil careers consist almost entirely of developing and refining such modes of adaptation. If, however, the teacher joins the pupils and looks at the world from their different positions and perspectives, the same cultural resources that are employed in strategic defence can be used for learning. This may involve a certain amount of bargaining.

Schools are, therefore, also trading-places. This is not just for cigarette cards or marbles, though that may be important in the pupils' social world. Trading is central to the main activities of school, to the establishment of the ground-rules which are to govern classroom interactions (*see* chapter 1) and work-rates (*see* chapter 6). These are most assiduously, though largely implicitly, constructed, and jealously defended. Breaking such agreements is a recipe for trouble. Each school, and teacher within it, has to negotiate their own mode of procedure. Some pupils will also trade one lesson, or one teacher, against another in order to pursue a rational line of interest that is not met by a more uniform line (*see* chapter 5). Trading assists coping, therefore, and obviates conflict and confrontation. It may help to establish a consensus.

These are the various themes developed in the book. Throughout there is an emphasis on reality as a social production, contrasted with views of attitudes and behaviour guided by deficit models; on the individual's construction of meanings on a rational basis, as opposed to pathological interpretations; on the emergent and negotiated character of interaction; and on how understandings are based on symbols such as language, words, looks, gestures, appearance, mood, laughter. I draw on a range of ethnographic work to illustrate these points. One of the great strengths of such approaches is their power to evoke the realities of situations from the perspectives of the participants. Further to that, however, the accumulation of such work in recent years reveals a number of theoretical lines and strategies. One of these is where a number of studies can be brought together to illuminate different aspects of a particular process or perspective, and thus suggest a general pattern. This is the case with 'initial encounters' and 'the ideal teacher', discussed in chapter 1. Certain findings have been replicated here; others have differed, and prompted a modification of the notions, a process that will no doubt continue.

Another line is where a theory has been suggested by one research study in a form that more pointedly makes it available for testing in later studies. The best example of this is 'differentiation-polarization theory', which states that academic differentiation by the school will lead to a polarization of sub-cultures among the pupils, between those championing pro-school and those anti-school values. A number of studies have followed up Hargreaves' (1967) and Lacey's (1970) initial formulation, and from them can be gained a developing sense of how this process works and under what conditions. Some have suggested alternative theories to account for Hargreaves' and Lacey's findings based on social structures and relations external to the school. But it is difficult to dispute certain aspects of the ethnographic work. This particular theoretical line and the relationship among these theories are discussed in chapter 2.

Also illustrated by the ethnographic method is the variegated nature of social life, with all its inconsistencies and contradictions, its multiplicity of roles, and layers of reality. It will be seen that it would be a mistake to formulate a theory pertaining to the whole based on research of only a part, though this is not uncommon. As knowledge of areas is built up, however, the degree of inter-relatedness of theories that have been suggested becomes more evident. This is considered in chapter 2, and in subsequent chapters.

Undoubtedly one of the main strengths of ethnography is in its power of cultural portrayal. Its present run of popularity in Britain began with those studies of the late 1960s and early 1970s of predominantly male youth. The chief motif running through these, apart from maleness, was social class (chapter 2). There were some graphic descriptions of these groups 'from the inside' which cast new light on their behaviour and what lay behind it. However, though these showed the usual detailed and faithful representation of the main subjects of study, others more peripheral, such as other students, teachers and girls, tended to be seen as stereotypical ciphers. The exclusiveness of what has been described as 'boys' own ethnography' was soon challenged, and studies of girls in their own right and differentiation by gender restored the balance (chapter 3). These showed how socialization, school processes and organization, the curriculum, teacher-pupil and pupil-pupil interaction and teenage culture all contributed to unequal chances between girls and boys at school. They revealed, too, the stereotypical nature of the passive, pliable, victim, female image, and showed girls as active, innovative, and constructive, in their own right, albeit often in different ways from boys. These studies do not simply add on to the end of the 'boys' own' researches, but require consideration of how gender relates to social class.

The same is true of 'race', equally largely left out of account in the earlier studies, but now gaining in popularity (chapter 4). Despite Britain being a multicultural society, many of Britain's schools, including multi-ethnic ones, are run on a monocultural basis. They offer a largely anglocentric curriculum. Pupils from most minority ethnic groups appear disadvantaged in the 'differentiation-polarization' process. They come into conflict with those teachers who operate a deficit model of cultures other than their own. Racism may pervade their relationships with white pupils as well as teachers. In the face of this, they develop and practise their own forms of resistance focused on celebrating the most prominent elements of their cultures, and fortifying their own identities within them. Here is the classic 'battleground' with opposing forces. However, not all schools are like this by any means. The study of non-racist, genuinely multicultural schools, enables comparative work to be done across the board in the continuous quest to find the conditions that promote the best education for all children. Again, a number of ethnographic studies, as well as providing rich description of their own particular subjects, can be brought together to fuel theory in a more general area. Similarly, all these studies are useful in considering the interconnections among social class, gender and 'race'. Some of the indications arising from these studies are examined in chapters 2–4.

If ethnography is strong on cultural portrayal, it runs an almost inevitable risk of painting a picture of individual subjection and of cultural determinism. But it contains its own antidote to this, for it is concerned also with individual interests, perspectives and volition. Chapter 5, therefore, shows some individual variations on a number of themes. It does not invalidate the themes, but shows how individuals weave a path through and among them, now borrowing, now contributing to them. There is a looser, more dialectical relationship between individual and culture in many instances. Such a view requires a more self-directed, strategical model of pupil development to place beside the more heavily externally directed models as in 'sex-role socialization', and such a one is also outlined in chapter 5.

The evocation of realities, theoretical advance, cultural portrayal, individual interests and strategies are, then, all aspects of the material presented here. There is one other, represented in chapters 6 and 7, which is to do with the unpacking and delineation of particular areas of activity, in this case 'work' and 'laughter'. Nobody would dispute that these are both prominent activities in school, in the sense that they constitute sets of behaviours that can be described in those terms, and they serve as focal points for the direction of other sets of behaviours. Most schools ring to the injunctions of teachers to pupils to work, and to occasional, and sometimes frequent, peals of laughter. But what are pupil perceptions of 'work'? How is it constituted in their minds? Given that most pupils say they want to work at school (chapter 2), what are their understandings of what is involved? Chapter 6 presents two prominent aspects of this as revealed in one study that lay emphasis on the nature of teacher-pupil relationships, and varieties of 'negotiation' between teacher and pupil.

'Laughter' as a theme runs throughout the book, from the 'sussing-out' activities of King and his henchmen (Beynon, 1985) in chapter 1, the 'havin' a laff' of Willis' (1977) lads in chapter 2, the 'resistance laughter' of Dubberley's (1988b) girls and McLaren's (1986) pupils, the intense association and 'running jokes' of Furlong's (1984) group of Afro-Caribbean boys in chapter 4, the creativity of excitement and their own life spaces by Lynn Davies' (1984) 'wenches'. Chapter 7 attempts to bring together from a number of sources and disciplines a range of work on pupil humour and laughter, and to indicate its main functions. Some of these are consensual in situations of high matching in the cultural areas discussed earlier, some are conflictual where clash and confrontation occur. Thus the 'peals of laughter' that one might hear resounding in classrooms and corridors might be being used as an aid to pupil development, a celebration of companionship, a teaching aid, a cultural defence, a test of teachers, an offensive weapon, a social balm or a social disintegrator. Given all these uses, and its high degree of effectiveness in all cases, it is not surprising that this contributes strongly towards the impression that 'schooldays are the happiest days'. For many pupils, however, this is little more than replacing the underlying reality with the antidote.

Some of the material presented here has appeared in various other publications, now largely out of print. I have taken the opportunity to update and expand this work while integrating it around the common theme of how pupils cope with school.

Chapter 1

Establishing Order in the Classroom

Our social behaviour is regulated by rules. Some of these are explicit. The grammar school that I attended as a pupil, for example, had a printed list of rules, rather like the Ten Commandments in tone. The last one of these I still remember as 'a breach of good manners is a breach of a school rule'. I remember it largely, I suspect, because it was not until the third year that I understood what 'breach' meant. I was perplexed, too, by another rule. This stated that if a pupil cut his finger while performing some woodworking task, then he would receive a 'signature' in his 'prep book'. Signatures (the initials of the person awarding them — a member of staff or a prefect) were marks for bad conduct. If you collected three in a week, you lost a 'merit' holiday (a free half-day); if you were unfortunate enough to assemble two lots of three, you were caned by the Headmaster. On one occasion I cut my finger rather badly while making creative use of the chisel in fashioning a dove-tailed joint out of a knotty piece of wood. I was hoisted on to the work-bench by the teacher, the finger was displayed to the rest of the class, and a *double* signature ceremoniously entered into my prep book. As luck would have it, this completed a set of three to add to another set already completed for various 'breaches'. I was duly caned as the law prescribed.

While, looking back, we might appreciate both the humour and the reasoning involved, neither were too apparent to me as a pupil at the time. I was as mystified as I had been by my mother's anger on one occasion when I was pulled out of the river half-drowned. Had she wanted me fully drowned, I wondered? The school's was an authoritarian regime. Rules were to be obeyed, not necessarily understood or agreed upon. Yet the length of the queue outside the headmaster's door at daily punishment time (waiting here was the worst part of the process for you could hear the stinging thwacks of the cane being administered to the bottoms of those ahead of you!) carries a suggestion that the system was not too successful. It operated by repression rather than consent, and, arguably, served to promote rather than remedy disorder. I certainly went on cutting my fingers with painful regularity until the woodwork teacher in despair transferred me to ancient history. This lack of efficacy, as well as the spread of egalitarian ideas, is possibly one of the reasons behind the growth of more cooperative regimes based on negotiation or bargaining in some form, either explicit or implicit. Pupils have considerable resources in this two-way process. They have collective strength (and parents!), and many varieties of recalcitrance, from rough-and-ready to finely-tuned. Above all, teachers are requiring something from pupils, and they are trying to change them in a way that might be perceived by pupils as an assault on the self (Geer, 1977). They invariably have to bargain to achieve these ends, for pupils are not passive, mouldable objects.

Consider, for example, classroom interaction. Teachers might try to establish rules on such matters as how pupils enter the room, where and how they sit, how they interact with each other and with the teacher, how and when to ask and answer questions, how to write in their books, work rates, appearance and so on. However, even if rules are laid out on tablets of stone, as those of my grammar school, they are not necessarily enforceable as such, nor may they be the best means to the desired ends. In most cases, in fact, rules seem to be negotiated. Thus a teacher might begin by introducing a rule 'no talking in the classroom'. This might be found impossible to enforce without sacrificing some other, more essential part of the teacher's programme (such as reasonably good relations with the pupils); or it might be found to run contrary to other valued aims (such as the production of work). The rule might become modified, therefore, in the light of experience to something like, 'I don't mind your making a noise in the classroom as long as it's a working noise', which leaves some flexibility to the interpretation. What actually constitutes a 'working noise' may not be a matter simply for the teacher to decide. It may be the product of a series of negotiations over a period of time which reflects the climate teacher and pupils have constructed between them. In this scenario, when pupils exceed a 'working noise' they are perceived as going back on the bargain, just as the teacher would be if the 'working noise' were disallowed. In both instances sanctions would follow. In this respect, pupils have considerable power — they can make life very uncomfortable for teachers, and on occasions bring about their downfall (Sikes *et al.*, 1985; Riseborough, 1985).

This is not to say that teachers do not play a strong part in the exchange. There is plenty of testimony to the skill of teachers in 'grooving' pupils in to classroom rules (Smith and Geoffrey, 1968), in promoting procedural activity conducive to a 'good working atmosphere' (Edwards and Furlong, 1978), in requiring cultural and communicative competence (Hammersley, 1977; Edwards and Westgate, 1987), in orchestrating the varied aspects of the teacher role so as to bring about a seamless web of teaching and control (Morrison and McIntyre, 1969), in establishing 'the ground-rules of educational discourse' (Edwards and Mercer, 1987). But, equally, pupils can, on occasions, have considerable influence, and this has increased as more authoritarian styles of teaching have receded. It is the pupils' part in negotiating rules that I wish to consider here — how they do it, what strategies and sanctions are brought to bear, what interests lie behind their actions, and what kind of teacher elicits the best educational response. I shall begin by looking at how pupils behave in new situations.

Initial Encounters

From the very first moment of starting school, children are active participants in the construction of classroom order. Davies (1983), for example, has challenged the notion that children are, in the first instance of initial encounters, passive. She quotes from a classroom observed by Wax (1971) in which no cooperation existed. It felt as if she (Wax) 'had been thrust into some scene from Alice in Wonderland. Never in my most anxiety-ridden professional nightmares had I imagined that a schoolroom could be like this one' (Wax, 1971: 253). In such circumstances, the basic importance of the pupils' willingness to talk and cooperate is emphasized in stark relief, as is the power of the students. Davies made a detailed study of videotapes she had made of several classrooms on the first day of school. Though her first interest had been in how teachers constructed order, she became increasingly aware, as she repeatedly viewed the tapes, of the work the children did in assisting the teacher. She illustrates the social competencies they displayed in the first few minutes without which the established order would not have emerged. They worked individually and in small groups before class began, and moved collectively when school was about to commence, all on their own initiative. Their collective response to the teacher's greeting confirmed the appropriateness of his approach. They listened, raised their hands, asked questions, providing the teacher 'with opportunities to display the kind of teacher he is and the kind of classroom this is to be' (p. 66). They discovered the nature of pupil competence, grasped a number of meaningful rules, and established an orderliness that all recognized. They showed an underlying considerable interactive competence that did not have to be taught.

However, the product of such interaction might not be 'learning' so much as 'coping' with the problems presented to pupils within the situation. Thus, a common pupil ploy observed has been that of 'pleasing the teacher'. Respect or liking for the adult, a desire to keep out of trouble, or simply getting tasks done as quickly and easily as possible can be the motivating factor. We noticed a young child of four years of age just starting school was more preoccupied with studying his fellows' responses than in listening to the teacher (Grugeon and Woods, 1990). Infants of 6–7 years old have been observed searching for clues to the right answers to teacher questions in teacher behaviour, and faking attitudes to appear to 'know' (Tuckwell, 1982). The chances are small, for example, that one will be picked out of a 'forest of hands' volunteering an answer, and if perchance selected, one can always have 'genuine' doubts. In any event, it is better to have been seen as being involved, and to have tried, than to sit unresponsive. Holt (1969) has given a range of examples of such behaviour, including 'guess-and-look' (studying the teacher's face for clues as to the nearness of one's guess), getting other people to do the work for you (asking, copying, trading), extracting clues or concessions from the teacher, winning acceptance of answers by subterfuge (for example, whispering so that the teacher might accept it if it sounds correct, perhaps clarifying in the process so that the teacher in fact answers his/her own question). Hargreaves (1972) gives examples of 'spotting the question' when the teacher is going round the class in a predictable sequence; duping the teacher by appearances and 'impressive language'; and of pupils who would write the date in pencil on their mathematics exercise books, so if the work was not marked, it could serve for work on another day. I was told in one school of pupils who re-used sibling's models in CSE examinations. Such strategies combine 'work-avoidance' with 'getting it right'.

However, such accommodating strategies assume an initial establishment of order in the classroom. This often has to be fought or bargained for. When pupils meet a teacher for the first time there are a number of unknowns (on both sides). Pupils do not know how strict or 'soft' the teacher will be, what behaviours and appearances will be permitted, how hard they will be made to work, and so on. Some regimens might attempt to establish rule by domination, and prescribe these things explicitly. In other situations they might emerge more inductively through a kind of bargaining.

Geer (1977, 7) describes a typical process:

> By listening carefully to what a teacher says he (sic) wants in class and comparing among themselves what grades or comments he gives for what kinds of work, and 'by trying things on' (mass shoelace tying, for instance) in the early days of a school term, a class may reach a consensus about its teacher's standards, both academic and disciplinary. It then transforms what the teacher says and does into rules for him to follow. He must not change these rules the class makes for him, and he must apply them to all pupils.

The emphasis varies, of course, from classroom to classroom, but in all such instances the agreement is implicit, and the teacher's behaviour is constrained, whether this is realized or not. Pupils can bring sanctions to bear, like sabotaging the arrangements for a visitor to the school. Teachers can use rewards, like allowing more time for a test. Geer argues that the basis of the teacher's authority for the pupil is the academic matter and the site of it is the classroom. Outside these areas, in corridors and yards, and in social and moral affairs, teacher control has less legitimacy. It is often in these areas that teacher-pupil conflict arises, as few teachers would accept the logic of these distinctions, considering that they teach the 'whole child', and that what happens in one arena affects another.

Bargaining can often be enjoyable for both teacher and pupils. It can be part of the joys of sociation, and, for the teacher, calls for considerable management skills, which recognize, for example, when and when not to give way. The establishment of a consensus which promises to yield near maximum education advantage given the conditions is a considerable achievement for all. However, the path to such a consensus is sometimes a difficult one. This would appear to be the case in the study reported by Beynon (1985). He observed a class in all their lessons during their first half-term at a boys' comprehensive school in South Wales. Among these boys was a core group who were the main instigators of 'mucking' and 'sussing'. Sussing 'revealed how individual teachers reacted to provocation and stress and whether they could uphold and put into practice (in acceptable, to the boys, ways) the claims they were making for themselves of being strict, ''no nonsense'' teachers, who were both interesting, worth listening to, and expert' (1984: 121). It was not a matter, therefore, of teachers unilaterally laying down rules by fiat, and of pupils following them, with perhaps some slight deviance. Rather, 'at this stage, pupils demand empirical evidence of each (teacher's) managerial expertise and a clear definition and demonstration of the parameters of the control s/he seeks to establish' (Beynon, 1985: 37).

Beynon identified six major groups of 'sussing strategies' among these boys:

(a) Group formation and communication. This was the essential basis of the challenge to the teacher, for there is strength in numbers and a common purpose. The group had 'a unity about it and an internal dynamism'. It was dominated by one boy — King — who initiated most of the challenges. They drew attention to themselves, created and exploited diversions and recruited others on occasions from elsewhere in the form and from outside.

(b) Joking. This provided both a good laugh in itself, and a stern test for teachers. The lads used *risqué* jokes, lavatorial humour, repartee and wit, 'backchat' and 'lip'.

(c) Challenges (verbal). These included asking stupid questions, giving pseudo information, 'build-ons' ('joining in with lip' and 'helping your friends'), unnecessary requests for information, 'third partying' (excluding the teacher from a conversation by placing them in the position of third party), answering back and open cheek, chattering and not listening, challenging comments and statements.

(d) Challenges (non-verbal). These included putting on a show, postural and gestural challenges, barging, hitting and spitting, splattering and inking, making noises.

(e) Interventions. These involved loud and dramatic interruptions, including shoutings-out, maniacal laughter, bellowed/guttural out-of-tune singing, 'parrots' ('insistent, repetitious and insolent demands made of the teacher'), dramatic entrances, and 'walk-abouts'.

(f) Play. The lads' games took the form of fidgeting with pens, ruler flashing, bag games, bringing things to school, finding materials, disc play (the plastic covers on the bung holes of beer barrels).

It is not difficult to recall from one's own school days and/or experiences as a teacher examples of these various kinds of behaviour. On the face of it, much of it may have been rather meaningless, anarchic and counter-productive. That is certainly how it seems to me when, as a pupil, I joined with my fellows in 2A in tormenting Mr English, to the point where he retired from teaching to become a librarian. Mr English was a gentle, sensitive, mild-mannered, cultured man, whom we all liked, but whom we never came to respect as a teacher. I recall the Deputy Headmaster reasoning with us for a whole lesson on how we should help Mr English, and our agreeing with every point. But the very next session with him was exactly the same. It was almost as if the 'sussing' was beyond our control. We could not help ourselves, and neither could he. He simply did not pass the test of the kind of teacher we had come to expect. Beynon's point about such activity, therefore, is that, at times at least, this is very important, indeed essential, activity, purposeful and skilful, and demanding considerable personal and professional abilities on the part of the teacher. Most of the activity, also, is almost intuitive on both sides. It is not planned. It arises almost as instant action and reaction out of the circumstances. 'Sussing' tested out the claims teachers made about themselves and the arrangements they made for conducting lessons. By these means, pupils discovered what sort of teacher they had, what meanings the teacher gave to certain statements, what degrees of flexibility existed, and, in so doing, exerted their own influence on the climate of the classroom.

This, of course, was a boys' school, and we would need to consider whether the analysis holds for girls' schools and co-educational schools. Also, the study was limited to a core group of boys. But Beynon argues that this group who perpetrated most of the sussing was performing a service for the whole class, and that in some shape or form it is an essential component of initial encounters. There is some support for this argument. Doyle (1979), for example, in his observation of student teachers in American classrooms, found similar behaviours which 'appeared to function as active tests of the ability of the student teacher to manage classroom routines and rule systems' (quoted in Ball, 1980: 111). He also noted, like Beynon, that the task of testing typically fell to a few pupils only in any one class. The rest, whether conformists or not, would watch the rebels doing the testing for them. Davies (1983:67) also found the collaborative work of her first-day pupils was done by a few, acting as 'representatives of the cohort'. Delamont and Galton (1986), whose research took place in six schools, were also convinced that 'other pupils were watching the testing to see where the lines were to be drawn by their new staff' (p. 58). Teachers must often feel that if only the ringleaders (like 'King' in Beynon's school) were removed, all would be well. While there might be something in this, the line of argument above suggests that if one group were removed, the testing would devolve to another.

Ball (1980), going on the evidence of his research at the co-educational Beachside Comprehensive (1981) and interviews with some students doing a Postgraduate Certificate of Education, also attests to the importance of what he calls 'the process of establishment.' He feels that the central question is one of how teachers and pupils 'define the situation'. Situations do not simply exist. They have to be interpreted. Different people may see different things in the same situation, or interpret the same things differently. They may try to manipulate aspects of the situation to influence others' interpretations. Situations are ultimately what we make them. In W.I. Thomas' well-known phrase, if people 'define situations as real, they are real in their consequences' (1928: 572).

'Testing out' is not necessarily a matter of conflict. Denscombe (1985) points out that pupils expect and hope that teachers will succeed in controlling them, though appearances in their behaviour might suggest the contrary.

> Without defying the laws of logic, pupils can dislike being controlled and, where possible, take active steps to undermine the teacher's efforts to obtain control, yet, at the same time, they can (and generally do) expect teachers to overcome such resistance and reserve respect for those teachers who can impose order on the situation even against the resistance they themselves might put up (1985: 33).

Even where pupils are intent on conformity, they still need to know what actually constitutes conformity in the teacher's mind and what does not. Ball (1980) draws attention to work as well as to general behaviour, and points out that the tasks teachers give pupils may be resisted or reformulated by pupils if they present difficulties. This is well illustrated by Blurton (1987), who describes a range of restrictive work practices in both higher and lower levels of the comprehensive school of his research. Band A English 4th-year pupils, for example, placed restrictions on work output if specific work was not stipulated. If they found a lesson boring, they had strategies for re-directing it. However if the work set was clear and offered tangible rewards, it was seen as legitimate, and work restrictions were lifted. By contrast, Band B pupils reduced the total amount of work they were prepared to do, whether explicitly stipulated or not. While Band A pupils worked overtime on what they considered legitimate work, Band B pupils were more likely to 'go slow', 'work to rule', and operate 'quota restrictions'. Interestingly, Blurton noticed these attitudes to work forming across the sets in the first year. To what extent did they emerge from initial encounters?

One perspective on this comes from our study of the transfer of a group of children from a middle to a 12–18 co-educational comprehensive school (Measor and Woods, 1984). First encounters at the secondary school saw a 'honeymoon' period, when teacher and pupils presented highly formalized 'fronts' to each other (Goffman, 1971). The pupils were ultra-conformist during this period which lasted a week, with no talking, high commitment to work, anxiety to please, though as noted earlier, we should not regard this necessarily as simply passive reaction. In class, there was the 'forest of hands' syndrome, as all strove for the privilege of answering the teacher's questions. After about a week, however, as pupils' apprehension began to fade, so did the front, and different identities began to emerge. Similar activity to that described by Beynon was now observed among both boys and girls.

> Pupils began to probe for 'living space' for themselves, testing around the edges of the sharply drawn rules, to negotiate the ground rules that actually operated . . . (they) soon began to discover priorities — important and comparatively unimportant parts of the school day, what they were actually allowed or not allowed to do in lessons, high and low status subject areas of the curriculum, important and less important teachers, and what adjustments to school uniform they could get away with. (Measor and Woods, 1984: 52)

This activity was not just a reaction to teachers and an evaluation of the teacher's credentials, but an active construction on the part of pupils in which they sought to establish their own preferred identities. In other words, they were not just 'making trouble' or 'testing out' the teacher, but trying out identities for themselves. These appeared in this case to relate mainly to intelligence ('bright' or 'thick', 'good' or 'bad' at a particular subject), orientation toward school ('teacher's pet' or 'menace'), and gender (boy or girl). There was also a question of establishing status within a group (also noted by Beynon). These factors meant that 'testing-out' was variable among the members of the form and among areas of their school experience. Here, therefore, we may note the possible multi-functionality of pupil behaviour during initial encounters, in which they seek to test out teachers' definitions of the situation in order to see how far their own might be established. These definitions might vary, not only between teachers and pupils, but among teachers, subjects and among pupils.

'Testing-out' therefore, seems a fairly common phenomenon, but the exact form it takes depends on a number of factors. For example, the behaviour of the boys observed by Beynon may be a comparatively extreme form influenced perhaps by such factors as the area the school was in (urban, industrialized); the intake (other children from the area went to a Roman Catholic comprehensive, a girls' comprehensive, a Welsh medium secondary in a nearby town, or private schools, and these other schools have not been researched); buildings and resources (the boys were accommodated in a particular building which was 'impoverished' compared to the rest of the school and had elementary-school origins); school organization (the separation of the building from the rest of the school cast the teachers and pupils in it 'adrift'); teachers (most experienced status-deprivation as a consequence of being cut off from the main stream and all its rewards); the ethos of the Lower School (the head and his deputy, the principal reality-definers, were both 'hard', coercive disciplinarians). It might also be argued that there is another factor behind this kind of 'sussing' deriving from a male culture (*see* chapter 3). There was certainly some of this, involving at its extreme sexual harassment of female teachers and violence with males. On the other hand, girls can also be quite disruptive. Delamont and Galton give the example of Annabel who tested the disciplinary regimes of her new teachers.

> Annabel keeps lifting the desk lid, and swinging the desk and her chair. Mrs Macauley bawls her out — offers her the chance to go outside the door if she is bored. It doesn't stop Annabel . . . . The bell goes, and Annabel who was fidgeting and yawning says 'Oh good'. Mrs Macauley tells them not pack up. Tells off Annabel, reminding her that she is Arlene's sister and 'She behaves much better than you'.

Annabel was unimpressed by this comparison. Her behaviour, and that of a boy called Dirk, was so disruptive that it coloured the staff's reactions to their form. Within a fortnight of the start of the school year, one of us wrote:

> ... At break it is clear that 1.6 are already the most unpopular form (which is tough for Miss O'Hara their form mistress), and Dirk and Annabel are unpopular already.

This class, 1.6, had two or even three teachers for basic subjects, and for English they were taught both by Miss O'Hara and by the deputy-head, Mrs Evans (whose husband taught the 'A' band form we studied). Annabel was not, however, overawed by Mrs Evans.

> Mrs Evans is asking them to tell her things about themselves and their families preparatory to writing an autobiographical essay. It is very noticeable that the class do not sit still even for the deputy-head. They swing in the chairs, and Annabel, at the back, is pushing into the back of the boy in front. (Delamont and Galton, 1986: 60)

Disorder was more variable and more muted at the schools studied by Measor and Woods, and Delamont and Galton, than in Beynon's school, and they introduced more variables. Measor and Woods, for example, describe how Phillip, an aspiring achiever, sought to restore order in a maths lesson, to bring the group into line with his own interests. And Delamont and Galton draw attention to other pupils who do not 'test out', but rather breathe a sign of relief that their new school is not such a bad place as they suspected, and begin to build 'shared meanings' with their new teachers. Here is one example they give of the establishment of shared meanings:

> During the morning, Miss Tweed has referred to 'Horace' on several occasions and each time the children have laughed. She says, for example, 'There's Horace at the window again.' One little girl's (stuffed toy) mouse is called Horace. Everyone giggles when it is mentioned. During the break Miss Tweed tells the girl, Yvette, to tell me why it's called Horace. The girl laughs, and Miss Tweed then explains that when she was writing on the first day Yvette spelled 'horse' as 'Horace' and another child called out: 'Look! There's a Horace outside the window eating the grass.' Then when she made a

mouse in needlework Yvette called it Horace. There is much giggling from the listening children at this explanation of the joke.

Later in the fieldwork, the observer wrote:

Anyone who mis-spells anything is referred to as Horace. For example, Miss Tweed says, 'It's like that Horace looking through the window' to another girl who has mis-spelt a word in her writing, or 'take it away and alter it — we don't allow anyone else to have a Horace in here.'

A few days later, Miss Tweed explained to the researcher why she was particularly supportive of Yvette.

She tells me more about the little girl with the Horace joke. Her parents are split up and she now lives with the Gran. She was very nervous when she came in and is more settled now.

All three of the observers visiting 1T recorded how Miss Tweed encouraged Yvette to paint her special pictures (sometimes even when other pupils were doing academic tasks), and how Yvette became a big fan of Miss Tweed. When Miss Tweed read aloud to the class, Yvette would move her chair next to the teacher's desk, and when praised she blossomed. For the whole class the 'Horace' joke is a sign that the initial encounter is over, and routine classroom life is in progress. (Delamont and Galton, 1986: 62–3)

Pupil Values and Teacher Offences

If pupils contribute towards the agreed definition of the classroom situation and the construction of rules written in it, what sort of principles do they bring to bear? How are these principles incorporated into the shared meanings? What can pupils do about it if those values are ignored or repudiated by teachers? In a classic article, Werthman (1984) studied some black, lower-class 'gang members' in schools over a two-year period. At the time, it was commonly felt that the problems such boys were involved in at school were a product of variations in their motivations and capacities pitted against middle-class school. Werthman showed this to be too simplistic a model. These boys did not all behave in the same way, there was little correlation between academic performance and 'trouble', nor were difficulties experienced in all the classes they attended. This suggested that the problems were not so much a matter of social-class difference or school phobia, but something more specific about the teachers and the pupils.

The matter rests, Werthman argues, on whether these boys accept the legitimacy of the teacher's authority. This depends on the teacher meeting four criteria:

(a) Conceptions of proper jurisdiction. Teachers do not have an automatic right to punish certain behaviours, though good reasons for ceasing them may be accepted.

(b) Matters like race, dress, hairstyles and mental capacities are outside the teacher's jurisdiction.

(c) How authority is exercised. Bland authoritarianism is insulting and demeaning.

(d) How teachers award grades and upon what basis. This was critical, for the evaluation could be used as a potent weapon against them ('grades' carry much more weight in the American high school than 'marks' typically do in British secondary schools).

Werthman shows that from their general experience, the boys reason that the rules teachers might be using to give grades are basically as follows: (a) they might be given fairly; (b) they might be used as sanctions; (c) they might be awarded as bribes; (d) they might be randomly distributed. They know then, when they receive a grade, that it is a single case of one of these categories, but they have to discover which one. Only the first is fully acceptable. Their objections to (b) and (d) should be obvious, and (c) is against their sense of morality ('kissing ass'). As for how they set about discovering teacher's rules, they 'behave like good little social scientists. They draw a sample, ask it questions, and compare the results with those predicted under alternative hypotheses' (p. 215). The teacher may already have given indications of the basis of the award, either explicitly or implicitly (for example, a good grade might have been offered for good behaviour). If not, the boy will seek clarification. If he feels he is being discriminated against, he will demand an explanation: 'What the hell did I get this for?' If he gets a bad grade and finds the teacher apprehensive, he might conclude the grades have been awarded randomly. If he gets no reply, he will feel insulted — and so on. After the teacher's response, the boy has all the evidence he needs to arrive at the rule

13

being used. All those except fairness are considered illegitimate, and thus cause the teacher's authority to be undermined. All behaviour that acknowledges the legitimacy of that authority will now be suppressed (such as cooperating in class, being polite, putting one's hand up, being punctual, waiting until dismissed, using deferential modes of address). Above all, the boys develop a physical bearing that communicates a 'causal and disdainful aloofness to anyone making normative claims on their behaviour' (p. 221). This is 'looking cool' — 'a walking pace that is a little too slow for the occasion, a straight back, shoulder slightly stooped, hands in pockets, and eyes that carefully avert any party to the interaction . . . ' (*ibid.*). The superb effectiveness of 'looking cool' lies in the unmistakability of the message to teachers coupled with their powerlessness to do anything about it.

A British study in two comprehensive schools similarly found that pupils reacted to teachers breaking the implicit rule structure they saw as governing their relationships. The main teacher offences were being inhuman, not knowing who the pupils were, being 'soft' and being unfair. They responded according to 'principles of retribution' which fall into two broad categories, 'reciprocity' and 'equilibration'. In the former, one pays back in kind, insult for insult, slap for slap — 'And if they turn nasty, well, we can turn nasty too' (Marsh *et al.*, 1978: 44). What is returned may not always be exactly the same: pupils may mess about 'to get back at the teachers for telling them off, and putting them in detention' (*ibid.*), or use physical violence if they are given a 'soft' teacher. The second category of pupil response involves tactics to neutralize possible loss of dignity and self-esteem as a result of the offence. 'Looking cool' would be an example of this. The most common example involved the pupil withdrawing, or switching off — for example, 'I just go quiet and that annoys them even more' (Rosser and Harré, 1976: 176).

Another common example of withdrawal, of course, is truanting, or, in pupils' argot, 'bunking off' 'dolling off' or 'going on the mitch'. Inveterate truants simply stay away from school, but others deploy more subtle strategies. They might turn up for the mark, and then leave; or present themselves for some lessons and not others; or appear for parts of lessons only. A gang of girls at Lowfield (Woods 1979) were particularly adept at 'slipping away for a smoke'. Bird *et al.* (1981) give an example of a skilful work-evader. Bob would 'skip lessons without being caught, wriggle out of work assignments with excuses and strategic absences, opt out of exam courses' (*ibid*: 16). Pupils can be present in body, but away in spirit. Thus Zena, 'When challenged she was able to outclass most teachers in her mastery of the English vernacular, but most of the time was content to sit chatting in the corner. Teachers soon learned that she was unwilling to work, but if not provoked she would cause them little bother' (*ibid*: 16–17).

Furlong's (1977) girls sometimes 'bunked off' as a form of mucking about. If a teacher was boring they would 'Run round the classrooms and the corridors or the toilets or something like that . . . ' (p. 169).

> *Carol*:   We had . . . that stupid teacher and he just sits there and gives us these stupid books to read, so I just sit there reading them . . . so Ann says 'Let's go out now', so me, Jill, Linda and Diane just follow her out. (Furlong, 1976: 162).

With strict teachers, the evasion was more serious and 'the girls had to stay out of sight, pretend they were absent from school and hope that no one would check up on them' (p. 169).

But withdrawal could be done by a more positive action:

> *Fay*:   Mr Potts, he was ever such a laugh; but when he got in a temper he used to really shout and nobody took any notice.
>
> *Rosie*:   Yes, his face used to go beetroot. He stood on the table in one lesson and went like this, 'grrr!' We just laughed. He looked so stupid. (Pollard, 1979)

Tattum (1982) found the pupils in the 'detached unit for disruptive pupils' of his research had similar motives to those identified by Werthman and Marsh *et al*. All pupils, regardless of sex, age or background showed remarkable consistency in how they accounted for their deviant behaviour. They did not seek to excuse it by 'appealing to unconscious motivations' (p. 93), or show much premeditation or calculation. They responded to situations which they saw as prompting a reaction. Tattum found five major areas of pupil motivation: (1) It was the teacher's fault (for example, by being ineffective at teaching or control — *see below*); (2) Being treated with disrespect ('Some talk to you like you're blinking dogs' — p. 98); (3) Inconsistency of rule application (for example, being 'picked on' unjustly); (4) We were only messing about — having a laugh (*see* chapter 8); (5) It's the fault of the school system (lessons all day of variable quality, badly organized timetables). All of these responses are situated within the school's own value-system. 'By the school's own values they expect to be treated with respect, shown care and concern, treated justly, permitted the leisure of a social life — all of which are features to which teachers give expression as being part of the ethos of schooling' (Tattum, 1982: 110). These accounts do not necessarily mean that the pupils concerned always thought that they were right and the teacher wrong. Several studies have indicated that pupils possess an acute sense of fairness (Nash, 1976; Davies, 1980; Furlong, 1977; Pollard, 1979).

Pupils, then exert an influence of their own on classroom interaction, and do have weapons they can use. Reynolds (1976), in his observations of ten South Wales secondary schools, concluded that good order in schools is a product of an agreement between teacher and pupils, a bargaining and nego-tiating, or what he calls a 'truce'. It is often argued that conflict is inevitable in schools (e.g. Waller, 1932). One way of handling the conflict is to tone it down by mutual agreement. Thus, a certain amount of limited rule-breaking might be permitted — perhaps smoking in the toilet, chewing in lessons, infringements of uniform regulations. Reynolds quotes the example of the 'pupil smokers' and the staff's 'smoking patrol', which followed them around the premises but always maintained a discreet distance, so they never actually caught up with them. Certainly it would not do for teachers to give too much away for, as we have seen, they would be considered weak. But, equally certainly, the weight of evidence we have supports the idea that negotiation is likely to produce the best results (*see*, for example, Hargreaves *et al.*, 1975; Grace, 1978; Reynolds, 1976; Denscombe, 1985).

Pollard (1979) came to similar conclusions about a group of pupils in a junior school. He found three broad groups — 'good' pupils, 'gangs' and 'jokers'. The last were by far the largest group, and they 'survive by negotiating a tacit set of understandings with the teacher which allows them room to develop viable adaptive strategies for themselves. In the right context they can have a laugh, talk, tease, run and play without incurring 'serious' penalties' (p. 91). Their acts take place within the 'working consensus', and will therefore include 'routine deviance, for these provide laughs and a release from boredom and routine, but they generally do not participate in unilateral acts of "disorder"' (p. 89). (*See also* chapter 7).

In working toward such a consensus, pupils may respond to teacher control attempts with a counter-strategy of humour and friendliness, or exert pressure in more oppositional ways. Concerning the former, they might try to neutralize a teacher censure, for example, with a palpably lame excuse which nonetheless is calculated to raise some sympathy because it strikes a common human note over and above the requirements of teacher and pupil roles (*see* Denscombe, 1980). Thus, some homework has not been done because 'City were playing last night'. The teacher was surely 'young himself, once upon a time?' Classrooms are full of such goodnatured banter and ribaldry, and both teachers and pupils use it to good effect to mellow the more abrasive effects of institutional life. It establishes a common bond, averts 'trouble' from pupils and heavy-handed authoritarianism from teachers, provides 'comic relief' from the rigours of working (Stebbins, 1980), and allows pupils to contribute towards the climate of lessons.

Denscombe (1980) draws attention again to the situated nature of pupil strategies, and shows how in 'open' classrooms, pupils gained a little more leverage. For pupils had more scope here to influence the content of the course, the amount of work done, and the manner in which it was conducted. 'From the pupils' point of view it blurred the boundaries between "proper work" and "having a chat" in a way which could be exploited in the negotiation of work' (*ibid*: 67). Denscombe maintains that thes pupils were more concerned with exploitation in this way, rather than in finding or making educational work more relevant and interesting.

The 'Ideal Teacher'

If all the pupils' principles are met and negotiation goes well, these presumably are aspects of 'good' teaching from the pupils' point of view. It is worth considering, therefore, what pupils regard as constituting 'good teachers'. This highlights further criteria pupils employ in assessing teachers.

For pupils in general the most important attributes of good teachers are that they should be 'human', should be able to 'teach' and make you 'work', and keep control. They should also 'respect' pupils if they wish the respect to be returned. This respect has to be earned — it is not an automatic right. Some teachers are felt to be inhuman. They interpret their role too literally. In pupils' terms, they are 'a load of rubbish' (Marsh, Rosser and Harré, 1978). 'Mostly . . . they're all straightlaced. Keep putting us down . . . . They go on as if they were never young and did the things we do' (*ibid*: 36). They are '9 to 4' teachers, not really caring about the job or the pupils. They might not even know who pupils are, thus depriving them of personal identities (*ibid*). Unpopular teachers' lack of respect for pupils might be reflected in their appearance. Payne's (1987) Barbadian pupils were very critical of shabbiness and uncleanliness in a teacher. Davies' (1984) girls were 'incensed by "dirty" teachers — any who wore scruffy suits, down-at-heel shoes, whose hair stuck up on end', or who showed a lack of propriety in appearance or behaviour (p. 29). Dubberley's (1988: 191) girls, similarly, criticized a teacher for being 'dead scruffy . . . filthy . . . Greasy hair — nobbut Oxfam clothes'.

In view of complaints of inhumanity and impropriety, it comes as something of a surprise to find that most pupils say that on the whole they 'like' school. Most of the pupils in the two Midlands comprehensive schools studied by Quine (1974) said they liked school, and this tendency actually increased towards the bottom sets or streams. However, we are given no indication of why they liked school, and if this differed among the pupils. Some may have liked it, for example, not because of the progress in work they felt they were making, but because of the opportunities for 'laughs' it presented. In my research, some like it because it was where they 'met their mates' (Woods, 1979). Davies (1982) discovered that one of her pupils liked a school because 'the tuckshop was better supplied with a certain variety of sweets than other schools' tuckshops'. In some studies (for example Furlong, 1984; Mac an Ghaill, 1988 — *see* chapter 4) there were contradictory feelings among some of the pupils. Expressions of 'liking' for schools, therefore, have to be tracked down. It cannot be assumed that they are in response to the official programme.

Pupils certainly like teachers to be human. Frequent mention is made of 'being able to talk to teachers'. Gannaway (1976), for example, found that an English teacher was liked and respected because 'you could really sort of talk to her' (p. 57). This contrasts with the following example where the root problem is seen by the students to be one of communication. The exchange is part of a conversation between a researcher and some fifth-form girls. It concerns a young, female, probationary English teacher and a group of girls whom several teachers found difficult. The girls were in a non-examination form, felt by them and by many of their teachers to be an irrelevance within the school. The teacher had slapped one of the girls across the face during a lesson, and a general riot ensued. The girls' account went like this:

Kate: You can't talk to her.

Others: No, you can't.

Kate: When she 'it you, it weren't even you, were it?

Deirdre: No, she 'it me for nothing.

Sandra: Then we all started shouting at her and she said 'Sorry'.

Deirdre: Yeah, she said 'I'm ever so sorry!'

Sandra: We all said 'You didn't 'ave to 'it 'er!' She went off 'er rocker, so she grabbed 'old of Deirdre, slapped 'er round the face, and she said 'You'll come down to Miss Jarvis' (senior mistress), got to the door and there was a riot.

Researcher: Did you all join in?

Beverley: Yeah, we all sort of went against 'er, shouting at 'er why was she 'itting Deirdre for nothing, and we just turned round, chucked our pencils all over the place, said 'Right! We're not doing no more work!' an' we sat there, didn't we? (Woods, 1984: 129)

This account was confirmed in almost every detail by the teacher concerned. She said she did her best, but found the group very difficult and felt she didn't understand them. They were not like any girls she was used to, and didn't respond as she anticipated. She admitted she overreacted in the incident in question. My interpretation of this is that the teacher was operating within a model of teaching and control that perhaps she was familiar with when herself a pupil but which was inappropriate in this situation. The incident brought matters to a head, but the underlying cause is perhaps conveyed in the girls' first statement: 'You can't talk to her . . . No, you can't!' these pupils above all, in their peripheral situation within the school, needed someone they could talk to, not someone who was going to try to enforce conventional teaching upon them and apply punitive sanctions. This incident is a further illustration of the power of pupils to influence the process of establishing and maintaining order.

Another of the criteria of humanity is whether teachers are able and prepared to 'have a laugh' with you. Jokes 'free things up', they are a way of making relationships more intimate (Walker and Goodson, 1977). Sharing a joke means making an alliance — against, perhaps, threatening aspects of work or the school. Humour eases interaction when it has got into embarrassing or otherwise difficult situations. It is a great leveller, for though the teacher is in authority over them, it shows that basically he or she is one of them. Over time, teacher and pupils may develop a common framework of meanings characterized by humour, which may seem rather recondite to an outside observer (as with the 'Horace' joke described earlier). Of course, there can be no guarantee that if the teacher 'had a laugh' with them, it would 'work'. If misused, it could worsen the situation. Connell *et al.* (1982: 101) quote a girl who disliked a teacher because he was 'boring. He cracks jokes that aren't funny. And then gets annoyed when everyone doesn't laugh.' As Stebbins (1980: 84) says, 'Using humour is like driving on a poorly maintained road; one does so at one's own risk. A practical joke may be carried off with the hope of generating amiability, but be defined by the subject as an aggressive, irritating act. Funning may turn into teasing where banter becomes ridicule'.

Nor does this emphasis on humour and laughter (explored in more detail in chapter 7) mean that pupils simply have a 'good time' orientation towards school. For the laughter has to be seen for the most part within a context where they expect to 'work' and to 'learn'. In fact, most pupils of all types say they want to work, and that a good teacher is one who makes you work and teaches you something. In Delamont's girls' private school, a good teacher 'makes you learn very, very hard . . . she really gets you to learn . . . She's especially well organized . . . keeps you working all the time . . . doesn't let you stop for a minute' (Delamont, 1976: 75). But the same was true for Furlong's low-stream Afro-Caribbean girls, who were considered 'difficult' by their teachers:

Q: Which are your best subjects?

Carol: I think the two subjects I work hardest in are . . .

Q: How much do you think it's the teacher or the subject — is it just 'cos you like the subject or what?

Valerie: The teachers, you know, you can't talk in Mr Marks' lessons, you just have to work . . . . So after a while you work and you enjoy it because you're learning a lot (Furlong, 1977: 173).

Definitions of 'work' might vary, but the activity is seen as important. Thus, the working-class Pacific island girls in Jones' (1989) research in New Zealand secondary school also rated teachers on their ability to provide notes to copy. They would reward or punish teachers who did not provide them with what they considered 'appropriate work'. The middle-class Pakeha (European) girls saw the teacher more as a 'manipulable resource' rather than just a provider of information. 'Doing school work' involved their active participation, and they, similarly, would use strategies to induce teacher conformity.

To Joanne in Connell *et al.*'s (1982) study (not herself an academic high-flyer), 'a "good teacher" is someone who is successful at persuasion, who stimulates participation . . . she doesn't like teachers who are completely slack, who just let the class rabble' — a view 'almost universally held' by the pupils Connell and his team talked to (p. 102). Lynn Davies (1984) found that girls of all abilities in the Midlands comprehensive school she studied preferred women staff to be mature, respectable and essentially conservative — not 'flighty' or inspired like Miss Jean Brodie. In Bronwyn Davies's Australian primary school,

> The constant concern of the children is that work should be done. The harassed [teacher] would probably have been astonished if he had realized how anxious they were to be getting on with their work. Linda . . . hankers after a more structured work situation than currently exists. Given more structure, she claims, she can 'work more solidly'. (Davies, 1980: 15)

Even the apparently most anarchic pupils may want to work. Davies and Munro (1987) show this in their analysis of the behaviour of Lenny, a young Aboriginal pupil in an Australian school, who seemed to be 'running amuck' and resisting all the teacher's efforts to teach him. Careful study of the videotape, however, revealed several indications that he knew that classrooms were about work. He attempted to gain the teacher's attention, albeit in some unconventional forms, though he used other, more conventional body signals. He showed disappointment at the lack of response (her preferred 'control' strategy), and explicitly stated at times that he wanted to work. At the bottom of the disjuncture between Lenny and his teacher seemed different perceptions of the classroom. The teacher envisaged a traditional situation with pupils getting on with their work and responding to teacher cues. Lenny referred to his teacher as 'Mr Kotter', a character in a book series who was once a 'Sweathog' like his pupils. When he returns to his old school as teacher, he speaks the pupils' language, shares their style, capitalizes on their unconventional behaviour, and responds to them with 'humour and wisdom'. This, Davies and Munro argue, holds the key to Lenny's perception of the teaching-learning situation. However, the teacher rejects Lenny's preferred style and only makes learning available to him under conditions which he finds intolerable' (p. 129). There is much dependence on 'relationships' and 'negotiation' in the activity of work, and these aspects are pursued in chapter 6.

For the moment we might note that one important factor governing relationships is 'control'. Interestingly, Mr Kotter, while entering the pupils' world, retains control. Rosser and Harré's pupils felt 'insulted by weakness on the part of those in authority who they expect to be strong, and this weakness, once established, provokes more playing up' (1976: 38). Furlong also found that the most important distinction pupils made among teachers was to do with their ability to keep order and to make 'trouble'. They were either 'strict', when they were taken seriously, or they were 'soft', when pupils played them up mercilessly. Gannaway's (1976) pupils were similar. They could make a 'non-starter' cry or 'a mad woodwork teacher' lose his temper. Though some might see such pupil actions as unfair and unfeeling, they are, as Gannaway points out, very moral actions since 'they are concerned with the basic quality necessary to establish a relationship with a teacher' (Gannaway, 1976: 55), as discussed earlier. Beynon's (1985) boys also believed in firm discipline, but thought that it was a male attribute, which made it difficult for women teachers unless they were old enough to be the pupils' mother. Foster's (1988: 382) pupils did not like teachers who tried to impose their authority too forcefully. They were 'pushing their luck' or 'getting above themselves'. Mac an Ghaill's (1988) 'Rasta Heads' (*see* chapter 5) did not like 'tough', authoritarian teachers, who ruled by fear, but nor did either set of pupils respect those they considered 'soft'. Davies' (1984: 32) girls, similarly, had little respect for 'saft' teachers. 'Soft' teachers, in fact, came bottom of the list with Dubberley's (1988: 198) working-class pupils:

> Pupils were contemptuous of 'water works', and insisted that staff should be able to 'stand up for themselves'. They were angry because they couldn't teach you anything and if asked whether they shouldn't feel sorry for such teachers, the retort was that they should have thought about that when they came into teaching.

There are clearly degrees of control, and teachers may be 'too strict'. In this, they may be 'unfair', which was one of the biggest offences teachers could commit according to Rosser and Harré's pupils (1976). Some of the worst sins they noted were unfair comparison with a brother or sister, being 'put down' or 'picked on', and suffering penalties unrelated to particular rule infractions.

As well as personal victimization, the cultivation of favourites and 'pets' is equally despised. Fairness also involves consistency and predictability. Lynn Davies (1984) found that the girls she studied were especially outraged at contradictions in teacher behaviour, for example when they demanded good manners from the pupils but showed bad manners themselves. Another example of inconsistency comes from Bronwyn Davies in an Australian primary school. She concluded that:

> Where punishment follows rule-breaking it is indeed critical for children to know precisely what each adult defines as right and wrong, and thus what they can expect will follow from 'wrong' behaviour. They felt angry if they made predictions concerning the normative pattern and these turned out to be wrong. If their predictions succeeded for some length of time and then failed, they felt the adult had betrayed their trust and was unworthy as a teacher: a highly-favoured teacher could in these circumstances, become an object of derision. (Davies, 1982: 121)

This is an important point. It is the teacher's unpredictability in such instances, destroying the pupils' sense of equilibrium, which leads to anger, not the fact that he or she may have punished them (*see also* Geer, 1977).

Teachers' rule, therefore, must be equable. They must allow a degree of freedom within an ordered framework and, as we have noted, be capable of 'having a laugh', and remaining 'human'. They must control in a way that makes sense to pupils, not necessarily applying the heavy hand. For example, two particularly successful teachers of disruptive pupils made their authority personal:

> I won't be regarded as the stereotype 40-year-old teacher . . . I don't keep the barriers up like some traditional teachers who say never be friendly with the kids . . . if I'm feeling awful one morning and I'm taking the register, I'll say "Look, I'm feeling dreadful this morning, so for God's sake, shut up" — not just "Shut up!" I mean I'm human and they've got to know it. And in that they see me as different — but not anti-authority. (Grundsell, 1980: 73)

Pupils said of the other teacher, 'You can talk to him like you want to talk to him. If you want to do something, he'll say you can do it or he'll say you can't.' Another said, 'Anytime you'd get mad, he'd get mad as well . . . that's how he used to teach — if I picked up a chair to hit him, he'd pick up a chair to hit me — though he never once done this. (*ibid*: 71).

The qualities of 'control', 'humour' and 'humanity' are also evident in Walker and Goodson's (1977) secondary-modern school teacher, who is a 'joker', but a serious one. He uses a lot of self-deprecatory jokes, for it helps the self-images of his kids, which are fairly low. But he never starts with jokes, but always establishes the formal boundaries and relationships first. He himself draws the contrast with another teacher who had difficulty with pupils, not because he joked, but because 'he was weak and he couldn't make things stick, and he was using jokes as a way out of that' (p. 207). Ron, on the other hand, is 'always' aware that 'I am the teacher . . . and that my fundamental job there is to be a teacher, I think it would be patently false to say I was a mate, and that's all, because I'm not. I'm a mate, I'll joke, but in the end I'm trying to get them to do something, and one knows that' (*ibid.*). This appears to be the sort of approach that most pupils welcome, for it recognizes the distinction between teacher role and person and tries to meet the responsibilities of both.

However, even if a teacher successfully establishes all these conditions to the approval of pupils, it cannot be assumed that they make the same sort of sense of lessons as the teachers. It is not always realized how recondite the teacher's lessons sometimes are, or what pupils understand by 'work' and 'learning'. The gulf between some pupils' and teachers' understandings is vividly illustrated by Grundsell (1978). Though his account derives from his work in a truancy centre, there is evidence that such perspectives are not uncommon among pupils generally (Furlong, 1977; Woods, 1979; Barnes, 1969). Some pupils do attach high currency to teachers who are capable of 'explaining' what they mean (Nash, 1976; Woods, 1979; Turner, 1983), and 'understanding' may represent the high point of learning. But for many it is a luxury they feel is not for them. Grundsell's pupils, for example, were not all interested in 'understanding':

> What they demanded was 'chalk and talk', the more chalk the better: plenty of writing on the board, numbered points one, two and three to be copied into their books. Lessons got their value rating according to the number of pages filled. A.J. loved the copying down — it was real progress to him. Asked to explain what he had written, he felt outraged — it was a double-cross. He had achieved the aim of the lesson by writing everything down. To be told that

the aim was something else, actually understanding, was a cruel deception. (Grundsell, 1978: 48)

Another pupil had an almost photographic memory. She learnt work, and whether she understood it or not was beside the point: 'I said it all right, didn't I? Well then, shut your face. What more do you want?' (*ibid*). One boy learnt — and understood — a great deal of geography from accompanying his lorry-driver father on trips. But this was jealously guarded as part of his non-transferable private life. To some, learning was a mysterious code, the key to which was understood by teachers and some pupils; but for them, they had to cover up their failings (and possible humiliation) as best they could. What the pupils at the centre wanted, therefore, was:

> Structure and safety — neat self-contained packages of learning where we taught and they learnt. With the 'worst' kind of teaching method they felt secure; a fixed target, a fixed time-span, results they could see and measure. Copying maps from the board of places they neither knew nor cared about, the kids settled in peaceful silence. We could watch their faces relax as the anxiety died away. The anxiety was that they would be asked to give and think, when they supposed they had nothing to give or think with. (*Ibid*: 49–50)

The curious thing about these habitual truants was that, although they had rejected conventional schooling, conventional schooling's rejection of them led them to seek security behind the strategies they had devised in 'proper lessons'.

These perspectives on teachers seem to be fairly widely distributed across the generality of pupils. Of course pupils are not necessarily united in these views, and there are many different shades and nuances of outlook among them. In some respects, groups of pupils are markedly different in their views, especially where these are associated with sources external to the classroom and school. I turn to some of the more prominent of these external factors in the next three chapters. This chapter has considered the part played by pupils in establishing order within the classroom, how it is done, the principles they bring to bear, and how they view teachers and teaching. It has been shown that, despite the sometimes conflictual nature of teacher-pupil relationships, including the rough and tumble of some initial encounters, the majority of pupils appear to have a basic orientation towards school which allows for some negotiation with the official programme. The main point is nicely summed up by Docking (1987: 79) 'Productive relationships in schools depend upon treating pupils with respect, being sensitive to their feelings and avoiding public, derogatory comments . . . Pupils respect teachers who are firm and who punish justly; but they also want to be treated as persons, individuals whose feelings matter and who are inherently responsible agents.'

Chapter 2

Organizing and Responding to Difference

Although pupils may share certain basic orientations, there are important differences among them. Some of the key differences arise from pupil cultures, especially those connected with social class, gender and 'race'. Some, it is argued, are induced by the organization and processes within the school. In the next two chapters I shall consider the implications of these cultural differences for pupil perspectives and school experiences. I shall discuss school organization and social class in this chapter, and gender and 'race' in chapters 3 and 4. This is for convenience of treatment rather than any real separation. As will be seen, there is considerable overlap among them.

Cultures

Dubbs and Whitney (1980: 27) define 'culture' as:

> ... cognitive, i.e. consisting of shared ideas, strategies, plans, and guidelines that are shared with others and learned from early childhood, not genetically transmitted. It forms the basis which individuals perceive and artifacts are the outward manifestations of these shared guidelines.

Cultures are thus social, shared, systemic, cognitive, learned. They include values and beliefs, rules and codes of conduct and behaviour, forms of language, patterns of speech and choice of words, understandings about ways of doing things and not doing things. Through ordinary processes of socialization people are inducted into many cultures, perhaps of a particular social class, religious, occupational, or ethnic nature. There will also be 'subcultures', distinct groups that, while being part of larger cultures in certain key respects, have their own particular refinements of them and their own particular concerns. One's part in cultures or one's use of them may not be consciously recognized. Rather one grows into them and may view them as a natural way of life. Contrasting cultures may therefore be seen as 'unnatural' or wrong. Thus the phenomenon of culture 'clash' or 'conflict' when two incompatible groups come together; and culture 'shock' when an individual enters a new culture for the first time. Much school and classroom disorder and disruption appears to be of this nature.

Culture clashes from my own experience include starting at the grammar school at age eleven, where I met a strange hostility from many of the staff (they had been forced to open their doors to all children passing the eleven-plus examination regardless of social class); and during teacher training, when I was sent to 'Toughboys Secondary Modern' where a peculiar 'culture of the stick' prevailed. The stick was the dominant symbol of this school, even more so than at my old grammar school. Every teacher had one, and replacements could be bought from the headmaster. It was essential equipment. As teachers left the staffroom, their stick penetrated fore and aft through their books, papers, boxes and other paraphernalia. One break time, a teacher who had mislaid his stick went into a frenzied panic exclaiming 'I can't teach without my stick!' However, while the cane was used frequently, it was only as a token or ritual tapping of the hands — nothing like the full-blooded swipes delivered to our bottoms when pupils for cutting our fingers. In theory, it seemed, the stick could easily have been dispensed with; in practice, it could not. It would have so undermined the teachers' confidence as to affect their whole performance, and pupils would have perceived teachers without canes as deviants, perhaps 'not proper teachers' (Sikes *et al.*, 1985). Teachers beginning at this school had to learn when and how to use the cane, and for what reasons. Deviations would invite penalty because that particular way of life had become so established in the school.

Uncommon behaviour is not the only, or main, cause of culture clash. What is important is what is understood. An example of this from my experience was when I moved from one school to take up an appointment in a school in a different area. The pupils at this second school seemed to me excessively familiar and rude compared to those in the first. My first thoughts were that this was some kind of testing- or sussing-out, and I responded with what I considered appropriate firmness. This rather upset them, because in fact they were only being friendly. I discovered this in due course from observing general relationships within the school and how other teachers behaved. Different codes of conduct prevailed in the two schools. The same behaviour was imbued with different meaning.

To understand pupil activity, therefore, it is necessary to explore the understandings that they attach to it and whence they arise. Two important influences are school organization and social class.

School Organization

Up until the late 1960s, sociologists of education in Britain, despite some great achievement in exposing the class-related nature of pupils' educational progress and attainment, had not penetrated the internal system and processes of the school. Studies typically focused on what went in and what came out, rather than on what happened in between. On some occasions when schools were examined, the input-output influence remained, as in Dale and Griffith's (1966) study of 'Downstream'. They wanted to know why some pupils deteriorated, and they took as their criterion demotion to lower streams. School policy and processes and teacher practices were not considered, and, not surprisingly perhaps, the researchers found a strong association between deterioration and parental background. The possibility that the school might have screened them out for that reason, and that teacher and pupil attitudes and subsequent interaction had been influenced as a consequence, was not countenanced.

The Manchester-based studies of Hargreaves (1967) and Lacey (1970) changed all that, giving strong indications of how social factors within the school contributed to pupil careers and achievement. I was a practising teacher on a master's course when Hargreaves' book, *Social Relations in a Secondary School*, first appeared. I can still remember the excitement we felt in reading about *real* pupils and *real* experiences. As with many such books that initiate new trends, there was a certain daring, risk-taking iconoclasm about this breaching of the sacred school walls. One concern was whether any more similar researches would be permitted. Nowadays, of course, they are commonplace, having survived a brief phase of 'teacher-bashing' in the early 1970s, when exuberance at discovering new terrain led to some of the natives getting trampled underfoot. Further, while, naturally, these studies have lost their novelty impact, their central message is just as relevant today.

'Lumley Secondary School for Boys' (Hargreaves, 1967) streamed pupils by ability and achievement. Hargreaves concentrated on the fourth year (then the final year of compulsory schooling), which consisted of some hundred boys divided into five streams, 4A to 4E. Over the year, he identified among the boys two distinct large cultures (or subcultures, since they were enclosed within the school), which he labelled academic and delinquescent. The former took shape in the higher streams, the latter in the lower.

They had contrasting value-systems. The academic subculture appeared to be in favour of academic achievement, dedication to school work, high attendance, punctuality and a high standard of dress and hygiene, and opposed to misbehaviour, physical aggression and copying. The extraordinary thing about the delinquescent group, by contrast, is that they are not just different but seem exactly the converse — opposed to academic achievement and school values in general, and for 'mucking about' and 'having a laugh', fighting, absenteeism, copying and so on. Why should this be so?

Hargreaves argues that within each class friendship groups form, pupils interact together, come to know what to expect of each other, and develop common values and certain patterns of behaviour. These, in turn, come to 'control and regulate the behaviour of the group' (1967: 8). For boys in high streams, school life will be a rewarding experience, as the school system confers status upon them. Society rewards achievement, and the school, with its emphasis on academic achievement and its importance for future occupation, reflects the values associated with that factor. High-stream boys are therefore geared positively into the system.

Low-stream boys at Lumley, however, were double failures, having failed the eleven-plus, and now being consigned to the bottom group of the initial 'failures'. It was thus being made continually more difficult for them to achieve and to acquire status through the official system. Their solution was to reject the values of the school, and indeed to stand them on their head and develop a culture of their own based on their exact opposite. Hargreaves thus saw the culture of a large number of pupils opposed to school primarily as an anti- or counter-culture, that is, as a reaction to the official culture of the school. In this, he was influenced by the deviance theory of A.K. Cohen (1955). Cohen developed his cultural reaction theory during his studies of gang delinquency in the United States, wherein he identified a delinquent subculture, which he saw as primarily a response to status problems associated mainly with the male, working-class role. Upward mobility is governed, he argued, by middle-class criteria of status — ambition, self-reliance, deferred gratification, good manners, opposition to physical violence, and respect for property. Working-class homes are less likely to produce young people with the ability to do well in terms of these criteria. They consequently experience failure in middle-class terms, and thus status-frustration, which they repair by inverting middle-class criteria and awarding status to values and activities which are their direct opposite — rejection of conformity, short-term hedonism, opposition to authority and so forth. This turning upside-down of middle-class criteria is the essence of the theory. Cohen emphasizes the importance of the group, whose members all experience the same problems and work out a joint solution. Hargreaves' study suggests how groups of pupils, initially predisposed to accept or reject values by their home backgrounds, may be encouraged both in their rejection of middle-class criteria and in the formation of a counter-cultural response by the organization of the school.

Colin Lacey's (1970) study was done in 'Hightown Grammar' whose boys had all passed the eleven-plus and thus were a fairly homogeneous group in terms of ability; yet a similar phenomenon was observed, i.e. the development of pro-school and anti-school cultures. Lacey argued that this development was assisted by the processes of what he termed 'differentiation' and 'polarization'. 'Differentiation' refers to the streaming practices of the school. After being in unstreamed groups in year one, pupils were streamed in four classes. This, therefore, emphasized differences in academic performance and behaviour, and allocated different resources to the two groups (the lower streams being given the poorer teachers, poorer rooms, etc.). The 'good' are rewarded, and the 'bad' punished. The two groups are faced with different problems, one of success, one of failure. 'Polarization' is a process which is then, over time, promoted by the pupils in response to these problems. For example, after six months of streaming in the second year, friendship choices were becoming increasingly confined to the form, and pro- and anti-school tendencies in top and bottom streams respectively were becoming increasingly evident. Lacey noted that already the bottom stream was regarded as a difficult form to teach, and was exhibiting some of the features of an anti-school culture. For example, symptoms of emotional disturbance, which in the early stages were mainly individual, were now being expressed mainly in group attitudes. This high priority given to collective behaviour and regard among the anti-school boys developed because, for them, the rewards of status can only come from the group, whereas in the pro-school cultures rewards came from individual effort in competition with others.

Hargreaves and Lacey made many qualifications to their argument, and they recognized the possibly strong influence of other factors, such as neighbourhood and social class. Lacey, for example, notes that 'As with all models, [his] is a simplification of reality . . . individuals operate with more than one set of norms . . . [and] behave differently in different situations' (p. 91). Much, for example, would depend on the teacher. The counter-culture would perhaps not be evident with an 'ideal' teacher. But such teaching is rare and/or difficult to sustain, and the basic pattern remains: the formation of two contrasting cultures within the school in response to its hierarchical structure, which opens up the pathways of success to one group and closes them off to the other. It is tempting to think that this research helped to modify streaming practices. However, streaming by no means disappeared, continuing to operate in subtle ways within mixed-ability groups, and more obviously in 'banding' and 'setting', the typical mode of organization in comprehensive schools. Did these adjustments affect the formation of polarized cultures?

Stephen Ball (1981) thought not. He almost exactly replicated the Lacey study nearly ten years later, but in a coeducational comprehensive school ('Beachside') which practised a degree of mixed-ability teaching. It also practised 'banding', dividing intakes into three broad groups on the basis of ability. The third group, largely remedial and smaller than the others, was not considered a disciplinary problem by staff. The real divide came between bands 1 and 2, and they seem to reflect perfectly the pro- and anti-school cultures of the previous studies. In turn, the teachers construct stereotypes. Ball presents these composites of teacher views:

> The band 1 child
> 'Has academic potential . . . will do O-levels . . . and a good number will stay on to the sixth form . . . likes doing projects . . . knows what the teacher wants . . . is bright, alert and enthusiastic . . . can concentrate . . . produces neat work . . . is interested . . . wants to get on . . . is grammar school material . . . you can have discussions with . . . friendly . . . rewarding . . . has common sense.'

> The band 2 child
> 'Is not interested in school work . . . difficult to control . . . rowdy and lazy . . . has little self-control . . . is immature . . . loses and forgets books with monotonous regularity . . . cannot take part in

discussions . . . is moody . . . of low standard . . . technical inability . . . lacks concentration . . . is poorly behaved . . . not up to much
academically.' (Ball, 1981: 38–9)

These two groups appear similar to those identified in the earlier studies. The
representation also suggests the reinforcing impact such teacher views might
have on individual pupils in the groups. Ball argues that these teacher
perceptions exist independently of any particular forms or pupils. Once
assigned, pupils are labelled accordingly. Moreover, it only needs a 'single cue'
in behaviour, real or alleged, for teachers to bring the whole stereotype to bear.
For band 2 children, this 'imposes certain limitations upon the sort of social
identity that may be negotiated'.

While Ball was at the school, the banding system was changed to one of
mixed-ability groups. This presented the opportunity for a 'natural
experiment' (Hammersley *et al.* 1985). If the development of polarized groups
is a purely organizational matter which the school can repair, one would
expect that mixed-ability classes would do it. If they do not, we must look for
some other factor. As far as the formation of a larger anti-school culture is
concerned, this strategy did seem to work. The social climate in lessons
improved and traditional band 2 type 'trouble spots' disappeared. The anti-
school groupings in the mixed-ability forms were neither 'large enough nor
coherent enough to dominate the ethos of any form' (pp.251–2). If they
looked as if they might become so, pupils could be moved easily between
classes. Ball argues that 'the absence of an anti-school subculture was related to
the removal of the fixed status structure embodied in the banding system.
Pupils no longer had to contend with the identity problems and threats to self-
esteem created by allocation to bands 2 or 3' (1984: 29). Furlong (1985: 98),
working in a 'liberal comprehensive', also found 'the lack of explicit
differentiation appeared to reduce the more extreme forms of disaffection'.
However, while there were no signs of a coherent anti-school culture at
Beachside, there was some social separation between groups, so that *some*
polarization occurred. For example, by the end of the third year, pupils were
choosing as friends others of the same social class and achievement level.

More recently, Abraham (1989a) set out to explore the extent to which
the theory was applicable to a setted comprehensive school in the south of
England. One of the assumptions in the theory is that there is a positive
relationship between academic performance and behaviour as judged by school
criteria. Abraham's findings supported this both within and between sets.

Further, he found strong evidence of polarization following the change from mixed-ability in the first year to streamed sets in the second using such indicators as time spent on homework, missed assignment reports, and regular teacher reports on 'good' and 'bad' behaviour. However, polarization appeared to decrease in the third and fourth years, though it was always greater than the first year and there is some evidence that differentiation between sets decreased in the fourth year, though not the third. He reasons that 'interset differentiation is not the sole agent in creating pro- and anti-school values which give rise to polarization' (p. 61). He suggests that the beginning of examination and career pressure in the third year exerted sufficient pro-school pressure on the middle sets as to outweigh any anti-school increases among other middle set pupils, the overall result being a fall-off in the indicators between second and third years. There was also a sharp increase in the indicators for the top band, which he feels is both a sign and a result of increased pressure on the pupils. A factor probably helping to reduce differentiation in the fourth year is the onset of subject options, producing an overlap between the two bands, and allowing pupils to some extent to choose subjects they like and to discard others (though see below for a contrary argument). Friendship patterns supported the general theory, though there were many more isolates in the class under examination than in comparable classes in previous research, even though some of them may have been anti-school. Overall, Abraham concludes that setting 'creates a more dispersed form' of polarization, which is exactly what would have been predicted under a less severe form of differentiation.

Troman (1988) however, disputes that setting is less severe. It depends, of course, on how it is operationalized. In his study of how pupils were allocated to maths sets in a 9–13 years middle school the criteria upon which teachers made decisions ensured the continuance of previous structures. The aim was to create homogeneous ability groups. But teachers did not employ measures of ability, such as results from NFER non-verbal tests and IQ tests, nor first school reports, preferring knowledge gained from 'pupil performance in class (behaviour, conformity to classroom rules, classwork), knowledge of siblings, knowledge of previous first year sets and in some cases the physical appearance of the pupil' (p. 420). Troman comments that such selection procedures 'made the former eleven-plus appear as an objective instrument of social justice by comparison'. He feels that there may be a trend towards more covert, but more efficient, forms of selection, in which teacher typifications based on such indices as described above prevail over more objective measures (*see also* Broadfoot, 1986). One would assume that in these circumstances polarization would develop apace, especially if the same criteria were used across the curriculum for all allocations. Since they seemed part of the general occupational culture, this was probably the case in that particular school.

D-p theory has inspired others researching other sectors and situations of the educational system. Burke (1986), for example, considered its relevance in a sixth-form college; Foster in a multi-ethnic comprehensive school working a declared anti-racist policy; while Rosie (1988) used it as a starting point for his study of the experiences of a group of school-leavers with special needs who underwent Youth Training Scheme training. Here, students were differentiated according to academic and behavioural criteria in college and on performance in work experience. However, Rosie found two forms of differentiation, one based on official policy lines, the other on a more integrated model involving more general principles of transition for young people across settings such as work experience, college training and home and family lives. Three student groups developed over the year — 'insiders, independence seekers and outsiders' — as the students developed cultural resources from home and among themselves to cope with the YTS course and their own needs, and they were fairly discrete and polarized, taking on identities of their own and rejecting the other groups. This, therefore, is another useful demonstration of the theory working under different conditions, and provides Finch (1988) in the same volume with an 'opportunity to highlight a wholly admirable example of ethnographers continuing to build upon each other's work' (pp. 197–8).

What if contrary indications are found? Some other researchers have indeed found lower-band boys as keen on the need to do well as upper-band (Quine, 1974, Stanley, 1989). But then, as Downey (1977: 22) observes, 'It would certainly be rash to assume that streaming in all secondary schools would necessarily have the same consequences ...' School organization, neighbourhood, school ethos, LEA policy, resource-provision — are all variables that might have a bearing on the theory. We have to continue to explore the conditions under which it works, and those under which it does not, seeking to account for the latter and thus progressively refine the theory.

Lacey himself, for example, found pupils who did not fit the general pattern. Priestley was a middle-class drop-out whose preferred subjects, commerce and economics, were not part of the school curriculum. Cready was a working-class success, whose participation in the school was secured through his great interest in singing in the choir. If the school had sponsored economics instead of music these boys may well have conformed more to type. As it is, they are good illustrations of how individuals can deviate from the general pattern.

Social Class

All of the studies mentioned so far in this chapter relate their findings to social class in some way. Hargreaves, for example, presents some evidence that high-stream boys at Lumley tended to come from homes more oriented to middle-class values than those of lower-stream boys; and that such values were indeed those espoused by the school (ambition, self-reliance, hard work, long-term aims, planning, good manners, control of aggression, respect for property — 1967: 166–8). In reacting directly against those values, the lower-stream boys were then in a sense constructing a social-class solution to the problem the school had presented them with.

In Lacey's school there was a clear connection between the internal selection processes and the social class of the pupils (counting manual workers as working class, and professional, business, clerical and non-manual as middle class). There was a higher proportion of middle-class than working-class pupils initially allocated to the higher streams, and this tendency increased over the years. One factor behind this tendency was working-class parents' lack of knowledge and experience of grammar schools, and their difficulty therefore in providing the same kind of cultural resource for their children as middle-class parents in that particular context. Parental encouragement was an important factor, and Lacey saw the conflict in schools as one between teams, consisting of pupils and parents, competing in the school for restricted prizes.

Ball also concluded that, at Beachside, 'working-class pupils tend to percolate downwards in the processes of academic and behavioural differentiation' (1981: 108). There was a high proportion of middle-class pupils in band 1, and friendship choices and academic and behavioural attitudes showed a strong connection with social class. More middle-class than working-class pupils improved in academic achievement between years one and two, and fewer deteriorated. The mixed-ability system did not bring about any marked increase in social mixing. Achievement and social class continued to be strongly related. Furthermore, middle-class pupils now tended to dominate the 'success' roles in all the school classes studied by Ball, whereas within the banding system working-class pupils had at least had access to such roles. Ball concludes that, given the school's emphasis on achievement and competition and teachers' encouragement of 'talented' pupils, 'the mixed-ability form-group appears to reproduce a microcosm of the banding system, with the processes of differentiation and polarization taking place within each form-group' (p. 273). Mixed-ability groups therefore may have solved a problem for the school, but not for the pupils. This point is emphasized by Furlong (1984: 98), who felt that mixed-ability groups only postponed differentiation until public examinations at the end of the pupil careers, and wondered if 'concealing the inevitable leads to even greater disappointment and hostility once the secret is out'.

Abraham (1989a), too, noted a social-class connection. 'Setting' technically allows for flexibility, that is a pupil might be in a high set for one subject, and a low one for another. However, there was a certain rigidity of setting across the important academic subjects of English, mathematics and French, yielding clearly identifiable 'top' and 'bottom' groups. The former showed a high correlation with non-manual and the latter with manual social class groupings. In Troman's (1988) study also, while he himself does not specifically relate his findings to social class, it will be seen that the criteria upon which decisions were made would militate against pupils from working-class backgrounds, that is, those with less cultural capital.

Dubberley (1988a), researching in an 11–16 mixed comprehensive school in a mining village in the Yorkshire coalfield, graphically illustrates the nature of such cultural capital, and the degree of cultural difference between the working-class pupils in the bottom sets and the middle-class staff. There were marked differences, for example, in pupils' and teachers' use of language, with teachers assuming a monopoly of propriety and seeking to correct pupils in arbitrary and deprecatory fashion. Pupils' own knowledge was discounted, and they were treated 'as though yer thick', which other ('posh') pupils were not. As in Hargreaves' and Lacey's schools, different resources were allocated to top and bottom sets, the 'style of teaching, content and commitment' varying considerably. Thus the capital of those who already had it was reinforced. The general feeling of teachers of the others seemed to be 'if yer not willing ter work I'm not bothered abaht yer' (p. 185). They saw the pupils' culture as defective, and, further, held them personally responsible. There was little appreciation of the very distinctive culture of the local mining community. Again, it was considered defective and 'parochial'. Teachers 'shouldn't go down to their level . . . they're too introspective . . . it's the club and pub syndrome' (p. 197). Dubberley concludes that 'working-class pupils fare as badly as ever in our schools if not worse . . . most teachers seem reluctant to appreciate or understand working-class culture with consequent disastrous results for the pupils' (p. 200). 'Setting', therefore, is no answer to the differentiation associated with streaming. Inasmuch as the aim of comprehensivization was to tackle such divisions, as Abraham (p. 75) notes, 'there is a glaring contradiction in a comprehensive practice which contributes to social class related polarization'. But then any such organizational device on its own seems weak beside the kind of cultural forces described by Dubberley.

This includes 'subject choice'. In my study of this process at Lowfield (Woods, 1979), I identified a pro- and an anti-school group, similar to those of the above researchers. These groups experienced different curricula, different teachers, teaching styles and aims which reinforced their differences in the fourth and fifth years, when they were allocated to 'examination' or 'non-examination' streams respectively. Their own 'choices' apparently had guided them in these directions. But what was the character of that choice? In their third year I had identified among them two broad 'group perspectives' which owed something to social class background. This showed the two groups employing different interpretive models, distinguished by instrumentalism and interest on the one hand, and social and counter-institutional factors on the other. In making their choices of subject, the conformist, pro-school pupils employed with some spirit the criteria of job-relatedness, their own ability at the subject, the learning situation, and interest. The 'counter-cultural' pupils, with some diffidence, considered whether the subject was hard work, examination-governed, 'nasty and horrible', boring, and whether it allowed them to be with friends and to have a certain amount of freedom.

Ball (1981) found teachers at Beachside Comprehensive operating with a notion of 'appropriateness', that is there were deemed to be appropriate routes through the subject choice process for different bands. Banding typifications in terms of 'suitable for "O" level' or different programmes of study held of individuals even when they deviated from the overall pattern. Ryrie *et al.* (1979) found something similar in Scottish schools. They concluded that 'the pattern of subjects studied by pupils results from mutually accepted assumptions on the part of pupils, teachers and parents about which subjects were *appropriate* for pupils of different types and abilities and that they tended to choose those subjects "naturally" as a matter of course.'

Closely linked to the notion of appropriateness is that of departmental and subject status and the hierarchy of knowledge. Ball related this to the time-honoured tripartite division, which goes back to Plato, and still remains, despite comprehensivization. Three types of pupils, it was claimed — the academic, the practical, and the general — required different types of curriculum. One can thus distinguish among academic ('O' level) subjects, practical (non-theoretical) subjects, and general (Ball terms the latter 'sink' subjects — they have little value in the job market). Teachers had the task of guiding pupils into appropriate channels. Connell *et al.* (1982) refer to these hierarchically organized bodies of academic knowledge as the 'hegemonic curriculum.' A vital feature is the organization of learning as individual competition, which was against the working-class family's practices of collective coping. One of its effects is to marginalize other forms of knowledge, and this is colluded in by pupils and parents. Thus a brilliant music programme at one school was regarded as a 'waste of time' by 'good' students. Highly creative children who do not fit the formal mould are regarded as disruptives. In dealing with such children, teachers develop an alternative curriculum, often containing a deal of practical and relevant knowledge; but it is also a subordinate curriculum. Other teachers have to struggle to establish and maintain their subjects (Goodson, 1983). This encourages the promotion of those students likely to enhance their subject and teacher status, and the discouragement of those who might have the opposite effect. It is possible to identify a range of teacher strategies to induce 'appropriate' choices by these various criteria — such as establishing pupil identities as successes or failures, 'frightening off', establishing 'fair procedures', 'weeding out' (*see* Woods, 1979).

The tension between individual choice and social selection is all too obvious. Hurman (1978) showed that subject choice did free up the system to some extent, but felt that it was more of a 'lubricant' than a radical change, devised in response to problems and tensions thrown up by comprehensivization, such as the desirability of treating pupils as individuals and the necessity of treating them in cohorts in mass processing and selection; and the perceived need for a 'balanced' education against the desire for qualifications in high status subjects. Thus, 'the option system acts as a lubricant in two ways: first, by appearing to satisfy many of the conflicting demands made upon it, it enables the organization to keep running; second, by officially handing over responsibility for choosing to the pupils and their parents, it eases the process of differentiation and selection which at 14-plus becomes actual and recognized in terms of differences in course and in examination targets' (Hurman, 1978: 306; *see also* Holt, 1975).

It is clear that the same kind of stratification by social class runs through all these schemes of school organization in some form or other — streaming, banding, setting, subject choice. They may involve a measure of progressive 'freeing-up' of the system, but the basic divisions remain. They continue in later developments. For example, since the institution of subject choice there have been considerable innovations in the 14-plus curriculum, notably the so-called 'new vocationalism' and a 'national curriculum'. Studying four comprehensives where the 'new vocationalism' operated, Evans and Davies (1987: 109) concluded that '... the option/selection system works by providing a framework of limited opportunity in which children are expected to recognize for themselves the limits of their own ability, and secondly to choose curricula appropriate to their 'status' and (post-school) occupational routes. Failing this, the school seems to act only in an *advisory* capacity, very often appealing to the help of parents (and the biographies of the children themselves) to ensure that any misrecognition of talents does not take place'. That pupils co-operate in this way is supported by Measor (1983a), who showed the influence of marketability on pupils' views (*see* chapter 4).

Moreover the divisions are likely to continue under the National Curriculum introduced by the Education Reform Act of 1988. In some respects a national curriculum has been seen as a natural step in line with the above progressive developments in school organization, establishing a general entitlement to learning, and setting out a clear agenda for all pupils. However, the secondary curriculum proposed seems to be based on that of a 1960s grammar school (Moon and Mortimore, 1989). It perpetuates the academic, subject-based approach, and the notion of a hierarchy of knowledge is preserved among the designation of 'core' and 'foundation' subjects, and even more by the subjects that are omitted. The proposals for attainment targets and the regular testing of pupils take little account of different rates of development. The old syndrome observed by Hargreaves and Lacey of some pupils achieving success and others experiencing failure and developing appropriate cultural resources to cope with their separate problems, is almost inevitable. Also, while the General Certificate of Secondary Education (GCSE) appears to have put an end to the divisiveness of GCE 'O' levels and CSE, it retains the divisiveness within, in that its top three grades (A, B and C) correspond to the top three grades of the old GCE examination. Selection is still done, therefore, in a fairly clear way at age sixteen. With attainment tests at 7, 11, 14 and 16, Moon and Mortimore (1989: 15) fear that 'this sort of pecking order — up to now created only by the public examinations' — will be reinforced 'through every stage of school'. The mechanics may therefore change, but the underlying structures persist. Why should this be so? We have to link what happens inside the school more firmly to the system of which the school is only a part for a satisfactory answer to this question.

Cultural Production

The social-class connection is fundamental in Paul Willis' *Learning to Labour* (1977). Willis spent a year studying a small group of anti-school boys in a Midlands comprehensive school. Among themselves, they were known as 'the lads' as opposed to the 'ear 'oles' (the lads' derisory term for conformists who seemed to be always 'listening, never doing'). Just as Lacey's 'counter-cultural' boys developed a culture in response to problems presented to them by the school, so Willis argued that his 'lads' rejected the basic idea of teaching as 'fair exchange' and formed a culture of 'resistance'. But he took the argument further, relating this culture to the structure of society, seeing it as a form of class struggle.

The 'lads' transformed aspects of normal school life into symbols of resistance. Borrowing from the wider system of commercial youth culture, particularly as regards dress and music, they developed a style of their own, opposing teachers with their manner of dress, their flouting of the rules regarding smoking and the consumption of alcohol, their unpunctuality, their general behaviour. In assembly they emptied the pockets of those in front of them, clipped jackets to seats, and ruined the collective singing. During films they tied the projector leads into knots and teased the conformist 'ear 'oles'. Outside they emptied litter bins, defaced signs, messed about with private property. On outside trips ('a nightmare for staff') they disfigured the coach seats, mauled valuable 'untouchable' items in museums, tested out antique chairs for 'strength', filched sweets, took a rise out of the general public. They had a great time (Willis, 1977: 31–3).

Most important is their dedication to violence:

> There is a positive joy in fighting, in causing fights through intimidation, in talking about fighting and about the tactics of the whole fight situation. Many important cultural values are expressed through fighting. Masculine hubris, dramatic display, the solidarity of the group, the importance of quick, clear and not over-moral thought, comes out time and again. Attitudes to 'ear 'oles' are also expressed clearly and with a surprising degree of precision through physical aggression. Violence and the judgement of violence is the most basic axis of the lads' ascendance over the conformists, almost in the way that knowledge is for teachers. (Willis, 1977: 34)

Willis, however, offers a different explanation from the 'cultural reaction' theory of Hargreaves. He saw the lads' behaviour as an aspect of the wider resistance of the working class to capitalist society. In this scenario streaming is almost an irrelevance, the lads' culture being a response to managerial authority, similar to their fathers' response to officialdom at work. The lads' culture is one that has strong associations with that of their future occupations on the factory shop-floor. Thus the denial of authority might be evidenced in the muck-about, whether by kicking away the leg of the chair of the person in front of you or by urinating in the teapot at work; masculinity and toughness is central to both cultures, as is the attempt to gain informal control of the work process; they have the same fundamental organizational unit — the informal group — and the same attitude to conformists ('cissies' or 'ear 'oles'); they both have the same kind of distinctive language and 'highly developed intimidatory humour' (p. 55) with 'pisstakes' or 'kiddings' or 'windups' and sometimes cruel practical jokes; they both champion practical knowledge and reject theory, school academic work and qualifications.

The lads' anti-school culture thus mirrors that of the wider working class in that area. But the lads are not just imitating their parents. They actively create their culture in response to the circumstances they are in and the problems they face. That it should come out the same is not surprising since school bears down on them in much the same way as the factory does on its workers. In a sense, therefore, the lads' creation of their anti-school culture is a preparation for work. As they celebrate their way of life at school and despise the 'ear 'oles', so they look forward to work, which promises a similar social climate. The nature of the work does not matter: it is something to be endured rather than enjoyed. What makes it bearable is good money, your mates, opportunites for skiving, few 'ear 'oles', 'having a laff' . . . and so on. This is cultural *production* rather than *reaction,* but the irony is that while celebrating their resistance they are conspiring in their own downfall in the sense that they choose low-grade manual work. Life on the factory shop-floor continues to celebrate freedom from conformist pressures, but at the same time ensures reproduction of the social class system.

Willis has the classic Marxist concentration on the prime importance of work and labour and on the way in which the economy influences the educational system. It is the work-plan that gives rise to certain predominant cultural forms, and the structural similarity of school to work that assists the development of similar cultures within school. However, this is no pale acquiescence to economic determinism on the part of the lads. They actively create their own culture, but they do it in a way that basically meets the requirements of the capitalist system. Willis' 'cultural Marxism', which acknowledges the relative autonomy of the education system and emphasizes the achievement of conformity through culture, contrasts with the political economy Marxism of Bowles and Gintis (1976), which sees closer ties between the economy and the educational system, and stresses the development of appropriate attitudes and relationships (*see* Hammersley, 1984).

The 'lads' are members of a collectivity (the 'working class') and practise resistance to the prevailing hegemony. But Willis argues that this involves 'penetrations' and 'limitations'. At times they appear to recognize their conditions of existence and the structures within which they are acted out — the Marxist process of self-realization or 'praxis', which 'realizes human nature at the same time as it transforms the world'. The lads' 'penetrations', however, fulfil the first rather than the second half of this, for they simply make space for 'mucking about' thus preserving the continuity of their own culture from school to work. Even so, this is a considerable achievement, and gives grounds for a guarded optimism, as opposed to the more customary pessimism particularly of political economy Marxists, who believe change must first occur in the economy before the capitalist system is changed. In the lads' *active* responses and in their penetrations, 'the counter-school culture helps to liberate its members from the burden of conformism and conventional achievement. It allows their capacities and potentials to take root elsewhere' (Willis, 1977: 130).

At other times, the lads encounter 'limitations' — their outlooks are ensnared within those conditions of existence, and they are 'alienated' from their true selves. The ultimate paradox of this alienation is when the lads come to believe that their way is the 'only way to live', and conspire in their own inequality. Their accommodation to their inferior position within the capitalist framework of society is seen by them, not as an accommodation, but as the condition that establishes 'right' and superior standards. This is how 'working-class kids come to choose working-class jobs' — in self-congratulatory triumph, not hopeless resignation.

Willis' theory has in some respects been associated with that of Miller (1958), who first expounded a 'cultural transmission' view in considering gang delinquency among boys in the United States. He argues that their main motivation for delinquent acts was their desire to follow forms of behaviour and adhere to values defined by the lower-class community. Focal concerns among these values were 'trouble', 'toughness', 'being smart', 'excitement', 'fate', and 'autonomy'. Whereas the middle-class community rates 'achievement' highly, in the lower class, status is often gauged along a 'trouble' dimension, both getting into it and staying out of it conferring status depending on the situation. 'Toughness', in a macho-masculine form, is highly valued and is seen in such attributes as physical prowess and a view of women as objects of conquest. 'Smartness' is not academic intellectual ability, which is regarded as weak and soft, but the ability to outwit others and avoid being outwitted oneself. A prominent feature of this concern is ingenious aggressive repartee. 'Excitement relieves the dullness of ordinary life, and deviant acts — such as annoying teachers, destroying property, stealing cars — might be perpetuated 'for the hell of it'. 'Fate' is represented by the idea of being caught because of bad luck. The emphasis on chance, Miller maintained, is reflected in the many forms of gambling popular in the lower-class culture. He argued that there are two other concerns that are achieved through those already mentioned — those to do with 'belonging' and those to do with 'status'. One achieves 'belonging' by adhering to the system of standards and values defined by the group; and one acquires status by demonstrating possession of the valued qualities of lower-class culture. Delinquent acts not only provide status, but also provide ways of satisfying the main concerns.

The comparisons with Willis are clear, as indeed are the contrasts with Hargreaves (1967), following Cohen's (1955) theory of status-reaction, and interpreting the anti-school culture as a reaction against the middle-class value system of the school. The policy implications of the latter might be read as that all that needs to be done is for schools to change their value-systems and all will be well. As Furlong (1985: 101) notes,

> Many would argue that the process of pupil differentiation has its origins beyond the boundaries of the school and at best teachers can provide lacunae to protect pupils from the inevitable. The ideology of opportunity for all may serve to legitimate what is presented as an open and meritocratic system, yet . . . the reality is that it is mainly working-class pupils who adopt deviant adaptations and subcultures. In this way the existing class structure is preserved . . . . Status deprivation theories provide us with little in the way of clues to analyze this contradiction.

Competing or Complementary Theories?

However, categorizing all this research too finely along theoretical lines may have its own 'polarizing' effects. Hargreaves (1981), for example, in reconsidering the Lumley study, acknowledged the relevance of 'control theory' (as well as 'reaction' theory) to this study, the nub of which is that deviance arises because of weak controls. If, he says, the pupils most prone to deviance because of weak family control are assigned to weak teachers (as those at Lumley were), then we would expect the controls on them to weaken further, and their deviance to increase. The nature of 'weak control' and whence it derives could lead to cultural transmission theory. Similarly, Lacey might argue that 'Hightown Grammar' is not closed to such an interpretation. As in Willis' study, the school here might be seen as a 'site of struggle'. Some might see the school as part of the system repressing working-class pupils, but the Manchester studies raise the question of 'whose side is the school on?' They present evidence to show that schools can help promote social-class divisions, or they can operate more as educational and less as social reproduction institutions by attempting to tackle them. Regarding this as the promise of only 'lacunae in protecting pupils from the inevitable' may itself be a limited and too pessimistic view, for one might wonder how the structures in society at the root of these divisions are ever going to be changed other than through human agency, some of which might have been educated accordingly within our schooling system.

Measures like de-streaming will not achieve wonders overnight. But they do contribute towards a changed situation from which not only fairer products might emerge but also, more appreciation of co-operation and participation and less celebration of difference. Together with these would go more reflective and critical attitudes that go on to challenge the system. Just one example of this comes from Stantonbury School in Milton Keynes. One boy writes, 'At 12 I was identified as having learning difficulties, but with the encouragement of my teachers I have overcome that. The interest taken in me as an individual saw that my talents were nurtured and my problems were given special attention. I am now applying for university'. Another describes the mixed-ability classes there as a forum 'where ideas and thought are informed by the different experiences of students outside school — differences in class, race and gender . . . this diversity of students has benefited us all, in challenging our attitudes and stimulating our thoughts. It transforms the classroom into a place of active learning and discussion — an environment that is relaxed enough to extend our perspectives and to encourage rather than intimidate. The pursuit of academic excellence does not sacrifice personal development; the achievement of one student is not at the cost of another' (Amos *et al.* 1989: 56).

Nowhere is it suggested that de-streaming is all there is to be done. Rather, the upshot of the message is that schools can aid or hinder certain messages. Inasmuch as schools differentiate, they aid social stratification on class lines. They could try to hinder it by attention to their processes and organization. This would not remove it from society. But at the very least it would not be reinforcing it, and if enough schools joined in, it might initiate a gradual chipping away at the structure. Lumley and Hightown Grammar thus could be subsumed under some of these structuralist studies.

A further link is shown when considering the charge that differentiation-polarization theory ignored the crucially important area of the content of the curriculum and its relationship to society and the way it favours middle-class pupils (Whitty, 1985). As Lacey (1986: 90) himself points out, he did not judge this to be a 'major factor in the success or failure of working-class children' at the time within grammar school education. The problem he tackled was why, when all had been pre-socialized to accept, and deemed suitable to take, the grammar school curriculum, did some succeed and some not. In a sense, the curriculum was a constant in this study. This is not to say that it is not important, and that for a full understanding of what happens to pupils in our education system, we need to consider the relationship between the two areas, as has been demonstrated. Lacey makes this connection:

> The study of the competitive process demonstrates the dynamic interrelationships between success and failure, based on the imposition of externally imposed values and knowledge systems. The development of opposed subcultures demonstrated the twin processes of alienation and incorporation. A study of the curriculum will demonstrate the nature of the imposed value and knowledge systems. Clearly the interrelationship between them is also an essential site for study. For example, the political power of the middle class in relation to the curriculum can be used to prevent changes that would endanger the success of middle-class pupils. However, if change occurred in the direction of a 'curriculum that would really be the in the interests of the working class' then Hightown shows that within the highly competitive learning situations that are typical of our schools at the present time, the middle-class parents would use their resources (cultural capital) to capture those rewards that led to academic success and the 'better' jobs. We would run the danger of producing a working class alienated from its own history as appropriated and taught in schools. (Lacey, 1986: 91)

One of the problems in looking at the studies by Willis and others similar on the one hand, and Hargreaves and Lacey on the other, as well as those by Beynon, Werthman and others (*see* chapter 2), is deciding which theory best explains which behaviour. On occasions, the same behaviour appears in different theories, and any seems equally plausible. But there are some guidelines. Lacey, for example, clearly demonstrates the influence of the institution in his longitudinal study of first to third years. Willis shows how resistance was an expression of collective counter-culture that built up during the 'lads'' school careers as they came to realize the gulf between themselves and the expectations of the school, and as they became more conscious of working-class culture as expressed through their father's experiences at work. This is more systematic and irredeemable than the kind of behaviour involved in 'testing-' and 'sussing-out' as discussed in chapter 2, though there could well be overlap between them.

Further commentaries on multi-causality are provided by McLaren,

Brown and Aggleton. McLaren (1986), in his study of an inner-city Catholic school in Toronto, Canada, where the students were largely Portuguese and Italian, also found strong parallels between the workplace of the factory and the school. For example, 'there was a distinct isomorphism between the use of space and time in the school and the daily itinerary of the factory worker. Instructional rituals were orchestrated by the teachers to facilitate (whether consciously or not) the inculcation, legitimization and credentialization of specific modes of work skills among students' (p. 222). They were perceived by teachers as understanding work only as hard and as 'drudgery'. These pupils were also seen as a 'they', that is as a distinctive group of children identified by their culture. The same kind of binary oppositions in teachers' minds noted in the British studies are apparent here, between, for example, the 'practical' thinking of the Portuguese students, and the 'abstract' thinking of middle-class students, between tough and unruly working-class students, and courteous, well-mannered, 'normal' middle-class students. McLaren feels the teachers here were using a cultural deficit theory 'as a rationalization for their failure to teach'.

However, there were some contrary indications which again give hope to those seeking transformation, and to developing a critical pedagogy, and provides substance to the 'relative autonomy' argument. There was, at times, a stress on spiritual growth and social reconstruction in the religious teaching in the school. Thus, 'a concept developed which stressed the important values of love, kindness, justice, generosity, self-denial and social action'. These values provided the context for questioning one's self, and for plotting the direction of one's spiritual life' (p. 226). One teacher, in fact, claimed they 'served to neutralize capitalism'. However, these values were subordinated to those in the major paradigm that emphasized subservience. This was strengthened by the instructional rituals through which the lessons took place, and by the counter-rituals with which they were met. In other words, the ritualistic form of the particular lessons contradicted their content and was felt to convey the major message. McLaren's study thus has much in common with that of Willis, showing particularly the strength and pervasiveness of rituals in sustaining the system — in symbols, clusters of symbols, metaphors, root paradigms, bodily gesture — and their relationship to the general social order; while holding out the prospect that 'cultural production' may not only contain seeds of promise for students, but offer teachers the possibility of developing a critical pedagogy.

Brown (1987) on the other hand, is critical of both differentiation-polarization theory, and of Willis. These leave large numbers of pupils out of account — in his research the larger majority of what he terms 'ordinary kids'. These are neither 'swots' nor 'rems' ('remedials'), two smaller, clearly identifiable groups in the three South Wales comprehensive schools of his research; and which might correspond to the pro- and anti-school groups of the earlier work. The majority of ordinary working-class pupils, he argues, neither accept nor reject school, but comply with it. This has to be understood in terms of their class background and their future aspirations, for these adaptations correspond to their perception of their entry into the labour market. Thus the 'rems' believe in 'getting in' (i.e. into working-class culture proper in the world of work, and hence rejecting school as irrelevant — these correspond to Willis' 'lads'); the 'swots' believe in 'getting out' (i.e. out of working-class culture by acquiring sufficient qualifications to challenge for middle-class jobs); and the ordinary kids believe in 'getting on' (those who believe in 'modest levels of endeavour and attainment' that would help them 'get on' in working-class terms). The thrust of Brown's work is addressed to the misconception of the 'new vocationalism'. 'Ordinary kids' draw on a working-class culture of long tradition, which directs them to 'getting on'. But 'getting on' no longer leads to attainable ends. 'Respectable working-class employment' has disappeared from the menu. Brown disputes that the pupils' attitudes are a reaction to school, and argues the connection, rather, with background working-class culture, among which there are important distinctions; and, more importantly, with the future, that is, the prospective labour market. Indeed, the latter he sees as the *basis* for the development of the working-class anti-school subculture, and not the result of it, as in Willis. Willis also, he feels, has too unitary a view of working-class culture.

Brown emphasizes the importance of working-class culture in the town of his research, which 'involves particular ways of thinking, feeling and acting, and which are the historical product of sharing the same location in a set of class relations' (p. 33). This culture is not all experienced in the same way, but is better seen as a set of resources which is used by people in the same class location in different ways. The gap between wider meaning structures connected to the class culture as a whole and the pupil identity is bridged by the notion of 'frames of reference'. This idea also involves drawing on the past and projecting into the future, and embraces the fact that pupils are active and creative agents. Thus, 'pupil FORS are creatively constructed, reproduced, and transformed drawing upon the raw materials of class culture' (p. 35).

However, while Brown adds an interesting new perspective to the study of pupil cultures, he does not dispose of the others quite as completely as he argues. For example, with regard to differentiation-polarization theory, there is little mention in Brown's study of school organization or processes; there is no sense of a longitudinal study following changes in pupils over time, no study of the origins of his pupil groups, and none of the rich empirical detail triangulated by various methods that figures in the earlier work. There is nothing to suggest that the authors of this would disagree that the school's socialization and selection processes are not the whole story, and that 'frames of reference' that have a past and a future might have something to add to the overall picture.

As for Willis' unitary view of working-class culture, based on a small sample of twelve 'lads', Gordon (1984) points out that the number is not important within a 'cultural studies' format. The group of 'lads' was ready-made, not pre-selected, and clearly identifiable at the outset. The task then was to understand their 'way of life', 'frames of reference' or 'culture'. 'Cultural production' was his starting point. Particular forms of this could be generalized to other groups in sites other than the school. But is is not claimed that this is the only working-class cultural form in schools, nor that forms of resistance elsewhere are the same as the 'lads' (*see* Willis, 1981).

Willis has also been criticized for neglecting the 'ear 'oles' — the far larger group of more conformist working-class pupils. But again, there was no necessity, nor was there time, for him to do so. It is tempting to regard these as 'ordinary kids', and indeed, these are potentially the greater challenge to capitalism, for like Brown's group with that label, they have expectations of the system that will not be realized. Correspondence theory (Bowles and Gintis, 1976) would suggest that they have been tutored with docile resignatory attitudes. 'Cultural production' approaches would suggest a more active, creative response.

Clearly, much work needs to be done on pupil cultures before some of these issues can be resolved. Almost any detailed case-study is bound to produce new information, suggesting modification to existing theories. Whether these are competing, alternative or potentially complementary has also not been fully explored. Clearly, some explanations do not belong together, and have vastly different policy implications. Others may have more mutual relevance than at first appears. Certainly the cumulative work done on differentiation-polarization theory shows that school organization does have a distinctive effect. This is not to say that it is the only, or the most important influence, on pupil careers and achievement. Nor that all pupils are necessarily affected in that way.

Brown has shown some important variations among working-class pupils. But there are considerable differences also among middle-class pupils. They are not all, by any means, pro-school and high achievers. Aggleton (1987), for example, shows that some middle-class pupils underachieve academically and practise resistance of a kind. He studied 29 students at a College of Further Education on a GCE 'A' level course. He investigated their homes, and both formal and informal aspects of their education. Student backgrounds possessed considerable 'cultural capital', with large houses, a high standard of living, foreign travel sponsored, a strong representation of parents in teaching, the arts and the media, strongly supportive of their children, prepared to intervene in school to secure the 'right' kind of education for their children, which included an emphasis on freedom and creativity rather than order and discipline, and an aversion to conformity. This was why these students were at a college, which had a more open structure than a school.

At the college, however, these students used their autonomy to avoid work, and indeed to devalue it, acting as if 'their own innate talents and cultural capital would *of themselves* provide sufficient basis for entry into, and success within, fields of practice associated with creative art forms' (1988: 218). As Willis 'lads' despised the 'ear 'oles' for their conformity, and Brown's 'rems' the 'swots', so these looked down on students who worked hard.

These principles were carried into and consolidated within the subcultural context, with their preferred sites, which allowed 'high levels of personal autonomy with respect to the negotiation of spatial and temporal possibilities' (*ibid*: 93). Thus in part-time work they valued the opportunity to negotiate with employers over how and when to work, and to be with their friends. They favoured exotic and unusual forms of dress and appearance. They preferred contexts which were friendly, informal, permissive, open-plan, providing opportunities to meet and talk to and about interesting people, and to engage in personalized modes of expression.

Aggleton argues that all this clearly illustrates the effects of early socialization. These students had hated the restrictions of school, and their transfer to college had been to find an environment more in line with the principles and values of the home. This extended to the curriculum, as well as to general disposition. Thus, 'subjects which failed to conform to criteria of cultural worth operating in the home were rarely studied. Furthermore, because opportunities for personalizing involvement in academic study operate discontinuously even within preferred subjects and because *effortless achievement* was so highly valued by students their chances of examination success remained limited' (1987: 81).

It was attacks on their 'personal space' and efforts to delimit their freedom that brought about resistance. But this was personal rather than political, it being restricted to personal contexts with no transfer to the broader power structure. Further, it is resistance which does not carry the same penalty as working-class resistance. Though fifteen out of the twenty-seven left college without adding to their qualifications, this had little significance. They were all in paid employment six years later, though youth unemployment was high nationally, 'working in cocktail bars and chic restaurants, as theatre staff, video and film technicians or as personal assistants to those in the worlds of fine and media arts' (1988: 218). They were not the ones being prepared for low-skilled training schemes. They had alternative channels of opportunity available, sponsored by influential parents with wide contacts. Aggleton proposes a grammar of modes of challenge in order to distinguish among different forms, and to avoid the problems arising when associating the concept with particular actions or individual acts of challenge (*see*, for example, A. Hargreaves' 1984 critique of the all-inclusive nature of some accounts of resistance theory). He suggests that many of the students' actions are best viewed as 'contestations' which 'are directed against localized principles of control, (and) may have as their object no more than the winning of degrees of personal autonomy within existing social relations' (1987: 125–6). This might be contrasted with 'intentional resistance' which might be directed against structured power relations of different kinds involving, for example, class, gender, and racial oppression; and which are based on collective strategies across a number of sites.

It is possible, therefore, to see some cumulation and convergence among these theories. Though they differ in emphasis and may have been represented as being in opposition, each seems to be commenting upon a different aspect of pupils' school experience, or a different factor bearing upon it, or a different group of pupils. Given the complexity of the social world and the time needed to do valid work, this is the only way research can be done — in pieces. These then have to be put together, if sound, rather like a jig-saw. Some, perhaps, will not fit, as they are part of another puzzle. But a large number of parts that seem quite disparate at first glance may have something to offer each other.

All those discussed in this chapter can be subsumed under two main strands — differentiation-polarization theory and resistance theory. I have suggested here and there how these might relate together rather than being exclusive. Broadly, the former can be subsumed under the latter, as long as no mono-causal claim is made by either. That there may be contradictions and inconsistencies here and there is to be expected. Such is the nature of social life. It is perfectly possible for pupils to be both culturally producing and reproducing from their own social class background *and* reacting to school processes. Similarly, it is not surprising that both middle-class and working-class contain groups of pupils of markedly different orientations. In other words, to explain pupil experience we need both to cast the empirical net widely and draw on a number of theories.

Some advances have been made. These seem fairly clear with regard to differentiation-polarization. Unfortunately, this does not guarantee a transfer into policy, as one might have been tempted to think from the changes in streaming practices following the earlier studies (though almost certainly other factors were also involved). In fact, the policy implications of this research are due for large-scale re-advertising as current reforms reverse the trend with regard to comprehensivization and differentiation between and within schools. Since the decisions that have promoted this trend cannot be informed by evidence, such as reported here, they would appear, as Hargreaves and Reynolds (1989: 13) point out, to be a matter of ideological preference.

> In this sense, it is somewhat disturbing that a group hitherto as impartial as HMI, should increasingly be seen to be adopting a language of differentiation in their reports on various parts of the education service. Moreover, these reports make no effort at all to distance themselves from possible interpretation of HMI's advocacy of differentiation as being support for grouping by ability in terms of streaming, banding or setting (Hargreaves, 1986; Campbell, 1989). HMI, under some pressure, one suspects from the DES, have helped insert and establish differentiation in the newly defined hegemonic discourse of current educational policy. They have helped make differentiation an acceptable, discussable, legitimate, agenda-setting element of normal educational debate, inside the school and out.

In such a climate, policy-makers need to be repeatedly informed of the hard evidence. Though political ideology is a weighty adversary, it has been modified, on occasions, if not altered by scientific argument and demonstration (*see* Woods, 1990a).

The same is true of resistance theory. While, currently, there would appear to be a growth in tendencies that will lead to a growth of resistance rather than a resolution of it in any transformation of society, there are contrary tendencies. McLaren (1986), for example, makes frequent reference to the development of 'communitas' in his school, which includes, on occasions, signs of fellowship between teachers and pupils on a plane outside the hierarchical constraints of society. There is, too, the growth of action and collaborative research among teachers, and the promotion of reflective teaching (Hustler *et al.* 1986; Lomax, 1989; Pollard, 1988), which might help develop such communitas. There is also growing support for political education within schools, and for democratic practices, both of which would objectify resistance and make it a subject for study, rather than part of a response. The Swann Committee (1985: 334) for example, were keen to see pupils encouraged 'to consider how power is exercised and by whom at different levels in our society, how resources are allocated, how policies are determined and implemented, how decisions are taken and how conflicts are resolved' (*see also* Stevens, 1982; Phillips, 1983; Lynch, 1987; Harber, 1989; Carrington and Short, 1989; Grugeon and Woods, 1990).

Democratic education involves power-sharing and collective decision-making:

> ... there is likely to be a sense of community amongst a group of learners; there has to be a working partnership between appointed teachers and learners; appointed teachers have to develop trust in the capability and creative ability of their fellow humans who come to them in the role of students; dialogue becomes an essential activity rather than an optional feature; unmandated or imposed learning is not seen as legitimate. (Harber and Meighan, 1989: ix)

Thought in these directions appears to be gathering pace at the same time as the 1988 Education Reform Act seeks to establish market principles in the system. In a curious way, it may give a boost to collaborative, reflective and democratic teaching by engendering resistance among teachers and helping to promote unity with pupils in common cause.

Chapter 3

Gender Cultures

As well as this polarization of pupil cultures fostered by school organization along broadly social-class lines, there is a polarization along gender lines. Again school organization and processes can assist this, though basically it is a product of differentiation on a wider scale and with a considerable history. Even as recently as the Crowther Report (1959) it was officially acknowledged almost without question that the education of boys and girls would be basically different, along the lines of boys as future supporters and providers of families and girls as wives and mothers. Thus

> ... all schools can and should make adjustment ... to the fact that marriage now looms much larger and nearer in the pupils' eyes than it ever has before ... there is a clear case for a curriculum which respects the different roles they (i.e. boys and girls) play. (Crowther, 1959: 34)

In fairness, this report did recognize that some girls would become workers as well as wives, and stressed the importance of post-school education for girls. But the general paradigm remained. It is one that schools can foster. As Shaw (1976: 137) argues

> ... the social structure of mixed schools may drive children to make even more sex-stereotyped subject choices, precisely because of the constant presence of the other sex and the pressure to maintain boundaries, distinctiveness and identity.

The divisiveness is engendered from a very early age when girls and boys are socialized through the home and a variety of other agencies into appropriate roles with their own attributes which are defined almost as much by the contrast with the other sex as by their own properties. As these develop, so more of the self is invested in the gender culture, with boys in particular 'policing the boundaries' making sure it reaches all boys and excludes girls (Hartley, 1959; Chodorow, 1979; Walkerdine, 1981). It is less generally recognized that girls and women also 'police the boundaries', graphically illustrated in Turner's (1970: 197–198) description of the traditional American family, where

> the wife characteristically made the kitchen her special province and, although submitting to her husband in most matters, contrived to convince her husband that only a woman knew what to do in the kitchen. The low prestige of kitchen competence made his invasion of her special province unlikely. But to protect her province more fully, she found it necessary to maintain an air of mystery about the kitchen, to prepare the kitchen with booby traps against occasional invasion by the male, and to inculcate in her sons a profound conviction of their own incompetence in the kitchen.
>
> Mystery is commonly maintained by the use of jargon and by insisting that personalized judgement and experience rather than a standard formula is the only way a result can be attained. The special language of cooking is akin to the secret passwords of children and the jargon of adolescents in supplying an air of mystery to commonplace transactions. In each instance a subordinated group is attempting to carve out its private sphere of activity in which it is free from surveillance. The insistence that a good cook judges how much of each ingredient to use by feel rather than using standard measures serves the same end. (Turner 1970: 197–198)

'Booby traps' are laid to confuse the straying male, private systems of arrangement and storing used. The myth of male domestic incompetence is assisted by folk literature, with comic strips, for example, showing fathers' and sons' laughable attempts to perform domestic tasks (though daughters' mistakes are treated more seriously). Turner's description conveys some of the subtlety and mystery engendered to legitimate, differentiate, imbue with worth, and defend roles. If it shows women imprisoned within the domestic arena, it also shows how women 'conspire in their own downfall' by making it difficult for males (husbands and sons) to participate in that arena.

This division is reflected, and at times exacerbated later in boys' and girls' experiences at school, in the subjects and activities they excel and struggle in, the informal groups they play or associate with and differentiate from (Shaw, 1977), in their general interaction with each other and with teachers, and eventually in the occupations they come to take up. This might be seen as the continuous creation and re-creation of gender differences over time related to structural divisions that run deep in society. The study of how they operate, however, again suggests points of challenge or resistance. The school can aid or inhibit the challenge. It can operate as an agency of the system, or seek to raise awareness of it.

The relationship between gender, social class and 'race' is complex, and there are various views on whether they are equally or variably important and in what order. However, gender does appear to be an important factor in its own right, in that there is a unity about girls' or boys' experiences; while there are also considerable differences among them, frequently owing to social class and/or 'race' influences (Acker, 1987a). These two aspects of unity and separateness are in considerable tension, but such is the nature of social life. I shall begin by looking at the nature of general gender divisions at schools, then the curriculum, followed by extra-school youth culture and its relationship to cultures within the school; I then examine some inter-relationships among gender and social class and conclude with a consideration of explanations and the prospects for change.

Gender Differences in School Organization and Processes

Gender divisions are fostered at school in a number of ways. There is, frequently, physical separation. Clarricoates (1981), for example, describes how many everyday routines of primary-school life are gender based, including proper 'line-up' formation. Ball (1981), also found two first-year forms in his comprehensive school typically dividing themselves into single-sex friendship cliques or pairs. So firm can the dividing line become that crossing it constitutes one of the biggest offences, with direct implications for one's identity. Boys who do not live up to full machismo standards and performances might be taunted with 'being a woman', or as a punishment be sent to 'sit with the girls'. In some all-boys schools it has been noticed that some boys have been assigned feminine roles, suggesting that it may be a necessary, or at least useful, contrastive procedure in formulating their own identities (Spender, 1982). Askew and Ross (1988: 160) conclude that such activity, 'while superficially directed against girls or against the teacher, is in fact directed at each other. They are proving through their behaviour that they are, in fact, 'real men' and very dependent on one another's approval.

There are no doubt ways in which some teachers seek to moderate the starkness of such separation between the sexes. There may, for example, be less these days of boys and girls lining up separately for certain activities. Yet research suggests that there are many other ways in which schools foster gender differentiation. Girls appear to receive less tuition in the mixed-sex classroom, boys getting more of the teacher's attention, both for behaviour and academic work, being given higher-level questions and more academic criticism, volunteering (often in the form of 'calling out') more answers, and occupying more physical and linguistic space (Clarricoates, 1987; Askew and Ross, 1988). Wolpe (1977) notes, for example, that boys monopolize the playground with their games of football, with girls forced to intermingle on the periphery. Clarricoates (1987) has observed how boys 'spread' into gangways and spaces around their own desks, whether girls are occupying those spaces or not. Boys tend to dominate classroom talk, talk rough, call out, move around, and it seems 'normal' for them so to do. Kelly (1988) claims that this is now 'beyond dispute in all age groups . . . , in several different countries, in various socio-economic and ethnic groupings, across all subjects in the curriculum, and with both male and female teachers (although more with males)' (p. 20). The differences are as large in teacher- as in pupil-initiated interactions, though Kelly observes that they are less marked where teachers have been trained in sex equity.

Mahoney (1985) describes how, in a class she studied, the boys denied girls' academic abilities, saw them as 'wives and mothers' (sources of materials to borrow, for example) and meted out verbal abuse and sexual harassment. Mahoney, in fact, regards the last of these as the most important, compared, for example to sexist materials or the distribution of time. She speaks of a teacher who complained to her of

> . . . the 'heavy teasing' that goes on in corridors, which could make the day wretched for girls. 'Boys', she said 'grabbed breasts, pinched bums or took things from girls so by the time they got them back they were late for lessons.' (Mahoney, 1985)

Verbal abuse was also common, with a large number of offensive words used by boys, 'slag' being the most widely used. Teachers were not blameless in some of their own interaction with girls, and their frequent failure to treat boys' behaviour in this respect as serious suggests a deep-seated acceptance of this kind of behaviour being part of the natural order of things. Spender and Sarah (1980) argue that girls are inhibited for fear of being 'laughed at' by boys. Stanworth (1983) describes how some girls adapt to school by developing an ability to melt into the background in lessons with boys, thus reinforcing the gender stereotype (*see also* Delamont, 1980; Connell *et al.*, 1982; Kelly, 1985). This 'quietness' and apparent docility might thus be interpreted on the face of things as typically female behaviour, indicating conformity in the main, though teachers often express a wish that girls would be more forthcoming in volunteering answers. Stanley (1986: 284) points out that this has brought a great deal of pejorative comment from teachers on 'quiet' girls — 'wallpaper person', 'faceless bunch', 'mouses', 'puddings', 'boringly well-behaved girls' — are some of the comments quoted. Quietness is often seen as a lack — of confidence and/or ambition (Stanworth, 1983; Shaw, 1984). Girls thus are perceived as defective in some way and as passive victims.

However, other interpretations have been advanced. Fuller (1983), for example, talks of girls 'bottling' their criticism. Stanley (1986,1989) argues that 'quietness' is a successful adaptation by girls to the situation that they are confronted with. In her research, it was an active strategy in order to facilitate their work, to avoid 'being shown up' and to protect their reputations, which were at greater risk than the boys'. Stanley's study shows that the strategy is used selectively, i.e. in some lessons and not in others, or in lessons but not in informal areas or activities. This variability was often not noticed by teachers, who did not see them in situations other than their own classrooms, but who nonetheless labelled such girls as possessing the quality almost inherently. Quietness, thus, can be an active response, and not an indicator of passive and bland conformity. Stanley (1986: 285) concludes that

> ...the quiet girls of 4T were not victims: their quietness was a response to a model of the 'successful upper-band pupil' which had become interlocked with conventional ideas about gender imported from the conservative community outside. Far from being weak and immature, Carol and her friends are mature and highly adaptable — perhaps another stereotyped image fits them better: that of the 'strong, silent type'.

Anyon (1983) and Buswell (1984) have argued that the surface conformity indicated by quietness may be concealing an underlying resistance, even though it takes a vastly different form from the rumbustiousness of Willis' lads. If the resistance surfaces in some form, it might be tackled by teachers reminding girls of the gender code. Llewellyn, for example, observed how the staff of a school encouraged certain views of femininity. A senior master tried to placate a rebellious pupil in this way:

> Just calm down, Sandy; with a temper like yours, my girl, you'll be lucky if you get a husband . . . and if you do, you won't keep him if you treat him the way you do your teachers. Come on, calm down, do you really want to end up like your sister? . . . back home no sooner out of it with two kids and bruises . . . (Llewellyn, 1980: 48)

The remonstration is put in the context judged to be most meaningful to the girl. If it does not succeed, the teachers might consider they have failed in one of their aims — to help shape a decent, respectable, home-loving person who will make a good wife and mother.

The Gendered Curriculum

The curriculum, also, reinforces these differences from an early age. Lobban (1987) has shown how traditional sex-roles are an essential part of the fabric of primary school reading schemes. Males in these schemes tended to be more active, innovative, instrumental and outgoing and to take the leading role, while females tended to have domestic roles, and to be subservient. Cooking and childcare were leading skills exhibited by girls. Boys were more independent, and had a wider range of motor skills, oriented toward a variety of future occupational goals. 'Dad' was shown in traditional ways as head of the household with Mum busy in the kitchen and doing housework. As Lobban (p. 153) points out, 'The world they depicted was not only sexist, it was more sexist than present reality, and in many ways totally foreign to the majority of children, who do have working Mums, and at least some experience of cross-sex activities'.

Though alerted to this in the mid-1970s, many schools continue to use reading schemes replete with gender and other kinds of stereotypes. 'Crown Readers', for example, have a king, a queen, and a baby in a castle, and are serviced by a 'big-guard' and a 'little guard', and a maid. Book 3, '*The Maid and the Mouse*' has on one page a picture of the maid on a shelf, a guard chasing a mouse, and a baby laughing on the floor. The maid earlier introduces herself thus:

I am the maid
I live in the castle
I brush in the castle
It is a big castle
I brush and brush and brush
I brush the walls
I brush the doors
I brush the windows

While at one level the heavy repetition is familiarising children with certain words, at another level it is, by the same token, imprinting upon children stereotyped views of how males and females behave. In the case quoted there is an ironic and symbolic touch of reality in the herculean task of housework confronting the maid (*see* Oakley, 1974). The stereotyping is not restricted to reading schemes, being found well in evidence in other textbooks, children's fiction, wall displays, and worksheets (Richardson, 1986; Browne and France, 1986).

It is not surprising that, in studies of subject choice at secondary school, these considerations should affect what boys and girls chose to study and how well they performed in them. In *The Divided School* (1979: 31–33), I noted some differences between girls' and boys' reasons for choices when it came to option-choice in the third year. Girls appeared to be more influenced by an affective factor especially *dislike* of other subjects, and boys put more emphasis on ability. Possibly this was a product of gender socialization, girls being more person-oriented and attaching more weight to feelings. It is quite possible that there were gender group perspectives there cross-cutting the social class ones, and channelling boys and girls into 'appropriate' routes. Girls favoured environmental studies, English literature, commerce and housecraft. Boys were more populous in chemistry, physics, technical drawing, metalwork and woodwork. They were evenly represented in other subjects such as history. This is not an untypical pattern (*see* Statham and Mackinnon, 1988). Differential socialization in early life, role-models as perceived in the family and the media, and peer reinforcement help to produce different gender identities which influence conceptions of self and career, and perception of abilities (Byrne, 1978; Deem, 1980). Consistent identities may exhibit variable personae among subjects. Thus, Carol (Stanley, 1989: 41) to several of her teachers was 'worryingly quiet'. But she was not at all shy out of school, nor in cookery, nor other lessons where she did not have to compete with boys.

> Her personal curriculum, designed to fit her for the role of matriarch, brought her into contact with like-minded girls in classes where she felt confident and relaxed. Like many middling-clever young women, Carol chose 'girls' subjects because she wanted a conventional women's job' which would fit in with family life, and because she thought it would be useful to learn domestic skills.

Though the National Curriculum introduced by the 1988 Education Reform Act might overcome some of this problem by removing much of the subject choice structure and process, it will not necessarily change perceptions of, and attitudes to, subjects revealed by that system. Gender identities can be reinforced by teacher attitudes and other school processes. This was certainly the case at Lowfield (Woods, 1979). The headmaster was keen on 'boys doing science'. Every morning and afternoon two fourth year girls would go to the staffroom to make tea for the teachers. And in countless interactions, boys and girls were reminded of their gender differences. Thus a girl's incompetence at games was laughed off — by pupil and teacher — as typically feminine, while boys' competitive instincts were encouraged. One male teacher, asked to describe the pupils in his class, showed much greater knowledge of the boys, admitting 'Now, the girls I don't know so much about' (Woods, 1979: 178). His remarks about them centred around a vague affective category of 'nice' or 'pleasant'. Gillborn (1990) also stresses the role of the school and teachers in gender differentiation. He quotes a science teacher who remarked aggressively, 'One thing I hate and detest is ignorant females . . . and this school is lousy with them these days . . . don't want to see that ugly lot in my lab' (pp. 11–12). A male craft teacher knew that he 'was not supposed to say this, but this is a *workshop* . . . It's a man's world in here . . . girls just don't fit in here, they don't understand it' (p. 12). Pupils who made non-traditional choices in the option-choice process nearly always had those choices queried, and in some cases physical appearance was taken as a guide to academic potential, 'attraction' and 'fashionable' girls being seen as dubious in that respect.

The structure of the curriculum can also assist this divide, where it is rigidly compartmentalized into traditional subjects. This is then promoted further by the genderization of certain subjects. Pupils opt out of some subjects and choose others along gender lines in a fairly regular pattern (Pratt *et al.*, 1984; Hargreaves, 1984; Smith and Tomlinson, 1989). Considerable attention has been given to science recently in this respect. Physics, chemistry and technical subjects appear to be something of a male preserve (Ormerod, 1975; Kelly, 1976, 1981; Statham *et al.*, 1988). Such subjects have a high market value, often leading to highly paid and influential careers; and the academic science subjects carry a considerable amount of academic prestige (Ball, 1981; Chisholm and Holland, 1986; Bridger, 1987).

Girls do not do as well as boys at science (apart from biology, which has its own characteristics). One suggested reason for this is their alleged lack of analytical and problem-solving abilities, which these subjects require. If such a 'lack' exists, some argue it arises not from inherent qualities but from differential conditioning in early life (different toys, household tasks they are asked to do, attitudes towards them, play-forms, role-models as perceived in the family and the media, relationships with others, etc.). Kelly (1976) lists eight main differences between boys and girls at age 11 relevant to attitudes to science: girls tend to be more verbal, less independent, more easily discouraged, more conscientious, more interested in people, less interested in science, less experienced in science-related activities and more restricted in their perception of their possible future roles than boys. Thus the GIST research project (Girls into Science and Technology) reported that 'scientific attitude and interests are already differentiated along sex lines by age 11', and further that 'girls' attitudes in particular decline over the three years of compulsory science' (Equal Opportunities Commission, 1982: 56). 'Girls' subjects' are traditionally the 'arts' such as English, languages and history; and, of the practical subjects, home economics, needlecraft, typing and commerce, but not metalwork and woodwork. Though more girls are now taking sciences than ten years ago, the gap between boys and girls is still wide along the basic science/arts division and among vocational subjects; and indeed in some areas, like languages, it appears to be widening. Also, the differences in achievement between boys and girls remain considerable in the higher stages of scientific education (Department of Education and Science, 1985).

As an illustration of how science ministers to boys' 'toughness' and girls' perceptions of feminity, Kelly gives the example of a chemistry lesson where

> ... the pupils were heating a chemical and collecting the gas which was given off under water, [and] there was a slight risk that the water could suck back into the test tube which might then crack and scatter its contents. The boys in the group commented 'great' when the teacher warned them of the danger, whereas the girls were obviously scared of the experiment. They approached it tentatively (which increased the danger) and panicked and squealed whenever a suck-back seemed imminent. The boys' greater confidence meant that their reaction to a potential suck-back was more positive — they heated the substance harder or took the tube out of the water. In the end several girls gave up their own experiments and joined the boys' group as onlookers. (Kelly, 1985: 139)

We also found in our research on school transfer (Measor and Woods, 1984) that girls reacted to science as an unfeminine subject. They claimed that the nasty smells made them 'feel sick,' 'gave them a headache' sufficient to cause one girl to miss a disco one evening; and they expressed considerable fear of equipment (such as bunsen burners) and chemicals (such as acids). They complained that they got dirty in these lessons, were subjected to revolting spectacles, and forced to spoil their appearance, (by, for example, wearing unisex goggles). Randall (1987) suggests that lack of self-confidence resulting from years of socialization leading to dependence on guidance but also reluctance to consult the teacher has particularly deleterious effects in practical work in the sciences and technological subjects. Significantly, none of this seemed to apply in areas of the curriculum considered more suitable by girls. One girl, for example, who could not understand how to use a microscope, was one of the first to grasp the principles of the double-electric sewing machine (Measor and Woods, 1984: 125). Similarly, though afraid of the bunsen burners, there was no fear of lighting the gas in cookery lessons.

For teachers this kind of classroom behaviour raises some fundamental questions. Presumably we would all agree that part of our task as educators is to teach all pupils to their maximum potential. Yet the teachers in Kelly's research seemed to operate within the parameters of gender differentiation. As one of them commented:

> If no obvious interest in the subject or topic is displayed, the male teaching staff often flatter the girls or are mildly flirtatious towards them, finding that this is often a successful way of encouraging

them. In the same circumstances male teachers will probably appeal to the boys' competitive instincts. We accept that treating the sexes differently in this way may well be encouraging them to see their roles in the world of science differently but are reluctant to abandon successful teaching techniques. (Kelly, 1985: 144)

We might note that this tactic works both ways. For girls learn to cope with male staff by cultivating their femininity and exploiting strategies for dealing with the opposite sex (Buswell, 1984). This kind of interaction between male staff and female pupils may make for a 'pleasant' social atmosphere, but inasmuch as it is ministering to gender roles, it is likely to be educationally counter-productive.

All this has contributed to what Kelly (1985) has described as the 'masculinization of science'. She argues that this is evident from: (1) the much greater predominance of males in teaching and studying it, and appearing in posters, advertisements, films, novels and text-books; (2) the way science is packaged and presented, in line with gender-differentiation, examples and topics appearing more to boys than girls; (3) classroom interactions which construct masculinity and femininity, and the former's positive relationship to the subject and the latter's negative, as in the examples above, thus leading to a 're-contextualisation' of gender from the family to the school (MacDonald, 1980); and (4) the masculine world-view embodied in scientific thinking (*see* Northam, 1983, and Walkerdine, 1989, for a view of mathematics as a male province).

Clearly, the developments referred to above lead to a belief that science is 'not a girls' subject' and that most girls will find it difficult. In fact, if they do like it and do well at it, they run the risk of being considered 'goodie-goodies' and unfeminine (Measor, 1983). The more this is subscribed to by the girls themselves, by parents, by the media and by teachers, the more the belief becomes a reality. The GIST team show clearly the prevalence of such a belief (Kelly *et al.*, 1984), and DES (1980) thought that some teachers felt physics was too difficult for girls. Harding (1983) comments: 'If teachers assume this, then girls will respond by lowering their expectations of themselves and perform less well, whatever their ability' (pp. 17–18). An associated outcome is that this will encourage girls to choose 'women's jobs', just as Willis's working-class lads choose working-class jobs. As Furlong (1986: 374) notes: 'As these impressions develop out of experiences, young people tend to come to incorporate fairly realistic appraisals of the opportunities which have been open to members of their particular class and sex within the local labour market'.

There have, in consequence, been attempts to promote a 'girl-friendly' science (Whyte, 1985), with, for example, more suitable topics, and projects. But Elliot and Powell (1987: 285) warn that this could lead to current stereotypes being perpetuated and reinforced, and a 'young women's ghetto within science', dealing with a restricted range of activities that may appear different but are still cast in the same mould (*see also* Measor, 1983b). They support a 'socially relevant and socially critical' science curriculum, though such criteria should apply across the whole curriculum, and this would create qualitatively better curricula for both sexes. They point out, too, that the emphasis on science tends to legitimize its status. Science is undoubtedly important, but so is reading and writing. Boys progress more slowly at this than girls, yet these have not received anywhere near the attention science has received (Askew and Ross, 1988). The values traditionally associated with science also become endorsed. But are these essential, let alone desirable? Perhaps the values associated with other, less high-status, subjects should be promoted. Applied to science, these might lead to a humanization (neither 'feminization' or 'masculinization') of the subject.

It is in these very subjects — the arts, humanities and social sciences — that boys in general have limited experience. They are less exposed to those areas of the curriculum that deal with human values, emotional matters, personal expression, caring and co-operative behaviour, and consideration of their own lives. Thus does the organization of the curriculum reinforce male behaviour and values, and the status quo. In fact, boys and girls *use* the curriculum for gender identity purposes. This means that overcoming gender divisions in the curriculum means more than opening up subjects to boys and girls, or making them both do certain subjects. Thus, Sweden made home management, typing and technology compulsory for both and the 1988 Education Reform Act in the UK made science compulsory for all up to age sixteen. But these measures do not mean pupils will do well at these subjects, accept them, or not appropriate them for their own purposes. Science, for example, is very useful to girls for they can deploy their feminine characteristics in response to the trials put upon them. Similarly, domestic science and needlework offer boys good opportunities to exhibit their maleness. For example, there are 'taps to turn on loudly, and electrical switches with buzzers attached to set off at inappropriate moments. There is food to steal and eat, cake mixture to throw around and daub on other boys' noses and hair' (Measor and Woods, 1984: 123). Similarly, in needlework, you can pretend that a sewing machine is a model train, seeing how fast it can go, and probably breaking it; give silly answers, or indulge in other forms of deviant behaviour that celebrate maleness and their basic disdain for a subject that represents the counter-image of their identity. One of them summed it up when he described it as

> Oh boring . . . don't like it . . . that's girl's stuff. I do think it's girls' stuff, needlework. When are the blokes going to do it when they are older? When they are not married that's about all, and if they do get married the wife will do it . . . they go out and get the money. (*ibid.* 38)

This indicated another factor in pupils' estimation of subjects, that of their marketability. Among the practical subjects technical studies and woodwork are considered quite useful potentially for 'jobs around the home', though that is less important than paid occupations. Needlework is perceived as being of no use to males. Cookery is less objectionable — there are, of course, many top male chefs — but this kind of 'life-skills' area is less important than the high status academic subjects which get the good jobs. The same is true of 'child-care'. Most boys will be fathers one day, but child-rearing is seen as the mother's role. On the other hand, the otherwise most deviant and difficult girls have been seen to become highly attentive and conformist during such lessons (Woods, 1979). Grafton *et al.* (1983) suggest reasons for this in their study of the subject 'Family and Child' in a coeducational comprehensive school. They found that nearly all opting for this were girls (a very few boys from a remedial group were involved but seemed to be 'time-filling' and left early), mostly from working-class backgrounds. The chief motives for choice of subject were utility and feasibility. It contained things useful for girls to know, like babies and children, food, diet and cooking, looking after a home, getting pregnant, playgroup activities. These were 'real' concerns to the girls compared to some other more 'boring' aspects of school. Boys did not take it, because, although most hoped to become fathers and have a family, for them it was 'sissyish or babyish looking after children. They think it's girls' work or women's work' (p. 166). The division of labour in society is affecting subject choices here in a fairly clear-cut way.

Measor (1983a) found in her research that pupils' evaluation of subjects was based on their instrumental value (*see also* Ball, 1981). Thus mathematics and English, and perhaps science (though choices should be allowed) were most important, for they secured the best jobs. Subjects like art and design and music were much less so, but these offered pupils sites and opportunities to indulge in minor deviant acts, to demonstrate that they were not too conformist, not 'goodie-goodies' or 'creeps'. There seemed to be a scale of priorities with pupils responding positively and conformingly to the formal demands made on them in highly valued areas; but bringing informal concerns and cultures into play in less valued areas. The two are in considerable tension within the pupil's everyday life.

Disjunctures between Teacher and Pupil

This can be complicated still further by teachers' expectations. Elsewhere I have argued that, for optimum learning to occur, there should be matching along a range of cognitive and social criteria including teacher and pupil interests (Woods, 1990). The problems involved are illustrated in a case study of sex education, where the teachers concerned believed they were adopting progressive methods in order to serve pupil needs. This is an area where schools are frequently judged to offer inadequate provision in the face of children's desire for more extensive treatment (Goldman, R. and J., 1982), so this school considered itself rather virtuous in that respect. Measor (1989), however, found a vast gulf between the official curriculum and adolescent needs and interests. The sex education provided was derived from the teachers' own culture and from their own adult status. Most of the twelve-year-old pupils appeared very embarrassed in these lessons. Girls, in particular, were very uncomfortable watching films on human reproduction and birth. There was something improper about it. For some of them, the subject was one of shared mother/daughter intimacy, not depersonalized public exposure. They were also uncomfortable sharing these lessons, given by male teachers about mostly women's bodies, with boys.

These teachers took considerable care in preparing their lessons. But they took no account of adolescent sexuality. In contrast to the school's fresh, hearty, open approach, the sexual world to these pupils seemed covert and mysterious, and it seemed right to them that it should be. At twelve years old, these pupils were at a crucial stage of development, many undergoing puberty, acting out male and female roles, experimenting their way into the world of adolescent sexuality. There was much discussion of these matters in small, informal groups. Status was to be won from knowledge, such that it was better to pretend to know than to exhibit ignorance. But much basic information was conveyed through the pupils' informal network — through jokes, stories, acted-out dramas — about the mechanics of sex, about the penalties for incorrect behaviour (for example 'losing one's reputation'), about emergency procedures, about the tactics of sexual signalling, involving, for example, complicated rituals of writing names on schoolbags, books, aprons and hands in such a way as to indicate one's desire without taking a public risk.

All this, pupils learnt largely by themselves. The sex education the school offered took no account of these matters nor of different rates of sexual maturing. It was distant, adult, unhelpful and actually violated some crucial elements in the pupil culture. If the pupils' world had been taken into account, the approach would have been less brash, there would have been less display of naked bodies, particularly less concentration on the female body, teaching perhaps would have been done in single-sex groupings, and reassurance given about the normality of pupils reaching puberty at different times.

McKeown (1985) came to a similar conclusion in her study of religious education. She asked pupils to comment on an educational filmstrip in which a Catholic priest aids a puzzled repentant boy who went to him after he had been in a fight with another boy. She found a variety of interpretations. One boy, for example, saw the act as one of counselling, but because what happened did not match his experience of counselling, it appeared totally unrealistic. Others saw the priest's role as representing adult authority. Within their own culture it would be most unlikely that the one who had started the fight would report it in such a way to an adult. The fight was their affair, and they would try to sort it out themselves. Telling an adult was in fact strongly condemned by the children's culture, so, like the sex education of our research, this mode of teaching religious education strongly conflicted with principles in their own world. Better were those lessons where their personal knowledge and experience were taken into account, where they were actively involved, and where they were given opportunities to reflect, and thus form their own personal philosophies (cf Stanley's [1989] 'personal curricula'), instead of reacting negatively to adult ones.

Such distance between teacher and pupil understandings and expectations only serves to aggravate the underlying gender differences.

Girls and Teenage Culture

There are, then, beliefs, attitudes and behaviours that contribute towards gender cultures. It is clear that male subcultures can be strongly constituted within the school. Are there female cultures or subcultures of similar strength of definition? To appreciate this, 'teenage' or 'adolescent' culture, which has its origin outside the school, must be considered.

Gender cultures in general stem from the sexual division of labour, which directs men toward main-line occupations and women toward 'servicing' and child-rearing roles in the home and in casual support labour (Newson *et al.*, 1978). This encourages girls to believe that marriage is the most important event in life for them, that they will need to 'find a man' and make themselves sexually attractive to him. Quietness and docility might also be seen as excellent qualifications for some of the jobs traditionally available to women, such as nursing, or becoming a secretary or air stewardess (Byrne, 1978; Stanley, 1989). Girls are also exposed to highly idealized and romantic notions of love, marriage and parenthood. Competence for a girl, therefore, may be measured in part by how well she projects this image. Hence the preoccupation among teenage girls with make-up, jewellery, perfume and fashion (Sharpe, 1976) and, among some, with having a steady boyfriend as the ultimate social success (Davies, 1984).

These concerns are reflected in 'teenage' or 'pop' culture, to which girls in particular become very attached. McRobbie and Garber (1976) argue that the so-called 'teeny-bopper' culture of the 1970s was popular among ten- to fifteen-year old girls because it could be easily accommodated in the home (the 'female's preserve'), with record-player and friends, was open to everybody and did not distinguish among them in the invidious ways that school did. There was no risk of humiliation, and the obsession with pop stars offered a 'defensive solidarity'. It enabled girls in a sense to 'negotiate a space of their own'; but the culture is nevertheless full of fantasy elements emanating from the romanticism of the traditional feminine role, which casts women in a surbordinate position.

The pop culture spans pro- and anti-school orientations and social-class considerations, according to Ball's (1981) research (*see also* Meyenn, 1980). Ball found that the 'pop-media culture, especially in terms of clothes, hair-styles, shoes, pop-group allegiance, knowledge of dances, etc., was important for all the girls [in one form] irrespective of their attitude to school' (p. 66). By the third year, the 'adolescent culture' was in full swing. Home-centredness decreased, and involvement in unsupervised activities with friends increased. There were concerts, discos, records, boyfriends and girlfriends. They went out to visit friends, to the cinema, cafés, pubs and parties, or just to hang about in the street. However, this emphasis on going out is partly motivated by the search for males; when one is found, the 'home-centred' orientation will focus on him (McRobbie, 1980). The values associated with this culture contrast with those supported by the school. Whereas the school promotes work and production, preparing for the future, intellectual values and self-control, the pop-media culture supports play and consumption, living in the present, and physical and emotional expression.

Ball found all kinds of pupils contributing to adolescent culture, but the anti-school pupils most, progressively so in the fourth and fifth years. Thus band 1 girls were certainly concerned with fashion and pop music, but their appearance differed from that of band 2 and 3 girls. The latter were more extreme — 'colours brighter, heels higher'. Many wore badges and favours for their favourite pop groups. There were also differences between the bands in the use of their own time, for homework and revision occupied quite a large part of band 1 pupils' spare time. However, for all of them participation in adolescent culture was an important criterion of status. Even the most conformist pupils looked to their peers, as well as to adults, for approval. If they did not, and just worked and conformed with school values without question, they were not popular. But if they achieved highly in school work and were rated highly on the pop-media scale — with fashion, pop and boyfriends — they could be very popular.

The difference between anti- and pro-school girls was mainly that, for the former, teenage culture offered an alternative value and status system to the school's, with an emphasis on freedom and social sophistication. For the pro-school pupils, the fourth and fifth years brought closer relationships with the staff, more participation in extra-curricular activities, as well as continued identification with adolescent culture. Though judged highly by teachers, they were held in low esteem by the anti-school pupils, who were now applying teenage values exclusively. Despite, therefore, a common identification with teenage culture, the two groups were driven progressively further apart.

Similarly, Llewellyn (1980) noticed a polarization of views on feminine propriety between top-stream and non-examination-stream girls in a secondary-modern school. The top-stream girls saw the non-examination ones as 'thick' and 'daft'.

> You wouldn't catch us clomping round the place like them.
> Eh — you hear the language on 'em.
> Eh-up, the way they stick together — it ain't natural, yelling at lads across park.

To the non-examination girls, the top stream were 'snotty' and 'keenos', but with no advantages:

> Exams won't get them nowhere, they'll be out with their prams next year — if anyone'll have 'em.
> You seen the way they dress? — wouldn't be seen dead in that.
> T'aint never seen them with a lad.
> (Llewellyn, 1980: 46)

This is an antipathy similar in some respects to that observed by Hargreaves (1967) between top-and lower-stream boys in Lumley secondary-modern school, and reflects again, the influence of social class cross-cutting considerations of gender. The girls are guided mostly by the code of femininity as they see it, the pro-school group emphasizing qualities of ladylike behaviour, the anti-schoolers mocking the others' orientation towards work (in the same way as Willis's lads did to the 'ear 'oles') and appearance.

McRobbie's (1978) study of a group of teenage working-class girls portrayed a similar polarity between groups and again the influence of social class and gender. These girls 'resisted' the 'official, middle-class ideology for girls in school', replaced it with one of their own — feminine, sexual — and reconstructed the school as an arena for their own anti-school activities. Their behaviour supported, therefore, 'a culture of femininity' which celebrates the concerns of getting a boy friend and getting married. McRobbie argues that this serves to reproduce class and gender relationships at the same time.

Similar polarization among girls was noticed by Middleton (1987) in her study of life-histories of feminist educators in New Zealand. The schools of their youth were streamed. The women noted that the 'commercial' streams (described by Taylor [1982], as a form of 'apprenticeship in womanhood') were seen by teachers and 'academic' girls as 'dumb classes', and frequently by 'academic' girls' as 'tarts'. 'Margaret' describes the 'intellectual' subculture of the academic girls, with dancing classes, debating societies, bohemian dress and habits, dating boys with exactly similar outlooks, romantic attachments, but no sex. They were straight, virtuous and virginal. The subjects of the curriculum also fed into their youth culture (for example, they would discuss poetry) but only as it offered a way of attracting men, rather than for its intrinsic value. Thus there was considerable continuity between family, school and peer culture for the 'academic' girls.

This was not necessarily the case with 'commercial' girls. As a child, Sharon had learned farming skills, and gender had not been an issue. She had had considerable freedom to work on her father's farm, but when she became a teenager, all that changed. Suddenly there was pressure on her from her parents to change her body image to ladylike elegance, and her behaviour to match. She was being groomed for marriage, and it was one in which intellectual pursuits were not seen as necessary by her mother. Though reasonably successful, she was aware of the low status of the commercial course, and felt she was in 'the dumb class'. The stigma remained with her and she retains a 'deep-seated sense of intellectual inferiority' and that she could 'never catch up with her peers in academic streams' (1987: 83). Thus Sharon did not enter fully into the 'commercial' girls' culture, but her life was considerably affected by it. Middleton concludes that 'the practice of streaming . . . was a central factor in the process of cultural reproduction' though family influences need to be taken into account. The case of Sharon also indicates how socialization is not complete and deterministic, but partial and influential.

Gender and Social Class

As noted earlier, girls have experiences in common, as do boys, but they also have considerable differences, as is clear from the examples above. Sometimes, social class seems the more influential factor in the formation of pupil cultures. Ball (1981), for example, in a detailed study of one form, observed 'a considerable amount of interaction between the (groups) of anti-school girls and anti-school boys . . . but only essential and unavoidable contact between these groups and the other boys and girls in the form' (p. 69). The girls approved of these boys. They were 'nice', 'funny', and 'modern'. The pro-school boys were 'weeds', did not wear 'the latest fashions or haircuts', were 'too serious and too involved in doing schoolwork'.

In this example, girls and boys in the same class location identify together. At other times, gender identity may be associated with a position of class subordination. This is well illustrated by Willis' (1977) 'lads' among whose culture sexism (and racism) were prominent features. The 'lads' show the concern for machismo-toughness and hardness, traditionally associated in the working class with being male. They have superior attitudes to the women. Girls are sex objects, the number of conquests a lad has had being one of the leading criteria in the informal status hierarchy. Yet sex, curiously, diminishes girls in the lads' eyes, and the 'easy lay', though sought after, is not respected. Not so the regular girlfriends, the 'missus', who is esteemed in the same way as mother. But she is still inferior, being 'a bit thick, like', and existing really to service the males, with cooking and housework. Such views, like their violence and aggression, are both rooted in the class system of society and linked to cultural concepts of masculinity. How this operates in respect of a mining community is illustrated by Dubberley (1988a), who makes a strong social-class defence against uncontextualized accusations of sexism among the males. He does not seek to excuse the sexism, but it must be correctly located, if it is to be combated:

> Coalton, like other pit communities, is a male-oriented community. In this respect it is sexist, but it is a sexism that has arisen as a particular manifestation of capitalism. The family unit is arranged and exploited so that coal can be produced. It is therefore offensive that some middle-class feminists should attack sexism in such communities while ignoring the very social and economic structures that force miners to dig coal and allow others the privilege of higher education and access to that cultural capital which enables them to make such criticisms . . . . (Dubberley, 1988: 122)

Gender roles and relationships have to be seen here within their social class context. This is also the case in instances of middle-class teachers seeking to impose their class norms and cultures upon working-class pupils. This is illustrated in the Lowfield study (Woods, 1979) where the senior mistress was incessantly trying to force girls into her own image of outmoded, middle-class, feminine propriety:

> That's what she's trying to get us to be like you know, trying to get us to be like her. But that's one thing I could never do, because ever

since I've been five I've been climbing trees, climbing on top of garages at the back 'ere — I don't think I could ever adjust to the way of Miss Sparkes . . . oh no!

(On the way they talk) you know if we go up and say 'Oh yeah, all right, we'll do it — they'll say, 'oh no, you don't say it like that', then they say it the right way, and you have to repeat it. But it doesn't make any difference, it's the way you've been brought up and the way you've spoken. You can't adjust really to the way of everybody else. (Woods, 1979: 198)

This is interesting for the reflective and analytical skills shown by the girls which some of their teachers deemed them not to possess, and for their portrayal and analysis of what the senior mistress stands for. They see it as an alien culture which they choose not to join since it contains values they hold of no worth, and in some instances despise.

A similar point is made by Dubberley (1988a). Among the examples he gives of middle-class teachers assailing working-class pupils' language in derogatory and superior fashion is one containing a racist, as well as a social class, sneer.

When we were in maths, we were like talking and she just came out with summat — 'even people in Africa can speak in better English than you.' We just looked at her and laughed. Yer know, she knows a lot more how to speak proper cos she probably comes from a different place. (Dubberley, 1988a: 181)

As with the Lowfield girls, these 'lasses' displayed an eloquence and an understanding of the 'arbitrary imposition of linguistic and cultural norms' (p. 182) sadly lacking in some of their teachers. But they fought for what they saw as their rights, and in this, their culture and its linguistic forms lent them considerable strength.

This notion of choice and active engagement with the world (as opposed to passive socialization) is central to the work of Anyon (1983), who illustrates another way in which gender and race intersect. She argues, from her research in five American elementary schools that for girls, gender development comes from coping with and accommodating to contradictory messages about womanhood; one emphasizing the domestic role, submissiveness to and dependence on males, non-competitiveness, child-rearing and caring; the other emphasizing a contrary set of values involving success in the non-domestic area. The former is more associated with working-class, the latter with middle-class women, but both involve contrary pressures. Working-class women need to be assertive and aggressive to some extent in the daily struggle for survival, while middle-class women, though encouraged to achieve in the world of work are also subject to pressures to be feminine and to prepare for domestic roles. Anyon found that girls responded to these pressures with a mixture of 'accommodation' (such as agreeing that men are more important, accepting the inevitability of the domestic role) and 'resistance' (effort, independence and perseverance at school work in excess of the obedience and neatness associated with the stereotype, being aggressive and assertive). She observed the complex reaction in intellectual, artistic and athletic achievement; in the appropriation of femininity and sexuality (that is, the conscious use of femininity to achieve their ends); being more assertive and intellectually aggressive especially among the girls in the middle-class schools; through 'tomboyishness' again more evident in the middle-class schools; and in 'distancing' and truanting — an 'internalized' form of resistance compared to boys' more open and demonstrative forms. However, Anyon concluded that these forms of accommodation and resistance take place within and do not challenge prevailing structures and 'trap women in the very contradictions they would transcend'. The major contradiction perhaps is that it probably requires collective political action to challenge those structures, but such action is not regarded as feminine.

Such work reminds us that the girls who do show devotion to schoolwork may not do so for the same reason as boys. Another formulation of class/sex differences in pupil attitudes drawing attention to a 'symbolic' factor is proposed by King (1971). He distinguishes between education's symbolic value (prestige, culture, knowledge) and its instrumental value (skills, qualifications, preparation for a job). He argues that middle-class boys value education for both reasons, middle-class girls only for its symbolic value, working-class boys only for its instrumental value, and working-class girls for neither. Where girls do show an instrumental approach, there is a distinct leaning towards those occupations that accord with the feminine image, as discussed above (and in Stanley, 1989).

Byrne (1978: 20) takes this 'compounding' of inequality further, suggesting five main factors that can come together in this respect: sex; lower social class; lower range of intelligence; residence in certain regions with a history of underachievement; residence in rural areas. Thus, 'girls who are less able, Northern, of lower social class and rural are quadruply disadvantaged' (p. 21). 'Race' could well be added to the list (*see* chapter 5). No doubt on occasions such factors do reinforce each other. However, as Fuller (1984: 37) points out, things cannot be so neatly aggregated. She points to the work of Epstein (1973) who relates how, in the USA, the potential double inequality of being black and female gives rise to *greater* educational and occupational attainment among black women than among either black men or white women. There are other examples, cited in chapter 5. Clearly the relationship between these factors is not a simple one.

While bearing in mind that models such as this cannot be applied to reality in a rigid manner, work by Burroughs (1987) indicates the general usefulness of the distinctions made by King. The following examples are adapted from Burroughs.

> Ruth, from a middle-class background, works hard enough for nine O levels, but not hard enough to get to a 'good' university; keeps pace with her friends academically, but not to be labelled a 'swot'; aims to get enough qualifications to leave open the option of a career, but in an acceptable 'feminine' field like acting or nursing; could win a prize, but probably not for academic reasons, rather for doing 'something different, like poetry, or reading, or a play . . . '

> Julie, from a working class background 'did not mention her job at all unless directly questioned about it. Given this low emphasis on future employment, the instrumental value of schoolwork is meaningless. It makes more sense to concentrate on preparing to be a wife (getting a boyfriend) than on preparing for exams, so that she can get a job that she really does not want, and only expects to have for a couple of years' (p. 247).

> Christopher (middle class) plans to study for scientific A levels in the sixth form, followed by university and a career in scientific research. He enjoys a lot of school, 'and the parts you don't enjoy you can usually see are going to help you . . . There's quite a lot of pride and challenge to it, and I always feel that I'm doing myself good if I'm slaving over something I don't like, it's really character building . . . ' (p. 250).

Alex (working class) accepts the ideology of the education system to work hard in return for a stable job. This is consistent with his construction of his future life style, based on traditional sex-roles — men should be breadwinners, women should be wives and mothers.

Ian's (also working class) 'mates' are everything to him. He likes 'having a laugh' at school, despises 'creeps', doesn't like being told what to do. He wants to work in a factory. His sex-role constructions are extremely traditional, and males in 'untypical' occupations are 'almost beyond contempt' (p. 261). This includes 'working hard at school'.

As well as illustrating King's basic model, one can also recognize some types here from chapter 3 (an 'ear 'ole', and a 'lad', perhaps?). Such models are, of course, extremely general, and disguise many individual and sub-group variations (*see* chapter 6). For instance from several examples already given it is clear that not all working-class boys have 'instrumental' attitudes toward school, nor are all working-class girls lacking it. Also, of course, the properties of the categories are not necessarily a permanent fixture. They are a social construct, and subject to change.

Explanation and Change

There seems a large amount of agreement on the nature of gender divisions within school, how gender identities are constructed through socialization, and how differential sex-roles are established and reproduced. There is less agreement on the underlying causes, and hence on policy for change. It has become customary to distinguish among: (1) Liberal feminists, who aim to bring about change from within prevailing structures, by, for example, giving boys and girls fair chances in all subjects, changing teacher and parental attitudes, use of female as well as male role-models, seeking more balanced and equitable socialization processes. (2) Radical feminists, who reject the above view since they see the underlying cause of female subordination in the structures themselves, a stratification by gender in which males are dominant, in other words 'patriarchy'. To these 'radicals' this is the major social division as compared to social class and 'race'. Women are seen here as an oppressed class, whereas 'liberals' see them as individuals struggling to cope. The hierarchy of knowledge, together with its hierarchies of school organization, also works against women. Proponents of this view argue that the changes proposed by liberals, though desirable, would scratch the surface of the problem, and that more profound change is required in society involving some transfer of power from men to women. (3) Socialist feminists, who also agree that a social revolution is necessary if women are to be liberated, but see social class rather than gender, capitalism rather than patriarchy, as the major problem. They draw attention to the diversity among girls and among boys, and to the communality between certain groups of girls and boys combined that is chiefly characterized by their social class position. Some males as well as females are oppressed in the system of power relations, and knowledge is differentially distributed to these groups, just as much if not more than to groups distinguished by gender. Attention is drawn to differences in pedagogic approach also between the open, questioning, stimulating, approach used in teaching high status subjects to pro-school, mainly middle-class pupils bound for professional and managerial occupations, and the more didactic, straightforward, teacher-directed approach used in low status subjects with working-class pupils destined for manual and low-skill occupations. Schools thus reproduce class relations by selecting and socializing and thus preparing students for their appropriate place in the labour market. Gender, and 'race', are also important in this, so divisions along those lines will feature prominently in schools also. But social class, it is argued, is the major factor. Some socialist feminists explore the ways in which all these factors work together across various sites, such as family, school, and place of work. Some recognize the separate existence of patriarchy, while seeing it as operating within capitalism.

This is only a brief sketch of these positions (*see* Arnot, 1989a, for a detailed account of developments in feminist theory). Few, I suspect, would hold simply to the first, liberal, view, any more than the proponents of differentiation-polarization theory would argue that changes in school organization would, on their own, secure radical changes in society. Nor would those who hold to the other views dispute the value of identifying divisions in all sites of activity and seeking to raise awareness about them. Therein lie the more immediate requirements for change.

There are signs that such a process has begun. Stanley (1989: 56), for example, found some lower-band 'lads' in the school of her research putting on a 'hard' show of bullying, racism and sexism, but she found their real attitudes less sexist than they appeared. Stanley points out:

> Times have changed, and in the Midlands as elsewhere, women have more power in these days of male unemployment; attitudes to 'men's work' have also changed in response to the devastation of heavy industry in the region, and the common experience of living off women's wages while the breadwinner is looking for a job. The Cato Park lads and their families also had less rigid ideas about 'women's work' than those described by Willis... and they were more realistic about this than many of their teachers'. (p. 56)

Two of the boys, in fact, were resentful that their teachers had not allowed them to take cookery. Of course one might take the view that this redefinition of an area as suitable, indeed desirable, for both girls and boys is driven by the enormous changes in work patterns taking place at the time with the decline of the traditional engineering jobs. Boys might be beginning to appropriate that, and other areas, if that is where the jobs lie. But that does not account for their underlying conformity and their opposition to blatant sexism.

Abraham (1989b) also noted some marked differences among anti-school boys in their gender value systems. One group, in fact, was strongly against the gender value system of the school, what Connell (1987: 120) calls the 'gender regime', and did not subscribe to traditional masculine values. The other group, of 'lads', seemed very similar to Willis' 'lads', equally strongly influenced by shopfloor culture, and by the domestic division of labour. But another group, known as 'the gothic punks', had a different set of values. Equally anti-school, they were, however, from lower middle-class backgrounds. They were a mixed sex group, and were distinguished by their all-black clothing. They rejected traditional masculine attitudes towards the curriculum (for example, that science and technology are important for boys, and home economics for girls), they rejected mainstream masculine sports, preferring music and socializing, complained about violence and macho hardness, and did not contribute to sexual stereotypes in their views of each other. Girls in the group were seen by the boys as companions rather than sexual objects. Unsurprisingly, there was some polarization between the two groups deriving from the gender differences between them. Abraham compares these to the 'Bloods' and the 'Cyrils' in an Australian upper-class boys' school, where the former persecuted the latter for their perceived effeminacy (Connell, 1987: 176–7). He concludes that while he did not observe them actively challenging the continuance of patriarchal relations, their actions did convey criticism of the school as a system; and revolved around rejection of traditional male values. This contrasts with forms of resistance noted among anti-school groups of boys in other studies that have the celebration of masculinity as a central theme.

Even though the two groups are of different social class, there is no straightforward connection with their gender orientations (*see also* Connell *et al.*, 1982). Many middle-class boys in the school held more traditional values, and some of the teachers' views on gender were aligned with those of the 'lads'. Also the 'Gothic punks' were more of a *counter-* school culture than the lads (p. 84). Thus hyper-masculinity is not necessarily a product of anti-school tendencies. Abraham concludes that his study shows 'the seeds of division between different types of men being sown', and offers a line of enquiry that 'could significantly inform initiatives in anti-sexist education for pupils and teachers' (p. 85).

The school in Abraham's study fostered conformity to traditional gender stereotypes by its insistence on uniform, its types of discipline, sports priorities, and views and attitude of staff. The question might be asked, however, if these were to change would it necessarily have any impact upon pupil values and cultures? Some studies show promising indications here. In one school's subject choice process, for example, Holly and Hume (1988) describe how a studied attempt to promote equal opportunities (by, for example, presenting subjects in terms of skills and how they related to careers, issuing notes to prompt pupils' thinking to counteract routine responses, using older pupils as counsellors, working hard to persuade girls to do science, promoting work experience for both pupils and teachers) in the space of four years produced significant results. The proportion of girls taking chemistry, for example, increased from 30 per cent in 1983 to 52 per cent in 1987. However, it is not easy to overcome thirteen years of gender socialization on the part of the pupils, nor the allegiance of some of the staff to a society organized by gender. This particular initiative owes much to the dedication and enthusiasm of one individual teacher who organized options. It is not, as yet, enshrined within school policy, nor does its major principle permeate the school in other ways. But it shows what can be done. Also there are signs in the study that the old stereotypes may be breaking down. Several girls, for example, were persuaded of their abilities and potential in science, and even more significantly, perhaps, boys *recognized* girls' prospective proficiency, whereas by the standard stereotype they might have been expected to contest it. Burroughs (1987) also noticed among her sample a strong emphasis upon 'caring' with boys who would not have been expected to show this according to traditional constructs of masculinity, and she wonders whether this 'may support the suggestion of an emergent and new definition of masculinity' (p. 256). This does not necessarily come just with adolescence. Davies (1987), in a study of Australian pre-school children, noticed that while some children seemed locked into traditional conceptions of gender, others were able to 'move partially towards a more liberated view' where their social environment had contained adults who espoused liberated views and offered liberated role-models (*see also* Clarricoates, 1987).

Arnot, (1989: 258) also reports on a London all-boys' school where teachers exploited the single-sex environment to try to change boys' gender orientations in a 'Skills for Living' project. Here

> ...boys are encouraged to think about such things as food preparation, shopping and baby care, to anticipate their future domestic lives. Classes discuss sexism in birthday cards, children's toys and books. The pupils are also encouraged to treat each other in a caring way. What the teachers are attempting is a redefinition of men's role in the family and a forum for boys to make themselves more aware of society's and their own assumptions about male and female roles. Such small-scale experiments point the way to a large-scale reform programme that could be developed within single-sex boys' schools.

It is more customary to stress the advantages of single-sex education for girls, since it is in company with boys that gender roles bite more acutely (Deem 1984). Thus, on their own, more girls might be encouraged to adopt more positive attitudes toward high-status and marketable subjects like science, and toward achievement in general, without fear of that coming under attack from boys as abnormal and unfeminine behaviour. It is thought by some that complete segregation would be detrimental to their social education, and these propose a compromise whereby boys and girls might be educated in the same institution, but engage in certain activities separately. Others (for example, Arnot, 1983: 87) feel that single-sex education on its own will not 'challenge the overall reproduction of dominant gender relations'.

The same might be said for a change of heart and mind by teachers, themselves not untouched (as indeed are all of us) by gender socialization, as Abraham's (1989b) study, for example, shows. But it is another factor that might help promote more general change. Here again, there seems to be a spreading of awareness. This is inevitably gradual since it involves deep examination of the self. As Skelton and Hanson (1989: 120) argue,

> It must be appreciated that to address equality issues is not to deal with external exercises restricted to the realms of the professional or the academic; rather it involves a challenge on a personal level. Confronting inequality involves the individual in self-examination. Personal assumptions, attitudes, expectations, behaviour are all called into question and may require change.

This is why there is such a great deal of personal reflection, examination, biographical work and life histories among gender studies (Middleton, 1987 and 1989; Aspinwall and Drummond, 1989; Evetts, 1989; Acker, 1989; Lyon and Migniuolo, 1989). Life histories take one back to early socialization, perhaps to domestic life not unlike that described by Turner at the beginning of the chapter. With the advantage of hindsight, a more mature mind, experience and knowledge, the mystification can be exposed and the division revealed as a social construct.

Such a technique can also be applied to pupils. Feminist educators are keen to promote teaching styles that take pupils' personal experiences and the way they construct their lives as their focus, as opposed to those styles that are more formal, impersonal and bureaucratic and that reinforce the status quo and encourage passive receipt of knowledge and socialization. Pupil-centred learning has a good foothold in British primary schools, though it proved impossible to implement the Plowden (1967) ideal (Galton 1987). What effect the 1988 Education Reform Act will have remains to be seen, but there is just as much chance that it will stimulate pupil-centred techniques (with the need now, for example, to teach all pupils a foreign language to age 16, formal techniques just will not do for new pupils caught by this), as it will traditional techniques.

Bringing pupils' lives and experiences to the forefront is not only a useful vehicle for teaching the pupil. It can be very instructive for the teacher and assist a wider perspective than school, as is shown by Arnot's (1989b) work. The talk that the teacher conducted with girls in her study

...reveals how paid employment (and domestic tasks in the home) are critical influences on these girls' lives. It puts into perspective attempts by teachers to try and break stereotypes and encourage girls towards wider horizons and less traditional routes. The limits and possibilities of educational reform are clearly demarcated by such 'evidence'. The reality of their parents' lives and work, their experiences of what young men and boys expect of girlfriends and wives, their own understanding of women's role in society militate against girls having any luxuries of academic ambition or non-traditional job expectations. (1989b: 189)

Arnot quotes Bernstein (1970: 120) to the effect that:

If the culture of the teacher is to become part of the consciousness of the child, then the culture of the child must first be in the consciousness of the teacher.

This applies just as much to boys as to girls, for if girls are oppressed by the structures that contain them, so are boys. This applies just as much to Willis' lads whose sexism is partly a product of their social class position, as to many middle-class boys who are launched on a conveyor-belt of ambition, competition and strain. Many of these will experience failure in terms of blockage or insufficient progression along career-ladders that are funnelled to warm them all up initially only to cool most of them down along the way (Woods, 1990b). Those that aspire to the top might experience stress they never anticipated. Males are also, therefore, to some extent prisoners of the structures within which they work (Connell, 1987; Hearn, 1987). Recognizing this, Nias (1989: 76) argues for the virtue of 'lateral careers' in teaching being regarded as more open and acceptable to men as well as to women, since their 'morale and enthusiasm might also be revived by the opportunity sometimes to move sideways (or out) as well as up'.

There is talk, too, of a 'new balance of values wherever power is being exercised' (Benn, 1989: xxvi), that places less emphasis on the stereotypical masculine qualities of hardness, ruthlessness, competition, objectivity and detachment, and more on qualities of humanity, gentleness, co-operation and social sensitivity.

Why shouldn't these criteria in which women are taught to excel be as highly valued for promotion or positions of authority in education as the capacity for confrontation and dictatorial dispatch? Why should so much academic research be funded for competitive 'male' industrial profit and the capacity to destroy rather than for 'female' environmental and nurturing goals? Why should the school curriculum be increasingly geared to the narrow, instrumental goals of 'male' employers rather than to more affective, social and cultural 'female' goals? (*ibid.*)

Such a recasting of the value-system upon which social relations in the occupational sphere are based would liberate and empower some males as well as females. A teacher in Lyon and Migniuolo (1989) wants to offer her boys 'some support in challenging the current oppressive definitions of what it is to be a man' (p.155), recognizes the need for 'space for positive alternatives' (p.157) and for a balanced (female and male) presentation of such courses as 'personal relationships'. It is argued that boys are poorly prepared for dealing with people and their own emotions, that they miss out on family life, being committed to a view of their lives as mainly life-long paid work (Arnot, 1989a). Many may feel torn between the pressures to work longer hours and wanting to play a bigger role in family life. Achieving masculinity for many boys is a struggle and it has to be re-earned every day. Thus 'boys don't cry' (Askew and Ross, 1988), they don't behave 'like women', and they revel in blood and violence. There is a 'masculine facade of hardness, toughness, imperviousness to pain and "objective" unemotionality,' probably also involving 'the rigorous denial of anything identified as "female" within themselves' (*ibid.*: 163). This may be why the boys Askew and Ross observed were rather rigid and stylized in their relationships with each other, did not seem to trust each other, nor to be very good at discussing their personal experiences, nor to listen to each other very well. Lacking such personal and social skills may be a concomitant of the need to appear masculine. It may also be connected with boys' slower development in reading (Barrs and Pidgeon, 1986), which may be both a product of, and a contributor to, the syndrome.

The difficulties of adhering to this masculine code were neatly shown in our study of school transfer (Measor and Woods, 1984: 25), after some boys had been boasting about how they were looking forward to cutting up rats, and some girls professing squeamishness:

An interesting footnote to this came during observation of the lesson in which the notorious rat was dissected. For it was a *boy* not a girl who fainted, and another boy fainted three days later during a film on the birth of a baby. The demands of the adolescent male code may not always be easy to fulfil by the lads who are subjected to it!

Chapter 4

Pupils and 'Race'

The term 'race' has become somewhat discredited since biological evidence has pointed to the non-existence of 'races'. 'Ethnic group' has become the preferred term, and this is defined by one author as

> a segment of a larger society whose members are thought, by themselves and/or by others, to share a common origin and to share important segments of a common culture, and who, in addition, participate in shared activities in which the common origin and culture are significant ingredients. (Yinger, 1981)

This is the sense in which I shall be referring to the pupil groups discussed in this chapter. However, though 'races' do not exist in a scientific sense, they are constructed in people's minds. When this amounts to attributing 'characteristics to social groups in a biologically and culturally deterministic manner' this may be described as 'racism' (Rattansi, 1989: 15). Where people engage in practices that discriminate among these groups, we have 'racial discrimination'. These beliefs and practices appear to predominate over scientific fact in society at large with the result that 'race' is just as big an issue, if not bigger, than social class and gender. It is certainly more explosive, with increasing incidence of racial unrest disorder, and violence, both in society and in schools.

The issue is, if anything, even more complicated to address than social class and gender. It is interconnected with those factors, but also more variegated. For example, at one level it is customary to refer to 'whites' and 'blacks', the latter covering all 'non-whites'. Though many of them are far from 'black', their inclusion denotes a common experience of oppression at the hands of whites. Not all 'blacks' are happy with this categorization, and this may be because there are large differences among them. The two largest groups in British society are those of Afro-Caribbean and of Asian origin or descent. These in turn contain large differences, Asians, for example, consisting of Indians, Pakistanis, and Bangladeshis. This could be taken further, groups of these, for example, originating from different geographical regions or having different religious affiliations or having different mother tongues.

This picture is even more complicated, since members within these ethnic groups are not always of the same social class (*see* Eggleston *et al.*, 1986); and one ethnic category may contain groups that have different experiences, whether as a consequence of higher social class position or not. This is the case with the Asian group, for example, where Indian and Pakistani pupils achieve considerably better examination results than Bangladeshis. The latter do have the lowest-paid jobs and occupy the lowest social class position. Yet 'Asian' pupils as a whole do nearly as well as 'white' pupils at schools, and considerably better than Afro-Caribbean (Statham and Mackinnon, 1989: 158). This does not mean to say that they do not experience racism and racial discrimination.

Thus, some elements of experience might be the same, inasmuch as all such groups might be considered 'black' (though some of them might not agree), and some might be different. My aim here is not to give a comprehensive account of the black experience in British or 'Western' schools, but rather to identify some general points that might be inferred from the detailed case studies of particular ethnic groups. Thus I shall consider the culture clash that can occur between teacher and pupils; following the 'differentiation-polarization' theme, the effect that school organization and teacher attitudes have on peer group formation and behaviour, gender and race; pupils' experience of the 'racial' curriculum'; and pupil relationships.

Culture Clash

Teacher Attitudes and School Organization

The misunderstandings and tensions that can arise between teachers and pupils of different ethnic origin because of culture differences have been well illustrated by Dumont and Wax (1969) in a classic article on teaching Cherokee pupils in the USA. They show how white teachers might totally misinterpret the behaviour of Cherokee pupils. The authors refer to a teacher of many years' experience who took the pupils' silence and docility as indicating well-mannered conformity — a model group no less — but who still did not manage 'to teach them anything'. She interpreted their conduct from 'within her own culture', rather than recognizing what the authors describe as 'the Cherokee school society'. Cherokees show a concentration on 'precision and thoroughness' though it is a 'congregate activity that is more often directed at social . . . relationships'. They are oriented towards relating to other persons (as opposed to particular scholastic tasks) and towards the tribal Cherokee community, where the basic three 'Rs' have little use. Their reactions within school to 'the pressures of alien educators' is to cultivate not a blatantly oppositional culture but one with 'exquisite social sensibility'. They do not reject tasks given them, but because these have 'no bearing on their tradition or experiences', they are unable to master them. They use silence as a weapon as conflict gradually escalates throughout their school career. Stress is likely to develop in such pupils, since tension and conflict is alien to their culture (unlike Willis's lads', or Hargreaves's and Lacey's counter-cultural groups, for whom conflict is central); stress will also develop in teachers unless they achieve better cultural understanding of their pupils, since tension can only escalate as they seek to achieve results as defined by their own culture.

Dumont and Wax go on to describe 'the intercultural classroom', i.e. one where there are more shared meanings between teacher and pupils. A distinctive feature of this is the teacher's willingness to negotiate, to talk with pupils, learn about them and adjust to them (as discussed in Chapter 2). The students have ways of facilitating such exchanges, for example, by providing spokespersons to mediate, who might head off potential conflict and provide cultural bridges. But this can only work if the teacher cultivates a more open and accessible role.

Since cultures equip us with ways of looking at the world, there is almost a 'natural' tendency to interpret others from our own perspectives. The Cherokee example is one of mutual misinterpretation, where the different assumptions of the two parties to the interaction led to there being no common ground on which exchanges meaningful to either party could take place — neither what the teacher saw as 'teaching' (something worthwhile) nor what the students saw as 'learning' (something worthwhile). There is no doubt, though, whose definitions prevailed. What counts as schooling is based on the dominant culture, in terms of which other cultures are considered deviant, lacking or inept.

McLaren (1986) noticed a similar gulf between some Canadian school teachers and a group of Portuguese students. For example, 'politeness and obsequiousness in responding to authority are not traits that fare well in the streetcorner state — yet these are the traits which teachers regarded as highly desirable in their students' (p. 169). The ritualized instruction which the teachers saw as 'a mission of sanity and love' some students saw as a 'ritual pathology'. There was also a world of difference between the Catholicism purveyed by the school, which came to be closely enmeshed with the secular aspects of work, and the logic of the student's existence and aspiration, mirrored in a central contradiction. They were urged, for example, to 'feel joyful and thankful for being loved by God', yet simultaneously encouraged to 'accept their sinful nature, be prepared to suffer and endure the banality of life, and accept the pains and sorrows that accompanied material existence' (p.182).

It is not surprising under such circumstances that school counter-cultures are produced among pupils of minority ethnic groups, some of which might prove more disruptive than the Cherokee pupils above. To what extent are these cultures formed and developed in reaction to the school, and to what extent are they a product of the ethnic group culture? A theme running through many of the studies on this issue is that it is a combination of the two, with the former providing the incentive and the latter the resource. In the process, the culture might become strengthened, and polarized.

Differentiation and Polarization

Wright (1986) made a study of the experiences of pupils from minority ethnic groups in the mixed comprehensive schools in the Midlands. She shows how classroom life for Afro-Caribbean girls and boys tended to be much more conflictual than it was for white or Asian pupils. Her observations led her to conclude that teachers' attitudes and expectations had much to do with this. There are clear examples of racism among them, including the attitude of the metalwork teacher:

> I had a black girl in my class. She did something or another. I said to her, if you're not careful I'll send you back to the chocolate factory . . . . It was only said in good fun, nothing malicious'. (Wright, 1986: 131)

Again contrary definitions of the situation seem to be in play here. Such a remark might have been 'good fun' for the teacher (cf. the countless jokes perpetrated through the media on racial types), but the pupils concerned and their parents clearly thought otherwise.

An English language teacher was observed to 'pick on' a group of Afro-Caribbean girls and to promote confrontation, blaming the girls for her inability to establish conducive learning conditions. She invariably expected them to be difficult so that she would be in confrontation with them, and played down opportunities for conciliation. She recognized their academic abilities, but these received only secondary consideration. This, in fact, seemed fairly common among the staff, with the result that the academic assessment of these pupils was influenced more by behavioural than by cognitive criteria. (It is quite common, in fact, for teachers to relate behaviour and academic achievement closely together, as in the Hargreaves, Lacey and Ball studies discussed earlier). Certainly Afro-Caribbeans, more than any other pupil group, were likely to be placed in ability bands and sets well below their actual academic ability. For example, at one of the schools of Wright's study nearly 20 per cent of Afro-Caribbean pupils were put in remedial groups on entry compared with 7.7 per cent of Asians and none of the white children, even though the Afro-Caribbeans' reading scores were as good as or better than those of the other groups. At the other school, 70 per cent of Afro-Caribbean children were assigned to the lower band at 13+ compared with 34.4 per cent of Asian and 47.1 per cent of white, despite having the best mean performance score and a mean effort score comparable to that of the other two groups. The teachers may have argued, and indeed believed, that they were treating all pupils the same and judging them by the same criteria, but close observation and analysis suggest they were not.

The pupils themselves talked freely of the insults, criticisms and directives that seemed to make up the content of their classroom experience. Inevitably, opposition was reinforced and pupils defended themselves by berating a teacher with a stream of Jamaican patois, which of course only confirmed the teacher's fears and sense of opposition. Afro-Caribbean boys also rallied into a strong sub-cultural group which took a delight in baiting the teachers. This seems another good example of the self-fulfilling prophecy or labelling process at work (Becker, 1963; Hargreaves *et al.*, 1975). The essence of this view is that deviance arises and develops as a consequence of being labelled as such. It also seems yet another contributor to 'differentiation and polarization', with some of the same institutional processes at work as those identified by Hargreaves and Lacey. This appears to be the case irrespective of whether it comes about through relatively formal means, as in one of Wright's schools, or as a result of an informal but pervasive derogatory stereotyping.

This recourse to cultural exclusivity appears to have been a coping strategy on the pupils' part. Not all black pupils take this line of action. Troyna (1978), for example, found a difference between black pupils in upper streams and those in lower. He set out to examine the degree of racial homogeneity among peer groups in a multi-racial (mainly white, Afro-Caribbean and Cypriot) London comprehensive school. As appears fairly general (*see* Mortimore *et al.*, 1988), a disproportionate number of black, and especially Afro-Caribbean pupils, were in the lower streams. All the pupils in the fourth year were asked to nominate three friends. The results (as with Hargreaves and Lacey) showed a high degree of stream-specific nominations, and also of racial homogeneity. When asked why they made their choice, some found it difficult to explain. However, the choosing by blacks of blacks as friends was a deliberate decision by most. Here are some of the answers:

'Because they understand more.'

'The white kids stick together because they do their own thing, y'know, they go to football on Saturday and all this.'

'I don't think that any of my friends are proper, proper English. I don't like the way they go on with their dirty jeans and their long, long hair. I don't like their culture.'

'[The white boys] do not understand our music. They say it's no good and we argue. But if it was in school like to muck about, it's alright, but if I was going to explain something to them about us, they can't really understand.' (Troyna, 1978: 63)

These pupils show here an appreciation of different life styles, the difference focusing on the crucial role of music in the lives of the black pupils. The life style of the white 'Rock music' follower, who is favoured with a variety of outlets, contrasts strongly with the 'Reggae boy' whose 'music received far fewer outlets and who is therefore committed to attend the local "Blues" (house parties) held by West Indians and to the specialist clubs' (*ibid.*). There is a certain hostility between the two groups, which helps promote differentiation, and music preferences aid both this and polarization within the separate groups.

Troyna, however, found a difference between black pupils in the upper streams and those in the lower, and social class appeared strongly related to the difference. Most of the 'Reggae boys' were in the lower streams. One high-stream black boy preferred going around with 'the top kids in the class', and only went with 'coloured kids' as a last resort. Another was also involved in a multi-racial peer group, and there was mutual contempt between these and 'D streamers'. This study therefore suggests that top-stream black pupils play down their intra-group loyalties, while bottom-stream blacks play theirs up and become racially exclusive. Troyna argues that 'this... results from the pupils' realisation of a common identity and shared destiny. These are the pupils who are most vulnerable to unemployment, police confrontation and other manifestations of normative racism in contemporary Britain. This realisation serves to differentiate them not only from the black pupils in the higher streams but also from their classmates' (p. 64). Here again, therefore, we see social-class influences cross-cutting the racial factor, and a very similar process occurring to that identified by Lacey. A similar kind of division was noted by Mac an Ghaill (1988) among the Asian pupils in his schools, with the small group of middle-class Asian pupils over-represented in the top streams and strongly critical of the anti-school subculture. This reflected the division within the wider Asian community between a black business class and workers.

Do these cultural divisions hold in more liberal, unstreamed situations? The answer is both yes and no. Furlong's (1984) study of a small group of disaffected Afro-Caribbean boys in an East London comprehensive showed some significant differences from these previous studies. These boys were seen as major problems by their teachers. Yet Furlong found contradictions in their attitudes. For example, they were both for school and against it; they wanted to achieve but were unwilling to work; they liked control, but revelled in its absence. To explain these contradictions, Furlong employs a similar theory to that used by Lacey and Willis, i.e. one of a culture of resistance. However, Willis's 'lads' had a clearer idea of their real situation than did Furlong's boys. For the latter, reality was obscured on the one hand by the liberal policies of the school, which deferred absolute academic judgement until their mock CSEs during the fifth year, and on the other by their families' lack of experience of the British educational system. A partial culture of resistance was needed, therefore, which would allow them both to accept school and its possibilities and to reject it, because they could see that they were failing.

The major theme of this culture was to establish a reputation as a man. It involved 'hardness', not in a simple 'macho' sense (as with white working-class youths), but through 'style' which informed the main themes in their lives — music, dress, girlfriends and relationships with the school. For example, their music was a derivation of Reggae, which they called 'Dub'. Bob Marley was too 'soft' and 'too commericial'; but Dub was 'cool, cool' and 'strictly rockers'. Unlike some other musical forms (e.g. 'Soul'), Dub culture 'eschews commodity fetishism, celebrates the West Indians' blackness for its own sake and emphasizes black identity and heritage' (p. 222). The theme of a reputation for masculinity pervaded their whole outlook on school life. Some other pupils were 'youtish' for doing things in a not quite manly way. Teachers who assailed their dignity were paid back in kind, even with violence. But the theme of a reputation, even if it brought conflict with teachers, committed them to school, for its concern with status involved skilled work requiring qualifications. Non-skilled work was 'shame, man, shame'. However, their concern for style within the school could not bring them to be wholly conformist.

The form of this culture of resistance, like Willis's' lads', was one of 'intense association'. Unlike white boys' groups, however, theirs celebrated language rather than action. There was 'a continual dialogue amongst the participants; they talked incessantly . . . spoke in a range of accents . . . used language creatively for running jokes amongst themselves . . . and as a demonstration of their own hardness (p. 226). The school was very important to the group. They hardly ever missed a day. However, they ingeniously appropriated it to their concerns, marking out their territory within it, and organizing 'private time' for themselves (e.g. arriving late for lessons and leaving early), during which they would engage in 'the most furious socializing' (p. 229).

The context of this culture was provided by the boys' parents' traditionally high expectations of education for their children, their own occupational aspirations and the school's liberal structure (no streaming, sets only for maths and English in the fourth and fifth years, compatible CSE and O level course, liberal examination entry policy, broad-based curriculum around a common core). Thus, though the boys knew they were failing within the school, they were 'shielded from the full reality of their public evaluation on standards established outside the school' (p. 232). When their lack of achievement became public — after the mock CSEs — they were gently 'cooled out' of the system (e.g. not having to attend lessons they were not taking examinations in).

We have seen here how cultural differences based on 'race' can lead to gross misunderstanding between different groups. These differences can be aggravated by racism which has the effect, where differentiation and polarization occur, of consigning a disproportionate number of black pupils to bottom streams or other underprivileged positions within schools. In this location they reinforce their togetherness both on a 'stream' and on a 'race' dimension and develop a culture of resistance which has racial, gender and social-class overtones.

Pupil Resistance

The syndrome of 'blaming the victims' in terms of a 'deficit theory' (that is, their 'underachievement' and uncooperative behaviour are a result of some cultural or biological deficiency), and then this giving rise to such outcomes has been perceived in a number of studies and across a range of ethnic groups. Teachers might interpret the outcomes as evidence supporting their views. An alternative, and stronger interpretation is that they are a form of resistance helping such pupils to cope with the problems they experience at the hands of the school. This would appear to be the case in the studies by Wright, Troyna and Furlong, discussed above. There is strong support for the argument.

McLaren (1986), for example, in his study in a Canadian Catholic School of lower-class Portuguese grade eight students, born of immigrant families, argues that school and classroom rituals, while comforting for some in parts, had similar effects to the subject choice process discussed in Chapter 3. Thus;

> Students were made to feel inadequate due to their class and ethnic status and hence the school offered to help socialize them into the 'appropriate' values and behaviours by tracking them into designated streams and basic level courses. (McLaren, 1986: 215)

He refers to a 'culture of pain' that was induced as they were subjected to dreary instructional rituals and routines, boring, repetitive instructional rites, banal subject matter, censure if they deviated from the official line. Resistance took the form of using 'pain' to construct counter-rituals. 'Staying cool' and 'bearing up' under pressure was one of these. 'Hitting back' against an oppressor was another, and there was much 'pretending to learn'. Humour also was a considerable resource, being a means of 'redefining the power structure of the class' and recapturing their 'sense of collective identity' (p. 161; *see also* chapter 8). All of this, interpreted by some teachers as evidence of a cultural pathology standing in the way of their educational advancement, was in fact a cultural strength in their efforts to manage. A different kind of educational ethos which attempted to requisition their culture as a pedagogical resource might have yielded better results for both sides.

Mac an Ghaill also discovered a similar syndrome in his study of black female and male youth of Afro-Caribbean and Asian parentage. Though there were differences among the teacher ideologies, they all identified the 'problem' as residing in the black students and their cultural background. They had become stereotyped over time into 'high-achieving conformist' Asian student, and 'low-ability, troublesome' Afro-Caribbean student. These, then, became even more polarized in the streaming practices of the school, Afro-Caribbean students being placed in lower streams, like Wright's even if they had 'higher ability' than Asian or white pupils. One teacher explained:

> The coloured boys always ended up at the bottom. It was not always because they weren't bright. They were the worst behaved ones. It was their aggressive attitude. They went wild if you disciplined them. You couldn't reason with them. The problem was there were too many of them, too many problems. (Mac an Ghaill, 1988: 44)

Another teacher commented that 'the Asians are better, you tell them to do something an' they are meek an' they go an' do it'(p. 65). The Asian students are judged by technical criteria (such as the measurement of academic criteria), the Afro-Caribbean by social/behavioural. Other students saw through the discrimination. Thus a group of Asian boys thought the Afro-Caribbeans no different from them, but suffering from teacher stereotyping and labelling. Even the more liberal teachers tended to work within the overall racist paradigm. Thus, one of these who claimed that he tried to treat his students all the same, was surprised to find out from the researcher that in one lesson he responded to a far higher proportion of interruptions from Afro-Caribbean pupils than from any other group; and that he used different criteria for different pupils. Operating these broad typifications of students, it should be noted, is not a pathological condition of teachers. Rather it is also a product of social pressures and constraints (the quote above makes this point) — a coping strategy that has become institutionalized in teacher practice and culture and school processes.

The students' response to this was to create their own culture around a form of resistance. With respect to the Afro-Caribbean 'Rasta heads', this was a visible form; with the 'Asian Warriors' it was invisible. Both, like Hargreaves and Lacey's groups (chapter 3), inverted some of the official values; at times, however, they accommodated the official ideology. They did have some common experiences. Pervading the Rasta Heads' subculture was a process of Africanization; particularly important was the influence of Rastafari, providing them with a distinct identity and life-style and a distinctive blend of experiences. But their subculture was not simply a response to school. Mac an Ghaill's analysis supports Brown's (chapter 3) argument about the importance of the local labour market. This had collapsed even for working-class kids, but it was worse for black youth. As one employer remarked, 'we pick our own kids'. What would be the point, therefore in academic success? The Rasta Heads' form of resistance developed during their third year in interaction with white teachers. The subcultural identification was accompanied by a process of dissociation from the dominant white culture, which developed with their growing experience and awareness of racism. Their visibility was due to their habit of grouping in prominent places; to their style of dress and appearance; to their habits of unpunctuality and lesson disruption; to their rejection of the official work ethic; and to their strategies of resistance, like 'sucking teeth' and 'bad looks'; to their use of Creole, which effectively excluded whites.

The 'Asian Warriors' were a group of nine students, two of Pakistani, seven of Indian origin, all born in England to working-class parents. They identified with the 'rude boy' subcultural form, projecting a tough image counter to the stereotype of passive conformity, and strongly anti-authoritarian (Hebdige, 1979). Again, this group came together during the third year, a central element of the association being resistance to racism. They did not think of themselves as English either, they were 'Asian' or 'Indian'. Among their strategies of resistance were collective threats to teachers' control — difficult to deal with since they could not be individualized; creating diversionary tactics was a game, with high status going to the more successful in the more boring situation; they also used their own language as a means of excluding teachers or as an act of defiance; used techniques of 'counter-interrogation' when cross-examined. This group, then, challenged the stereotype of the achieving, conforming Asian students, in a way not dissimilar to the Afro-Caribbean 'Rasta Heads'. However, by contrast with the latter, they remained largely invisible, the behaviour of middle-class Asians, who identified more with whites and who *were* more conformist, being assigned to them all. Clearly, the social class element is of some crucial importance here.

Mac an Ghaill's main argument is that differences in academic achievement between these groups and others cannot be explained solely by intrinsic cultural differences. The major problem lies with racism. He claims that his research shows that

> ... racism operates through the existing institutional framework that discriminates against all working-class youth ... through 'race'-specific and also gender-specific mechanisms such as the system of racist stereotyping. There may be no conscious attempt to treat black young people in a different way to white youth, but the unintended teacher-effects result in differential responses which work against black youth. Different strategies that are informed by class and gender are adopted by different sections of the youth in their resistance to a racially structured society. These collective responses, which are linked to the wider black community, are seen as legitimate survival strategies. (Mac an Ghaill, 1989: 186)

Pupil-teacher Integration

Not all pupil-teacher interaction takes this form. Foster (1988), for example, studied a small, neighbourhood co-educational comprehensive in a working-class area in a declining industrial conurbation, and the attempt of the teachers to put a multicultural anti-racist policy into practice. There were about equal numbers of Afro-Caribbean and white pupils in the school. His conclusion was that they largely succeeded. In his two years' association with the school, he saw very few examples of racism, heard no derogatory remarks, witnessed no examples of inadvertent differential treatment (cf. Driver, 1979), or of teachers categorizing pupils in terms of race. Pupils were seen as individuals. It was considered important to understand their ethnic backgrounds, and teachers were keen to identify positive elements deriving therefrom. Interestingly, two new members of staff who had held racist views previously and had been warned to 'watch out for the black kids' were inducted by the staff into the anti-racist ethos. At other times and places, as Foster points out, it could work differently with the transfer of racist myths from one institution to another.

Similarly, there were few indications of racism among the pupils. Complaints made to him about the staff were common to both ethnic groups and related to such things as outlined in chapter 2 — teaching methods, being 'soft' or 'boring'. There were slightly more Afro-Caribbean boys proportionately among the anti-school group, but their views that school was 'rubbish' and a 'waste of time' were shared by girls and boys from both main ethnic groups. Many of these, especially the Afro-Caribbean pupils, like Furlong's, retained a strong belief in the value of education and planned to go to college to 'get qualifications'. There were few complaints of anything approaching racism from teachers. 'None of the teachers here are like that', said one black girl. Foster concluded that the hostility of the Afro-Caribbean pupils derived from 'more general dissatisfaction and poor prospects after school' — similar to their white peers.

As for school organization, there was no evidence of any inequalities or unfairness arising as a result of it. Differentiation did take place from the fourth year, but a complicated system of block timetabling, setting, option groups and mixed ability avoided any marked differentiation and polarization. Pupils were allocated to groups by ability and 'motivation', indicated by behaviour. Since Afro-Caribbean boys were slightly disadvantaged in the arrangements, this latter criterion may have worked against them, as it did in the other studies discussed earlier, since they were more likely to be seen as behaviour problems. Foster also found a mixed-ability class 'very equalizing'. The teacher did work to an 'ideal type' student, but there were no racial criteria involved, and no sponsorship of high status children. Equal treatment was reflected in examination results, the Afro-Caribbean pupils doing just as well, if not better (especially girls) than white pupils. The anti-school pupils had not been labelled failures and rejected. Foster preferred to conclude that

> It was more plausible that students with anti-school attitudes, derived from and developed outside the school in class, ethnic and youth subcultures, by their behaviour in school secured for themselves allocation to low status groups in the fourth and fifth years. (Foster, 1988: 394)

There seemed to be no disadvantage for ethnic minority pupils in the option system, though there was one on social class lines, bands 2 and 3, predominantly working class, not being represented evenly across the choices, and working-class parents being less likely to intervene. Studying one mixed-ability class in detail, Foster found teachers differentiating quite strongly on grounds of ability and behaviour. There was no significant tendency for Afro-Caribbean pupils to occupy the lower rankings, though there was for all *boys* as compared with all the girls.

In short, the 'race' element, it is claimed, has been effectively handled here to mutual benefit. It is the social class factor that is dominant in this particular situation. Why should this school be so different from those studied by Wright and others? Assuming the methodologies were comparable, there were some significant differences. Foster's school served a community with a long history of co-operation. It had a most liberal organization. Its staff had a high level of awareness about 'race', and were actually implementing an anti-racist programme. Above all, perhaps, it was most generously staffed. Though it had declining numbers (500 in 1982, 363 in 1986), the LEA wished to preserve it, so maintaining a staff of 40, the minimum thought necessary to preserve 'comprehensive' education in the school. This gave a teacher-pupil ratio of 1:9 in 1985–6, making it 'the envy of many schools in the city'. Contrast this with the teacher's comment in Mac an Ghaill's school, given earlier: '... The problem was there was too many of them, too many problems'. There are limits to the changes that can be made in schools while teachers work under such constraints (Hargreaves, 1988).

Gender and Race

A consistent finding in research is that some groups of black girls do well at school though boys from the same ethnic group, often in the same school, do badly. Mac an Ghaill (1988) studied a small group of young black women, some of Afro-Caribbean, some of Asian parentage, at a sixth-form college. Supporting Anyon's (1983) formulation (*see* chapter 4), he saw their response as one of 'resistance within accommodation'. They valued academic qualifications, but rejected the racist curriculum. They were pro-education, but anti-school. However, unlike some of the Afro-Caribbean boys described earlier who were 'pro-education' but thought the school rubbish and did not try, these girls largely went along with what they were asked to do in lessons, even nationalistic history lessons. Judith explained

> . . . I'll put it down for them, so that we can tell them that black people are not stupid. In their terms, we can tell them that we can get on. In their terms, I come from one of the worst backgrounds but I am just saying to them, I can do it right, and shove your stereotypes up your anus. (Mac an Ghaill, 1989: 180)

A similar response was made to teachers' assault on their language, which 'really got to' Leonie. She felt that 'it was rejecting another part of you, being black you know, being part of you' (*ibid.*). When, at junior school, the whole class including the teachers, laughed at her when she went to see a 'filim', she 'felt so bad inside, you can't understand . . . . I mean they're laughing at me, they're laughing at my parents, they're laughing at everything associated with Patois, with everything black' (p. 181). The point recalls the experiences of the working-class girls described in chapter 3 (p. 75), but here a 'race' dimension is added. Some of the friends reacted by talking Patois even more, and for some of them, this was not only defiance but it was a considerable resource also, as we have already seen. Leonie and some of her friends, however, coped in a different way, by pretending to change, but remaining the same 'deep down'. This is therefore hidden, but no less real resistance. Like the Cherokee Indian children, described earlier, things are not what they seem in such responses.

Other features of their 'resistance within accommodation' included sympathetic, not polarized, attitudes to other anti-school groups of students who chose different routes, especially the Afro-Caribbeans. They coped with teachers by accepting their instrumental value, but not allowing their assessments of them to penetrate too deeply. Their main aim in school was to gain high-status academic qualifications. These would be the public testimony to their own worth, a salutary expression of their abilities in the face of general expectations of black, working-class women. Mac an Ghaill points out that these are collective strategies, though they might seem individualized, in the sense that they are mediated by a peer group network which, in turn, is linked to the wider black community.

The Black Sisters, in the schools they had attended, had experienced and witnessed similar forms of racism to the boys' groups. There were similar kinds of hierarchical racist stereotyping, with white students being seen to be treated with more respect and having more expectations made of them; and differences being seen to be made between Asian and Afro-Caribbean students (as above), with the former hard-working and conformist, the latter troublesome. Yet in one of their previous schools where there had been a majority Asian student population, the teachers used negative stereotypes of the Asian students, assuming deep cultural differences between them and white students, and classifying them as 'alien, sly and over-ambitious' (Mac an Ghaill, 1988: 16). This grading was reflected again in the streaming practices of the schools, with Afro-Caribbean students being concentrated in the lower streams in the schools where they formed the majority, and Asian girls in the school where Asians were in the majority. Clearly 'race' seems a potent factor in the differentiating functions of these schools, and helps to support the view of all three student groups in Mac an Ghaill's study that racism, not gender or social class, was the main problem in their schooling.

The Black Sisters were oppressed but not defeated by the racism they experienced. You were treated 'bad, really bad as a black person' but 'it's still good, better to be black' (p. 20). They were not caught in two minds between two cultures, as is sometimes argued. They were progressively minded, and proud of being black and female. There is, in fact, a considerable amount of evidence to show that young black women resist the implications of the standard gender stereotyping. Fuller (1980), for example, described a group of aspiring black girls in a London comprehensive, who were well aware of being at risk of being 'double subordinate', but strongly refused to accept the academic and career implications. They were determined to do well in these spheres, and recognized the value of education in their search for greater freedom and control. They had a strong sense of their own worth, which they considered undervalued by others in comparison to boys. However, while strong academically, their behaviour in class was not a model of propriety. Fuller argues that their behaviour was linked to their positive identity with being black and female. Thus they conformed to the behavioural standards of the peer group sufficiently to retain their friendship without sacrificing their own academic aims. In arriving at their adaptation, they had come to rely on their own judgements and evaluations of themselves, rather than on those of others, including teachers.

Riley (1988), also, found that the group of fifth- and sixth-form Afro-Caribbean girls in her research saw themselves far from being 'at the bottom of the pile'. They had strong opinions in three areas:

Firstly, they had firmly held and clearly articulated views on gender and sexuality. They did not consider themselves peripheral to male black culture, nor did they consider themselves to be passive sexual objects with little involvement in the 'real' male world. Secondly, they had a sense of political awareness and a determination to challenge political decisions which might restrict their future prospects. Thirdly, they were well able to analyse their own experience of schooling. Although a number of these young black women were justifiably critical of many aspects of this schooling, they were also able to evaluate and use creatively, the more positive aspects of their school life. (Riley, 1988: 223)

In another example, McKellar (1989), a black teacher educator, recalls her experiences at school, after failing the eleven-plus examination:

> ... there came a point when the negative attitudes of the teacher actually served to increase my determination and motivation. I began to carve out clear goals and ambitions. Instead of accepting the academic downfall signalled by failing the eleven-plus, I sought avenues for achieving status, both in school and the world outside, as well as in the future that lay ahead of me. (McKellar, 1989: 77)

Her determination brought swift results and she was soon transferred to grammar school. She felt that such experience meant that 'at an early age an awareness of one's overall position in society develops' (*ibid.*).

This suggests a possible explanation for this reaction which has not been found to the same degree of generality, for example, among white, working-class girls. This is that, as the potential degree of disadvantage increases, so does the individual's sensitivity and consciousness. In the denial and/or denigration of the background culture and of one's own identity is a catalytic quality of reaction that lies at the heart of the formation of many of these school subcultures. This is well illustrated, again, in Middleton's (1987) study of New Zealand women by the case of Tahuri, a Maori girl of parents who were 'working-class' in terms of the 'pakeha' (white) world. Her parents, and other relatives, encouraged her, and she grew up strongly pro-education. But at secondary school 'her enculturation as a Maori was viewed as inappropriate and the devaluation of her culture made explicit' (p. 86). As a bright student, she was put in the top stream, where she was prevented from taking Maori language classes, in favour of French and Latin. Maori was for the bottom streams. Tahuri's response was to join up with other top stream outcasts in a show of resistance, which included an 'exaggerated display of sexuality,' 'black pants, black shirt with jerkin . . . coconut oil in hair . . . . It was unacceptable. It was totally atrocious. We were just walking catastrophes, us three, we were just not allowed through the door. I mean, it was so dreadful that we were in that class, degrading its quality like that' (*ibid.*). This linked them with the other Maori girls concentrated in the lower streams. In this instance, therefore, streaming does not act as so much of a constraint on peer identification as it did in Troyna's study.

As Middleton (1987: 87) observes, 'Perhaps (finally), it is the experience of *marginality* — in terms of being working class, black, female or a combination of these — which is radicalizing'. This point is also noted by Phoenix (1987), who added a further comment that black children are used to black women participating in the labour market and dominating households, in a way not expected of white women, and that, therefore, their acquisition of gender identity is qualitatively different from that of white children. These points might help also to explain why these black girls' attitudes and experiences differ from some black boys'. As we have noted, some groups of these boys are equally as able and pro-education (*see* Furlong, 1984, Mac an Ghaill, 1988) but they accommodated in different ways. Mac an Ghaill, for example, emphasized collective unity among the 'Rasta Heads' which had led some of them with high ability to reject individual social mobility within the school, and teachers' efforts to divide them. They had thus become congregated in the lower streams. Why should their adaptation differ so markedly from those of the young black women's groups discussed earlier? As males, they were, arguably, slightly less marginalized. A gender factor merged with race and class to promote more 'visible' resistance. But possibly a more important factor was their future job prospects, which they saw, realistically, as poor.

Pupil Relationships

The research considered so far in this chapter suggests a strong tendency for ethnic groups to differentiate and polarize to some degree on their journey through secondary school. The process seems to be aided by school organization and teacher attitudes, not forgetting the influences of background factors and future expectations. Pupils draw on their ethnic culture as a resource, and develop it in celebratory style in a similar way to Willis' lads. This further distinguishes the group and marks it off from others.

At Willis' (1977) school, for example, each of the three groups of Caucasian, Asian and Afro-Caribbean pupils had their own classrooms in the fifth year for 'friendship groups', where they engaged in different activities in different ways. 'So much for integration!' declared the Head of Upper School (p. 47). The polarization is evident, at least from the 'lads'' point of view by their condemnation of the other groups as 'the fuckin' wogs', or the 'bastard pakis' (p. 48). Willis chronicles the nature of the 'lads' prejudice, Asians receiving the worst treatment as 'alien, "smelly" and probably unclean', and on account of their conformity and success both because it was not rightfully theirs as interlopers and because it was a degrading attitude (as with the 'ear 'oles'). The Afro-Caribbeans at least had the good grace to be troublesome at school, have low status, and certain macho elements and musical tastes that were not dissimilar to the 'lads'. But they were 'foreign', 'smelly', probably 'dirty', 'stupid', and there was a pronounced sense of sexual rivalry and jealousy. Clearly these divisions are as complete for the 'lads', if not more so, as between the 'lads' and the 'ear 'oles'.

Several studies point to this process being well in train long before secondary school — as early, in fact, as four years of age. Most research done in Britain since the 1970s suggests that pupils prefer to mix with others in their own ethnic group. Jelinek and Brittan (1975), for example, showed that both Asian and Afro-Caribbean children had established a pattern of own-group friendship by age eight. Davey and others (1982, 1983) in another large-scale study (of 16 schools and 4000 children) again showed this pattern, (61 per cent of children had established own-group preference by age seven) though where there was an opportunity to choose friends from other ethnic groups they did. There seemed to be more antipathy between Afro-Caribbean and Asian children, than between those and white children. These children were aware of ethnic distinctions on a hierarchical basis which accorded minority groups lower status. Friendships in this respect were thus 'more determined by category membership than by personal characteristics' (Davey and Mullin, 1982: 91). Kitwood and Borrill (1980) concluded that the young Muslims in their study, used school to promote their own feelings of solidarity, rather than for mixing with other pupils. Other, similar research led Tomlinson

(1983) to conclude that 'pupils in multi-ethnic schools do not appear to form inter-ethnic friendships to any great extent, being 'racially aware' and preferring their own groups from an early age, becoming even more ethnocentric at secondary level' (1983: 129).

However, there are some exceptions to this general trend, and a challenge to the general argument. Denscombe *et al.* (1986), for example, found that a number of primary school teachers in their project were sceptical of much of the evidence pointing to discrete ethnic friendship groupings and developing racial prejudice at primary school. Teachers' observations can be misleading, as we have seen. But Denscombe *et al.* decided to test these views in two multi-ethnic classrooms using a range of methods, including extended fieldwork observation. The sociometric tests, which involved pupils naming their three best friends in class, and which is a popular method in this kind of research, seemed to indicate the usual pattern of ethnic grouping. But the long-term fieldwork observation of priority and actual contacts between pupils during free association in both class and playground showed a high degree of racial integration, supporting teacher's own observations. As Denscombe (1983) points out in an earlier article, if one black child mixed with three white in a friendship group, this could be taken as indicating an absence of prejudice. But a quantitative measure might expect a more 'balanced' level. Further, there is no evidence of motivation in the earlier studies. In other words, when in-group preference exceeds expectation we cannot assume this necessarily indicates ethnic preference or bias. To underline his point, he shows that in one of his schools with a white/Asian mix most of the white pupils included Asians among their friends, and he concluded that while children tended to stick with friends of the same ethnic group, they were equally prepared to include a pupil from a different ethnic group among their friends. This raises the question of the validity of sociometric tests and quantitative surveys as methods of investigating pupil relationships. Pupil interaction is too complex for such broad measures. Observations, Denscombe *et al.* argue, are better *indicators* of friendship, though we need to know more about how pupils understand 'friendship'.

My own research supports this view, and, indeed, in one multi-ethnic primary school classroom of seven-year-olds, pupils freely nominated friends from other ethnic groups, this actually counting as a desirable qualification in some instances. From their comments in writing and in discussion, and from observation, the chief things they felt about friends was that they spent time with each other, helped and cared about each other, were 'kind', shared and gave each other things, found each other attractive, played, and had fun together. They provide physical, intellectual, emotional, and moral support for each other (*see also* Davies, 1982). Friendships were for the most part gender specific and multi-racial. Malcolm's friends, Surdip and Rajesh, are 'both helpful, we all like playing football I know that if I fell over they would fetch the teacher'. Warish likes Darren 'because he does not fight with me. I give Darren lollipops and he comes to my house'. Mandy liked Rashan because 'she is pretty and she is indian. She is kind and helps people. We share sweets and time together. We play with my ball we play tickie as well. Rashan has got black curly hair and brown eyes I like her. I like her because she is indian and I have never had an indian friend before' (Grugeon and Woods, 1990: 99).

Here, ethnic difference is proving an attraction. This was also the case among the pupils of another class of seven-year-olds in the same school, and those of an all-white rural school, with whom their teachers arranged an 'exchange', with visits to each other's schools. From the very first exchange of letters, these two groups of children developed a strong sense of friendship. This included those pupils considered 'difficult' by their teachers, including one who had been known to use racial abuse to an Asian teacher (this boy made friends with an Afro-Caribbean boy in the other school). Individual links were forged and they identified with each other, these personal liaisons causing a certain amount of excitement which acted as a catalyst for the curriculum work done around the project, as well as giving a boost to personal and social development. These friendships were important to them and they had a certain amount of emotional investment in them. They were the project's prominent feature, and the main motivation behind the children's efforts.

One might assume that, if such inter-racial relationships are attended by a lack of prejudice in that respect, they might be positively encouraged by rejection of prejudice and conscious awareness of racism and knowledge of each other's experience. Carrington and Short (1989) tested this knowledge among children in two all-white primary schools in the south of England. Using picture techniques and asking children to 'describe what was happening', they discovered some sophisticated ideas about 'race' among the older children in their sample (8–11 years) though the young (6–8 years old) were more limited in their understanding. Concerning a scene where a black boy approaches a white boy and girl playing with a ball, and is rejected, all recognized it as unfair, a frequent comment among the older children being 'people are exactly the same except for colour', or that '(the boy) can't help being black'. Some identified more important factors, like 'It's how friendly they are. It's what they're like inside that's important' (p.63). A majority thought it wrong to reject the boy on racial grounds as 'he's just the same (as us) except a different colour' (p.64).

The authors also tested the children's racial preferences, and here they found a high degree of in-group preference. However like Denscombe earlier, they considered 'this not a straightforward matter as a majority of children said they were 'not bothered', and those expressing a preference usually gave it a context, preferring, for example, to be white in 'England' or black in 'Brixton' because that was the majority colour, but 'If most of my friends were black and I went to a black school, then I wouldn't really mind (what colour I was)'. These older children showed a fairly full appreciation of the impact of racism on the lives of black children operating in a wider context, subject for example to immigration laws, victims of stereotyping, and various socioeconomic constraints, such as employment and housing patterns. There was, however, a certain amount of xenophobia among these pupils, arising from an ethnocentric historical view, which Carrington and Short thought amenable to antiracist teaching.

As for secondary school, at least one study has shown that ethnic separation is not inevitable. In Foster's (1988) 11–16 comprehensive school of almost equal numbers of Afro-Caribbean and white pupils, pupils of all kinds argued that racism was insignificant in the school, and that black and white pupils got on very well, and had few conflicts. Cultures were mixed here also to some degree, as well as people. For example, white students sucked their lips also to signal dissent, and some of them used a form of Patois. Girls especially pointed to a large number of ethnically mixed friendship groups. The only name-calling was confined to 'young' and 'cheeky' 'little kids', and, curiously perhaps, to black students among themselves. One Afro-Caribbean girl said

> I say it's equal in this school ... You think when you hear of prejudice in the school you think it's the whites callin' the black or ... the Pakis, or whatever ... but it's not, it's the black people callin' the black, they're always callin' each other black this and black that, it's ridiculous really. (Foster, 1988: 385)

How do we account for such results that contrast so strongly with those studies stressing ethnic differentiation? The different methodology can hardly be held totally responsbile here. Rather, I suspect, in the case of my research at least, it has a great deal to do with the well-established, strongly integrational community served by the school, which was reflected in the school ethos, and its strong commitment to multiculturalism. This is not to say that the school, or the community, were devoid of racism, but that there was an openness and a tolerance that had left these children comparatively free of prejudice as yet and that enabled them to interact with their fellows on an equal basis regardless of ethnic groups.

Foster (1988) identified three reasons for the lack of racial clashes in his school: Firstly, the area had been multi-ethnic for a long time, and there was a long history of fairly co-operative and tolerant relationships between two main ethnic groups (as with my school, above). Secondly, some white students who were racist kept their views quiet as they were vastly outnumbered by pupils, both black and white, who were anti-racist. Thirdly, the teachers had 'succeeded in conveying the importance of Anti-Racism'. However, rather ominously perhaps, the only two Asians in the school were subject to abuse and name-calling from both Afro-Caribbean and white pupils. Were they the *real* minority in the school and area?

Such cases, however, are still few and far between in the literature. More typical seem to be the schools involved in Cohen's (1987b: 10) project. In one (all-white) the 'children exhibited a high level of colour prejudice . . . sometimes articulated with great emotional intensity, and often backed up by quite sophisticated arguments . . . and "rich" repertoires of racist images, jokes, stories and ritual insults'. Purely disciplinary methods and 'rationalist' pedagogies would appear to be of little avail against this kind of ingrained racism.

There are few other signs, too, of any such integration at secondary school level other than occasionally in top streams. Racist stereotyping was common among the pupils of the 12–16 co-educational comprehensive school studied by Figueroa (1985). Racist name-calling was widespread among them, and were an expression of racist 'frames of reference' (cf. Brown in chapter 2: 49; also Chapter 7) — taken-for-granted, largely implicit but deeply influential sets of beliefs and values through which people interpret the world. These FORs are socially learned and collectively sustained. 'Whites', 'Asians', and 'Afro-Caribbean' pupils tended to see each other in a negative and narrow way. Whites were the most prejudiced. They thought all blacks 'smelly', 'dirty' and 'noisy'. They were particularly denigratory of the Asians, who had 'got fleas', were 'wank-heads', 'breed like rabbits', and were 'annoying and donkies' (p. 6). Both of the other groups were more positive about the Afro-Caribbeans, though Asians did think they 'pick on you, swear and talk behind your backs'. Both Asians and Afro-Caribbeans considered the white English prejudiced and racial. Racist comment was part of informal classroom discourse. An Asian boy was told by a white boy 'Shut up you top-knot black dick! This isn't Brixton'. A second-form Vietnamese boy was called 'Chinkie', a Sikh boy 'turban dioxide', an Afro-Caribbean boy 'rubber-lips' and 'gorilla'. There were more signs of integration and harmony in the top streams (cf. Troyna above), suggesting that school organization again was an important variable. But Figuera argued that the name-calling and racist FORs have to be seen in a wider context. This includes the local community, which, unlike that of my research, had a negative view of the school, partly at least because many of its pupils were black, and the wider society where racist FORs are common. Figuera concludes that 'Despite simplistic assumptions about the power of informal pupil interaction to lead, unguided, to cross-cultural understanding, it is largely through informal pupil culture and inter-action that racism is reproduced' (p. 14).

Meanwhile the general trend in large-scale survey work continues. Hallinan and Williams (1989), for example, in research that covered 59,000 American high school students, could only find a few hundred interracial friendships. Major factors in establishing friendships were 'proximity, similarity, status and reciprocity'. Divisions based on sex and race thus continue through secondary school. School organization again plays a part in this, inter-racial interactions taking place by chance as well as choice where students are freely distributed, tracking (streaming) having the power to 're-segregate a de-segregated school'. This usually results in a 'disproportionate number of whites in the academic track and of blacks in the general or vocational track'. The conditions for polarization are thus set as 'Black and White students are denied the chance to recognize existing similarities between them and to develop new ones that would foster positive inter-racial sentiment' (p. 77). The most important factor in friendships was 'reciprocity' — and for this to happen, students had to have opportunity to interact. Tracking clearly works against black-white interaction. However, preference does not necessarily imply rejection and/or prejudice, though the circumstances are not conducive to combating it if it exists.

The Racial Curriculum

School knowledge is stratified in terms of 'race', just as it is in terms of social class and gender. The case of Tahuri, the Maori girl, above is one illustration of this. The curriculum is racially influenced in terms of organization, content and process.

The Organization of Knowledge

Tahuri shows how the allocation of subjects to different streams can militate against certain ethnic groups. Mac an Ghaill (1988) relates how the Asian young women in his study claimed that at critical points of their school careers they were offered low-status, often practical, subjects, in the expectation of their finishing their education at sixteen; while Asian boys were encouraged to take science subjects, and were seen more positively. Two girls, for example, who wished to take 'O' level physics were told the course was full, and that girls normally chose biology. These 'race' and gender divisions were exacerbated further by teachers who encouraged girls, but not boys, to make Asian food in their home economics lesson. Teachers seemed to work with the notion that these girls' futures considered of 'arranged marriages'.

As with the schools of Hargreaves and Lacey, the distribution of resources among the streams was unequal, top streams receiving better classrooms, more experienced teachers, more resources, first choice of subject and so on. Once the allocation to stream was made, there was little chance of upward mobility for the lower stream. At the end of year three, the top stream had first choice of subject and were encouraged to take science, other streams having non-academic subjects and 'general science'. Streams were further differentiated in terms of examinations. As already noted, this scheme of organization affected the Afro-Caribbean pupils disproportionately, since they were over-represented in the lower streams, even though some of them were acknowledged by all to have high ability. They had been demoted on the grounds of perceived 'troublesome' attitude.

That option choice procedures discriminate against minority ethnic groups is supported by research by Tomlinson (1987) in a study covering eighteen multi-ethnic schools. Given that teachers are in a powerful position in this process, and keen to see 'appropriate' choices made (*see* chapter 2), if they do hold stereotypical views, they could steer some pupils in directions not to their best advantage. This is apparently what happened. For example, pupils of Afro-Caribbean origin were less likely than other pupils to be studying a minimum balanced curriculum, and more likely to be studying social studies rather than history and geography, and more practical subjects. Bangladeshi pupils, mostly girls in one of the schools, were more likely to emerge with a different curriculum from all other pupils, with biology, typing and a course in textiles prominent. There were large differences in level of examinations the various groups were entered for. Pupils of Pakistani, Afro-Caribbean and particularly Bangladeshi origin were less likely to be entered for 'O' levels. Thus, like pupils in the lower social class, pupils in some minority ethnic groups are disadvantaged in this process in terms of developing the critical skills that come from studying the higher order subjects.

Gender and class were also prominent discriminators in Tomlinson's study, as they were in that by Kelly (1988b) of pupil take-up and achievement in science. This showed that black and Asian pupils are less likely than white pupils to take physics, and that black pupils leave school less well qualified in science than white and Asian pupils. However, these ethnic differences disappeared when social background was taken into account, suggesting that class is the major factor. Kelly points out that this may be a false distinction since the class factor may be disguising the extent of racial disadvantage. Asian boys did particularly well, while white girls were the least interested in physical science. Kelly concludes that 'Different aspects of science seem to have different cultural meanings in different communities, so that the sextyping of interests which is evident among whites is not so marked in other groups' (Kelly, 1988a: 125).

Knowledge Content

As regards content, the bias is by now well-known. Surveys of literature used in primary schools have revealed a racial as well as a gender-loaded emphasis in favour of 'whites' and 'males'. Thus one London study of the most popular reading schemes revealed that over half of them

> . . . had no black characters appearing at all. Of the remaining books the majority have only the occasional black character appearing

tokenistically in the illustrations but not in the text. Books where black characters play a positive and central role are a rarity indeed. The impact of this is to deny black children and their community a voice, and . . . to reinforce those post-colonial and supremacist ideas about the Third World that are a part of mainstream British culture. (Richardson, 1986: 33)

Some geography books represented the view that people could be divided up into 'races', and by their choice of words to describe them implied that white people (positive words, for example, 'fine, straight, fair') were superior to black (negative words, for example, 'coarse, woolly, thick'). Many books still present people in other countries and cultures as objects rather than subjects, emphasize difference rather than similarity, and exoticness rather than simple basics (*ibid.*).

The subject of history is an important one in these debates. Traditionally, this has been taught from an English, nationalistic, and mono-ethnic point of view even though Britain has been a multi-ethnic society since at least the sixteenth century. It celebrated victories, conquests, explorations, the acquisition of empire, the beneficial and paternalistic effects England had on colonized countries, the achievements of great men, parliamentary history, and so on. The influence of social Darwinism from the nineteenth century onwards contributed to a view of the British as a superior 'race', with feelings of moral superiority and xenophobia (MacKenzie, 1984). As Dance (1960) observed, this view was 'obsessed with the white man's burden, and with the corollary conception of the historical unworthiness of races which are "coloured".' It had very little relevance to the lives of black pupils, or working-class pupils, and less to girls than boys. Other ethnic groups in British schools, therefore, were denied a history of their own, as well as being subjected to racism (*see* Cohen, 1987b; Shah, 1988; Taylor, 1989).

The Swann Committee in consequence called for 'a fundamental reorientation of the attitudes which condition the selection of curriculum materials', to help pupils 'analyze critically and rationally the nature of British society in a global context' (DES, 1985: 324). This emphasis on critical method, and providing pupils with skills and evidence to make their own discoveries and draw their own conclusions, has been countered with another concern — about the richness of British culture and tradition and the desirability that pupils should learn about it lest it be lost (Joseph, 1986). To others it is a culture that has been prejudiced and discriminatory and is best revealed for what it is. These are the poles of the current argument about the history programme of study under the National Curriculum. Whatever emerges, it is unlikely to have shaken off all the old ethnocentric values. As Tomlinson (1989) shows, the beliefs connected with such values have become deeply ingrained within British society, settling 'like a sediment in the consciousness of the British people' (Mackenzie, 1984: 258).

They certainly seem behind the Education Reform Act of 1988 and the new National Curriculum. What sort of 'National' Curriculum was this to be? As noted previously, its subject-centredness and exclusivity ensured a strong traditional and conservative line. There was little recognition of ethnic diversity or the need for a curriculum that reflects the multicultural nature of British society in the initial consultation document, and the provisions have been much criticized by minority ethnic groups (Haviland, 1988). However, the actual programmes of study devised by the working groups may hold some promise. Thus, S. and T. Turner (1989) feel that the plans for science give teachers considerable freedom to develop programmes of study which include an international dimension. The emphasis on social, economic and environmental factors in the attainment targets provides a basis for such studies (and also for wider appeal among girls and boys). They identify four important elements in the science proposals for these purposes — 'international science', development education, cultural diversity, and cross-curricular links. The report of the working group on English also strikes a balance, recommending that all pupils be taught to write standard English, but only taught to speak it if motivated to do so, pupils choosing when and where to use it (Cox, 1988). Pupils' first language, or dialect, should be respected. Creole varieties of English, for example, 'are highly complex . . . governed by rules in their own right, and it is a political/ideological question as to whether they are dialects or languages in their own right'.

Similarly, in the guidance offered to the teaching of mathematics (National Curriculum Council, 1989), mention is made of utilizing the pupils' own interest, mathematics reflecting the real world, making use of the local environment, striking a balance between application in everyday life and more abstract ideas, employing different modes of learning, giving thought to communication, and seeking opportunities for cross-curricular work. All of these figured in the 'multicultural mathematics' project we described in 'Educating All' (Grugeon and Woods 1990). This whole-school project, gradually built up over half a term, developed a 'street' that the children could actually walk down with houses, shops, pubs, dentists, church, a trailer site for the traveller children — in short a representation of the neighbourhood with which all ethnic groups could identify. Authentic figures, complete with turbans where appropriate, populated the street. Things could be added, handled and moved, and a dice game with numbered squares was devised for moving. The fact that they could stand and move in the street helped develop their sense of progression and of probability, as well as their conceptualization of number. This, we thought, was not just an example of effective multi-cultural teaching, but effective teaching in general. The important factor might be, therefore, not the National Curriculum itself, but what teachers make, or are allowed to make of it.

The Process of Learning

Reference has been made earlier to a qualitative difference in teachers' perceptions of pupils in top and bottom streams, and in their teaching. The former are able and aware, and taught to think. The latter are restricted and troublesome and taught by rote. Imani Perry (1988), a fifteen-year-old black student, experienced both in American schools. After ten years in private schools, she decided to go to public (state) school, because she felt isolated 'as a person of colour'. She 'yearned to have a large, strong, black community be a part of my development'. However, her public school was no less isolating for her. It was less concerned with thinking, creativity, analyzing and processing ideas and more with accuracy, memory and detail. A good student here was one who was well-behaved and hard-working, not thinking independently. Because of the absence of teacher-pupil contact, there was no other way of determining intelligence except by grades, appearance, and behaviour. We are not surprised to discover, after earlier examples, that 'Black and Hispanic students who retain strong cultural characteristics in their personalities are most negatively affected by teachers' emphasis on behaviour, appearance, and respect for authority' (p. 334). The routes to these qualities are culturally based. For the middle-class, upper-school pupils, 'good behaviour' was 'natural'. In Black and Hispanic cultures, respect has to be earned. It comes from the relationship. Where there is none, there can be no automatic obedience. In such a situation, the merest gesture or innuendo can be visited cross-culturally with mammoth significance. These pupils thus gravitate to the lower-level classes, where 'bad textbooks are used without outside resources, the reading has less content, and the point of reading is to perfect reading skills, not to broaden thinking skills' and where books are 'more often stripped of any content' (*ibid.*). After three months in this school, Perry found herself just as isolated as in her former school, intellectually as well as racially. For she was in upper-level classes, with few black students other than Asians, and with little intellectual stimulation. She values her experience at this school, for through it she 'learned one of the most blatant forms of oppression and inequity for lower-class students in American society' (p. 336).

Perry's comments draw attention to different, social interpretations of 'intelligence', to different conceptions of pupil learning and teaching methods. The ethnocentric nature of the main understandings here not only discriminate against minority ethnic groups, but obstruct the learning processes of all children. Until recently, British primary schools, for example, were thought to be almost perfect models of their kind, where all things 'were bright and beautiful' (King, 1978), children were still largely 'innocent', and proceeding steadily through their 'stages of development' which did not as yet admit them to the inner mysteries of abstract and conceptual thought, such as are involved, for example, in notions of social justice and racism. Such things were not as yet children's concern in the comfortable, cosy world of primary school, and they were as yet best protected against evils in the outside world and not outreached in terms of intellectual development (Ross, 1984).

However, it is becoming clear that young children do have considerable capacity in this respect (Donaldson, 1978; Blenkin, 1988). Lee and Lee (1987) give examples from their study of visits between schools contrasting strongly in terms of 'race' and social class, and the teachers' attempts in both schools to introduce multicultural/anti-racist programmes. The children showed a clear grasp of 'race', gender, and social class. As in Francis' (1984) classroom, when a situation is constructed wherein pupils can discuss these issues freely through talk, they develop their ideas. The black childrens' consciousness of 'race' was particularly acute. But when they spoke of the children of the other school, social class was most prominent in their perceptions. They referred to how they talked, dressed and behaved, and where they lived. The authors explain the lack of reference to 'race' by pointing out that their reality necessarily involved consideration of a white perspective, so they had no need to 'state the obvious.' The (white) children of the other school, however, did produce comments on 'race', but few on social class. They showed an appreciation of the problems of black children ('... if you keep on being teased on your colour... you may be a bit more aggressive than white people'), and the beginning of understanding of the structural nature of racism ('... estate agents... just dump the black people in one area') (p. 215–6). Lee and Lee advocate a teaching method that involves a 'democratic process underpinned by a progressive pedagogy... (which) values co-operation and collaboration through talk rather than simply individual exploration' (p. 219). Some versions of 'child-centredness' pin the child within his or her own gender, class or 'race' perspectives, when they need to be taken out of them to appreciate others' view and others' perceptions of their own, and to discover 'group' perspectives. They also differentiate by stage of development ('childhood' as a separate state) when other more relevant continuities of differentiation ('race', class, gender) might be stressed.

These points are supported in a study of an anti-racist iniative in an all-white primary school by Short and Carrington (1987). They present similar evidence from a project carried out as part of the normal curriculum of a fourth-year class to show that young children can cope conceptually with individual racism and appreciate structural features of racial inequality. Their project, called 'In Living Memory' examined economic, cultural and social change in post-war Britain, through constructivist learning techniques which involved consulting parents and grandparents, group discussions and problem-solving, archive photographs, documentary evidence, imaginative exercises (for example, a letter home from a recent immigrant), class discussion, written work, and reading and discussion of a well-known novel about life in a multiracial junior school ('Donovan Croft'). Such methods ensured a grounding in history and in the children's own personal histories and life-worlds. It was not, for example, 'preached' at them, which seems to achieve the contrary effect to that desired (Verma and Bagley, 1979). Thus, just to give one example, while several parents might have agreed with Jenny's father that 'it is all the Blacks here that causes unemployment' (p. 225), the children were able, through an exercise where they were asked to solve the acute labour shortage of the immediate post-war years, to work out amongst themselves a different conclusion. The apparent success of such anti-racist initiatives might be contrasted with the more limited attempts that have been made, now largely discredited, in 'multicultural education', that celebrated cultural diversity by focusing on exotic features of different cultures, and so emphasized strangeness and separateness. The emphasis is on acceptance and incorporation, which implies a reinforcement of the status quo in which prevailing injustices and inequalities are preserved untouched. It is seen by some, in fact, as a liberal ploy to insulate the system from black unrest (Mullard, 1982 and 1984).

Even in situations where teachers have more awareness of the possibilities of culture clash, and indeed are working to a more sophisticated multicultural policy, there can be profound disjuncture. Moore (1987) illustrates this with the case of Khasru, a fourth year Bangladeshi boy born in the Sylhet, who was set a task by his teacher of writing a 'love story' for his GCSE folder. His first draft was corrected by the teacher for grammar and style. The second draft was discussed with the class's support teacher (strongly committed to a multicultural approach that 'condemns the Eurocentrism that has always afflicted compulsory education in this country' — p. 4). This time the criticism continued the comments on style ('getting rid of some ''I saids'' ''she saids'', 'adding a bit here', 'maybe . . . '), but was mainly about content. At one point in the story, the girl had said 'I love you. Then I said ''I love you too''.' The teacher thought that sounded a bit sudden. Then 'All this stuff about relations . . . . This isn't really necessary is it?' However, in response to the teacher's occasional question 'Would they say that?' Khasru says 'Yes'.

Moore argues that there are two realities in play here. The teacher has a conception of how people talk and behave in these matters and sees it as *the* way of telling a story.

> These are the ways, the conventions, the discourses the teacher has been brought up with, and there is no question but that they are the right ways, the right conventions, the right discourses. The possibility of linguistic diversity in the broadest sense, that embraces genre, perception and form — and that is suggested by the whole-school policies he believes he supports — seems not to have entered his consciousness. In short, for all the teacher's anti-racist convictions, Khasru's *alternative* way of telling a story has been perceived by him as deficient . . . (Moore, 1987: 8)

As Moore points out, it is one thing to incorporate 'black exemplars' with curriculum content, and to establish a policy for dealing with racist incidents in the school. These can be done within existing pedagogies and anglocentric views of the world. Promulgating linguistic diversity and language tolerance is a different matter. In practice this amounts in the school to the provision of

Bengali language tuition and the development of a World Language Programme, which again can be done within prevailing curriculum understandings. There is no recognition, however, of different discourses or linguistic traditions, and no room for Khasru's diversity of style and form. Bengali, his strongest language, is thus effectively marginalized.

The battleground of much culture clash is language in some form or another. Heath (1982, 1983) contrasted the kinds of questions black children were given the opportunity and required to answer at home and at school. At home questions were concerned with whole objects, events, causes and effects. At school, they were often asked for 'labels, attributes and discrete features of objects and events, in isolation from the context' (1982: 105). These were strange questions to them, which they inevitably struggled to answer, yet teachers were amazed that 'They don't seem able to answer even the simplest questions'. As a black parent remarked about her child's silence in the classroom, 'Nobody play by the rules he know'.

A similar example comes from Mac an Ghaill's (1987) work in a Midlands Supplementary school, staffed and populated by black teachers and pupils. The students here felt a polarization between their mainstream state institutions, staffed predominantly by white teachers and the majority black student population. They, too, amongst other things, pointed to the cultural break over language. Their mainstream school teachers saw Creole as a form of sub-standard speech. These students had developed considerable linguistic skills, both oral and written, but they were not appreciated at the local school, where they were more likely to be ridiculed. Speaking about the supplementary school, one student said

> Ye feel what is different about here in the whole place, don't ye. Ye see black people don't own anything in this society. They don't belong anywhere. Ye just feel better when it's yer own place, like our church. Ye feel proud. Ye can be yerself, the pressure is off, ye can learn. (Mac an Ghaill, 1987: 6)

The difficulties for teachers, however, are illustrated in a project in our research involving a well-intentioned attempt by a Church of England all-white junior school to incorporate a multicultural perspective into its curriculum (Grugeon and Woods, 1990). This was in response to the Swann Report, and an *aide-mémoire* from the LEA. The term-long project on 'Living and Growing' involved a vast amount of work for both teachers and pupils, 'research', reading and reporting, However, our conclusion was that the teachers

> ... still seemed to be operating a traditional programme that equipped children with a number of facts which gave them no real understanding of other cultures, but simply reinforced traditional stereotypes. This was evident in the way the children reported their findings and experiences. At times, they were merely filling in workcards, and some reports were phrased in the same kind of style. (Grugeon and Woods, 1990: 226)

On a few occasions, however, the knowledge gained was more clearly *theirs*. They had written about it with more enthusiasm in their own idiom. Significantly, however, these opportunities had not been capitalized on by teachers. Not being built into the planned structure of the project, there was no time for pause and reflection. The relentless pace of the programme squeezed out the activity with most potential for the matter in hand. One example of this was the pupils' visit to the Commonwealth Institute, where a Nigerian teacher excited their interest in his country and culture. They talked at length and with enthusiasm among themselves and with the researcher about this visit, but it was not followed up by the teachers. The Headteacher, in fact, had been more concerned about their *behaviour* on the visit. On another occasion their feelings and imaginations were fired by a television programme some had happened to see about the Kalahari Bushmen. They had learned a number of facts about these people in their project, but the television programme brought home to the children the plight of these nomadic hunters, who had been deemed by South African official policy to have been 'overtaken by civilization'.

> In the morning they were queueing up to express real feelings of outrage to their teacher. The school secretary, fired by their enthusiasm to do something, telephoned the BBC and was given an address which the children could write to. Their teacher thought that they might do this if there was time. The relentless pace of the project meant that they did not. There was no time for unscheduled events in the programme. (*ibid*: 198).

Nor was there time to pick out and discuss the different kinds of ethnocentricity that cropped up continuously in the children's talking and writing;

nor the meaning of some of the things they copied; nor the stereotyping they fell prey to as a result of the selected methods. However, we thought this a useful start by the teachers rather than 'a superficial irrelevance' (Mullard, 1984). But it does illustrate the difficulties confronting teachers who are willing to implement change. School knowledge and teaching methods have long historical roots with a firm hold on the very ethnocentricity they now seek to alter. They are not unshakeable, as is shown in the same study in the whole-school 'multicultural mathematics' project discussed above, and a school exchange. The 'Living and Growing' project does not appear to be untypical (Troyna and Ball, 1985; Troyna and Williams, 1986), though the latter projects hold the promise of change (*see also* Tomlinson and Coulson, 1988).

Conclusion

The emphasis on culture draws attention to pupils' collective constructions, and how they negotiate 'race' and gender as members of a group. It moves away from stereotypical views of pupils as deficient in some way, such as girls as passive victims, 'lads' as mindless vandals, Afro-Caribbean youth as dumb and obstreperous, boys as natural scientists, and so on. Looking at the world from the perspective of their various groups fosters a more active view, which sees much of their school response as a form of resistance of some kind or other against a system which does not work in their interests. 'Visible' and 'invisible' resistance, 'resistance within accommodation', a 'partial culture of resistance' are some of those dealt with here.

Many of the subcultures formed around the resistance appear to have a central organizing feature. With Troyna's Reggae boys it was music; with Furlong's 'association'; with the Maori girls, it was sexuality; with other groups, language. Though the medium may vary however, depending on what cultural resources pupils have at their disposal, the message is the same. The outer manifestation is but a symbol of the defence or resistance against assaults on their culture and identity coming from teacher attitudes and school processes and organization. These themselves may be mediatory forces of wider influences operating in society (Brah and Minhas, 1985).

Major influences bearing on pupil school experience are social class, gender and 'race'. The relationship between these is intricate and diverse.

There is both unity and variability in the experiences of girls as compared to boys, blacks as compared to whites, working as compared to middle class. Just as the unity of women's experience is fractured by class (Acker, 1987), so the 'black' experience has been shown here to differ according to ethnic group, class and gender. Yet all 'blacks' may be subject to racism in some form or other, at some time or other, in some situation or other. Plenty of evidence has been advanced in this chapter to demonstrate this across a number of minority ethnic groups in a number of countries. Yet, here and there, cases can be found where 'race' does not appear to be a factor at all, yet would be expected to be, given the general pattern. In these circumstances, class and gender seem to assume more importance, though the former may mask a 'race' factor. Members of certain ethnic groups, for example, may be allocated to the lowest-status jobs, or find it most difficult to find employment, and hence be assigned to the lower reaches of the class structure on the grounds of their 'race'. Such structural factors are not always evident in personal interactions between individuals or groups in particular situations.

Having said that, there is a considerable contrast in the institutional climates presented among some of the studies discussed here, between for example, those of Wright, Mac an Ghaill, Troyna and Figueroa on the one hand, and Foster, Denscombe, Carrington and Short, and Grugeon and Woods on the other. Differences in methodology and focus of study may account for some of this contrast. But there also seem to be other, possibly more significant factors like school ethos, school resources, school organization and structure, staff culture and ideology, neighbourhood factors like mix and stability of ethnic groups in the community, relationships in the community, and the local labour market. Variation among these yields a variety of patterns which attach variable importance to class, race and gender in different places at different times to different people. Some of the complexity — and the importance of context — is illustrated by Cohen (1987b):

> . . . in one social context sexist imagery adds further injuries to the repertoire of racist insults; yet in another setting the same terms may unite white and black boys in a 'multi-cultural' celebration of macho norms, and in common resistance to anti-sexist initiatives. More positively the shared experience of boys' sexism may bring black and white girls closer together, and this alliance may shift the latter's attitude on race. Finally the sexual double standard may get trans-

lated into a racial one, in which Afro-Caribbean cultures are positively associated with masculine and proletarian values, whereas Asian cultures are despised as 'effeminate' and 'petty bourgeois'. (Cohen, 1987b: 7–8).

As we have seen, in the research of Lee and Lee (1987), the black pupils focused on class, not 'race', in discussing the white pupils in the other school. In other circumstances, 'race' might have been more to the fore (*see* Mac an Ghaill, 1988, for example). However, it does seem that to most black pupils, 'race' and racism appears to be the primary factor operating on their lives outside their homes. As Hameeda told Mac an Ghaill (1988), 'the first thing that people notice immediately, I don't think that they are going to think, a woman. They're going to think a black and then they're going to think a woman' (p. 15).

Moving on to policy, there would appear to be limits to what schools can achieve in combating racism, as with class and gender inequalities. There are wider historical, social, political and economic forces at work. However, as with class and gender, they can serve to reproduce such divisions, or, as several studies here suggest, work to provide a 'cultural interruption', or a window on the world through which these matters might be objectified. They can do this in several ways. First, by attending to those aspects of school organization that promote status differences and encourage polarization of pupil cultures. The social class differences encouraged by streaming and tracking are lent an extra dimension when 'race' is added. Secondly, by making the curriculum less ethnocentric, and more reflective of and relevant to the life-worlds of its pupils, and more representative of Britain's breadth of history and of its position in the world (*see* Lynch, 1989). This may involve challenging some assumptions about what is considered 'normal' and 'natural'. Thirdly, by teaching methods that seek to 'critically engage students at the level of their own cultural literacy' (McLaren, 1986: 252). McLaren argues for an 'emancipatory politics of culture which will help to render problematic the meanings embedded in the cultural forces and content of classroom instruction' (p. 253). Such 'cultural cartography' goes well beyond the superficial touches of some multicultural approaches to mount a critique of 'contemporary social life in all its cleavage and continuity, rupture and bland consensus . . . ' (p. 255). This involves democratic, collective, collaborative and participative procedures (Harber and Meighan, 1989; Carrington and Short, 1989; Grugeon and

Woods, 1990). Fourthly, by revising theories of learning to more constructivist modes which see pupils less as vessels to be filled and more as human beings, each with their own personal qualities, skills, knowledge, experiences, and schemes of relevancy to be developed. This is not a bland pupil-centredness, but one that is structually embedded, where pupils are encouraged to see themselves as part of the world in all its divisions and inequalities, and to identify and appreciate some of the dialectical exchanges between them. This may involve a revised view of pupil abilities, be it the ability of young primary school children to handle abstractions and concepts, or that of different ethnic groups who may have different ways of expressing their ability. It may also involve revised teacher-pupil relationships, with pupils having more control of their own knowledge, and more freedom to express it.

Fifthly, teachers might consider their own attitudes. As with gender socialization, many of us have had a racial socialization, being brought up through ethnocentric paradigms of the world, which have inbuilt defence mechanisms against revision and demystification. We ourselves frequently require a 'cultural interruption' to arrive at new understandings of the world and of ourselves. This may be helped to be brought about by investigating our own life histories (Middleton, 1987, 1989); by inservice courses focusing on pupils' lives (Arnot, 1989b); by curriculum development (ALTARF, 1984; Gaine, 1987; Cohen, 1987a and b; Carrington and Short, 1989; and see the journal 'Multicultural Teaching'); by teacher reflectivity (Pollard and Tann, 1987; Pollard, 1988); and by racial awareness courses. Though some of these courses have been heavily criticized for being superficial, individualized, misplaced irrelevancies, some have given cautious support to some forms of them as one of a range of strategies that might be used, supported by structural linkages (Gaine, 1987; Lynch, 1987; Galliers, 1987; Abbott *et al.* 1989; Carrington and Short, 1989). In reply to those who argue that it is structures, not attitudes, that need changing, one might reiterate the point made by Allport, as did Carrington and Short:

> It really is not sensible to say that before we change personal attitudes we must change total structure; for in part, at least, the structure is the product of the attitudes of many single people. Change must begin somewhere. (Allport, 1954: 506)

Chapter 5

Pupil Interests and Strategies

The Subcultural Critique

Subcultural approaches have been criticized on a number of counts. Chiefly, they seem unreflective of the complexities of social interaction. Some representations present a picture of cultural determinism, that is of individuals being shaped by cultures. But individuals do not slavishly follow subcultural norms. They do not always and in every respect, for example, imprint masculinity or femininity upon themselves without reflection. They do have choices. These certainly vary according to one's position within the social structure, but most people have some degree of choice. Not all boys in the same structural location behave like Willis' 'lads'. Not all girls aspire mainly toward motherhood and the kitchen sink. Not all Afro-Caribbean boys take the line of action pursued by Mac an Ghaill's 'Rasta Heads'. One might argue that this kind of group is a local adaptation to a general issue, and that it has both local and general properties. But here there is another problem, which is to do with the concept of subculture itself. Subcultures are both part of, and different from, more general cultures, that stand distinct from them in terms of values and behaviour patterns. As Phillipson (1971) notes, the problem is to identify where one ends and the other begins. Subcultural theorists tend to draw a very firm demarcation line. This, after all, is almost an inevitable corollary of differentiation-polarization theory, as it is of resistance theory. It can be a consequence of studying pupil groups in terms of how they are distinguished by such factors as social class, gender and 'race'.

The most trenchant critique of subcultural theory along these lines has been made by Matza, addressing himself to theories of delinquency. He views the typical delinquent as, in essence, no different from normal youth.

Frequently, many delinquents do experience guilt or shame, admire law-abiding persons, distinguish among their victims, and are subject to pressures to conform. They are thus at least partially committed to the prevailing order. Much delinquency, claims Matza, is based on the deviant's justifications for the deviance, which are not recognized as legitimate by the rest of society. However, the justifications are embedded in, or extensions of, the prevailing legal framework, rather than emanating from a different or 'counter' code. They *precede* the deviant act, and make deviance possible. Matza, in an article written with Sykes, called these justifications 'techniques of neutralization'. The youth becomes delinquent by learning these, not by induction into some counter-culture. Five techniques are described in the article: the denial of responsibility, the denial of injury, the denial of the victim, condemnation of the condemners, and the appeal to higher loyalties.

> 'I didn't mean it.' 'I didn't really hurt anybody.' 'They had it coming to them.' 'Everybody's picking on me.' 'I didn't do it for myself.' These slogans, or their variants, we hypothesize, prepare the juvenile for delinquent acts. These 'definitions of the situation' represent tangential or glancing blows at the dominant normative system rather than the creation of an opposing ideology; and they are extensions of patterns of thought prevalent in society rather than something created *de novo*. (Sykes and Matza, 1957: 668)

Many 'delinquents', then, or by the same token, deviant or supposedly 'counter-cultural' pupils, are perhaps not so different. There is an implicit criticism of all subcultural theory, and more of an emphasis on human will. At the same time, such an approach on its own will not explain the uneven distribution of deviance among the social classes. In a later paper, Matza and Sykes turned to delinquent values — the search for excitement and thrills, toughness, disdain for work — and argued that these also were not as deviant as subcultural theory implies (Sykes and Matza, 1961). They maintained that these are typical values of the gentleman of leisure, and are held to some degree or other by all of us. They are 'subterranean values' which are present in the leisure activities of the dominant culture — in competitive games, drinking, gambling, cynicism and 'concealed deviance'. We all indulge in these now and then. The delinquent simply suffers from bad timing. They are not *counter* values, therefore, but values very much *shared* with the dominant culture and helping to bind the delinquent to it. During the brief responsibility-free era of adolescence, the 'delinquent' expresses these values, inverting them as adulthood approaches. This paper by Matza and Sykes has also been criticized for failing to account for the differential access to leisure and opportunity to express these values of different social classes. However, this work at least helps to explain the attractiveness of delinquency as an end in itself, rather than a reaction to, or compensation for, some deficiency or deprivation.

In his later books, *Delinquency and Drift* (1964) and *Becoming Deviant* (1969), Matza developed a more comprehensive theory of deviance. The delinquent is seen as rather ambivalent, oscillating between conventional and deviant value systems, 'neither compelled nor committed to deeds, nor freely choosing them', in a state of 'drift'. This state is affected by the youth's social situation, so that working-class individuals' long periods of boredom (e.g. at school) give rise to desperation and frustration, which aid the drift into delinquency. Thus during 'drift', a boy has the option to commit deviant acts; whether or not he does so depends on whether he wishes to, or decides to, which depends on whether he finds himself in the mood and this, in turn, might be a consequence of his position in the social class structure.

Thus Matza breaks away from the determinism of subcultural theory and its parcelling of groups and sub-groups, segments of life, and cause and effect. He shows the interactional and relational elements between the delinquent culture and conventional culture, as opposed to the differential and contrasting aspects. He emphasizes the importance we should attach to the delinquent's own construction of meanings. In his later book, *Becoming Deviant*, Matza moves even further in an antideterministic direction.

> Man(sic) participates in *meaningful* activity. He creates his reality, and that of the world around him, actively and strenuously. Man *naturally* — not supernaturally — transcends the existential realms in which the conceptions of cause, force, and reactivity are easily applicable. Accordingly, a view that conceives man as object, methods that probe human behavior without concerning themselves with the meaning of behaviour, cannot be regarded as naturalist. Such views and methods are the very *opposite* of naturalism because they have molested in advance the phenomenon to be studied. Naturalism when applied to the study of man has no choice but to conceive man as subject precisely because naturalism claims fidelity to the empirical world. In the empirical world, man is subject and not

> object, except when he is likened to one by himself or by another
> subject. Naturalism must choose the subjective view, and
> consequently it must combine the scientific method with the
> distinctive tools of humanism — experience, intuition, and
> empathy. Naturalism has no other choice because its philosophical
> commitment is neither to objectivity nor subjectivity, neither to
> scientific method nor humanist sensibility. Its only commitment is
> fidelity to the phenomenon under consideration. Thus, in the study
> of man, there is no antagonism between naturalism and a repudiation
> of the objective view, nor a contradiction between naturalism and
> the humane methods of experience, reason, intuition, and empathy.
> Naturalism in the study of man is a disciplined and rigorous
> humanism (Matza, 1969: 8).

This meaning-construction is a continuous process in which people manage or
negotiate their identities and interests. This might be contrasted with the
interpretation of action as a consequence of psychological attributes or
structural or cultural determinants. This may be already evident from some of
the studies examined in previous chapters. But the emphasis there on the
whole has been of group solutions. The point being made here relates to the
individual both vis-à-vis the general culture, and the various subcultures to
which he or she may be affiliated. Cultures certainly influence identities, beliefs
and actions. But a number of studies suggest that individual pupils have a
degree of autonomy, and considerable skills in coping with contradictory
pressures.

Pupil interests

Furlong (1976), for example, saw no evidence in the London comprehensive
school where he did his research of pro- and anti-school cultures, or indeed of
any consistent pupil grouping, and was more impressed by transient patterns
of interaction among pupils which depended perhaps on time of day or who
was present. Furlong claims that there is no consistent pupil culture as such,
and that it is individuals who construct their own actions, not the group that
dictates them. The key point, he argues, is that the individual defines the
situation. When several agree on a definition and can communicate this
agreement among them, we can talk meaningfully of a group, but the fact that

different pupils take part in different groups at different times 'simply illustrates the point that they do not always agree about what they know. Teachers, subjects and methods of teaching mean different things to different pupils . . . ' (Furlong, 1976: 169). Furlong prefers, therefore, to talk of 'interaction sets' and shows the great variety of these that exist within a single lesson as pupils move in and out of a number of interactions defined not by cultural norms, but by common understandings. The guiding definition is that the members of a set see things in the same way and agree on how to act. Thus 'shouting out' can be an example of interaction if the pupil is aware of support from others (there are several other illustrations in chapter 2). In a sense, therefore, this is 'joint action' (Furlong, 1976: 162).

Furlong, in turn, has been criticized for not tackling the reasons for a pupil's variable actions, and not relating pupils' perspectives either to their goals or their values, or to the structure of the school. Hammersley and Turner (1980) in considering 'conformity' and 'deviance' argue that there is no single set of values presented by the school and all the teachers, but much inconsistency, and often 'official' and 'subterranean' values appearing side by side. Exactly what anti-school pupils are 'anti-, or what 'deviant' pupils are deviating from therefore has to be explained with some care. Totalising them in this way may be misleading. They also argue the need, as Furlong did, to take into account pupil intentions and definitions. Once this is done, we can see a pupil is faced with a range of options. Many factors govern the individual's choices, including possibly their own shifting goals and the impact of different contexts. The resultant picture is one not of a consistent reaction like 'conformity' or 'deviance', but of variable behaviour.

The intricacies of pupil decision-making which lead to variable behaviour have been studied by Turner (1983). Some of the factors are illustrated in this conversation with a pupil who had articulated the major school goals of getting a good job and working for examinations. But now he had this to say:

John: In geography you can mess around at the start then you can get down to it and do all the work, then you can mess around at the end.

R: Why are you disruptive in geography?

John: Because I don't like Mr Thomas. Because I used to have him in the third year, he said John is not capable of doing CSE and I got really [untranscribable] . . . went into Mr Green's group. Mr Green said I

> was top 'O' level material. It just shows what Mr Thomas did, and
> then I got chucked back into Mr Thomas's class because Mr Green
> left which is really annoying. It means I'm back where I started
> from, just thinking how I'm going to pass 'O' level . . . The thing
> is with friends [pause] if you don't join in you run the risk of losing
> all your friends . . . You get classed as being a teacher's pet or
> something, if you work too hard, so you join in or they think
> you're afraid of the teacher or something. It makes you look stupid
> if you are the only one working and everyone else is messing
> around, so you join in just for the sake of it. (Turner, 1983: 93)

This illustrates some of the different and contradictory pressures
operating on pupils. While conformity to the school's ethos is John's ideal in
terms of his major expressed aim, he does not feel that the school provides him
with the appropriate resources (i.e. a good teacher) to achieve that aim. This
affects his attitude and leads to occasional non-conformity, especially in
geography lessons. In other words, his conformity is conditional on the school
meeting his own instrumental aim. Other resources that have a bearing on
pupil decision-making are the school itself in its general ethos or in its
organization; equipment and facilities, such as inadequate books; and non-
school based resources, such as the home. The extent to which these are
available, and the quality of them, affect the extent to which pupils pursue
their academic goals. They are also affected by 'alternative interests' such as
combating boredom through illegitimate talk and activities, or through the
need to 'have a laugh'. These may come to the fore in situations where
resources are lacking, or where their quality is dubious, for example where
school tasks are irrelevant to their own goals. They might thus 'juggle their
interest' (Pollard, 1980) depending on the exact composition of the situation
encountered.

However, the peer culture clearly has an influence, as can be seen from
John's comment above on his 'friends'. They have guidelines for appropriate
workloads. The majority of pupils are unwilling to go against these for fear of
being seen as a 'swot' or 'creep' or 'teacher's pet'. They prefer to be seen as
one of the crowd, that is, the group with which they are affiliated. The
question is, how deep do these affiliations run and how do pupils handle the
matter when they conflict with their own personal interests? John resolves the
dilemma by exhibiting both forms of behaviour in the lesson — conformist

and non-conformist — a similar strategy to that employed by certain pupil groups discussed in chapter 5.

Some individuals appear to have the ability to make the most of their options by delicately balancing between a number of alternatives, some of which appear to be in opposition to each other. Thus one boy, a 'good academic', in a study by Stanley (1989) avoided being labelled a 'stiff' or a 'creep' by his peers by indulging in a certain amount of unorthodox behaviour in his capacity as 'court jester', exploring the boundaries of what teachers would put up with. He 'cultivated a role as "sitter on the fence" which enabled him to mix with all sorts, good and bad' (*ibid.*: 46). Birksted (1976) presents a portrait of a boy who experienced a similar dilemma at school between 'being sensible' and 'having a laugh'. He managed, through careful adaptation to different contexts, to achieve great popularity with his teachers and with his peers, the central values of whom stood in opposition to each other.

'Knife-edging'

Interactionist approaches are distinctive in that they emphasize this ability of some individuals to make the most of their options by delicately balancing between a number of alternatives. This shows the fallacy of rating pupils as entirely 'deviant' or 'conformist' (though there may, admittedly, be some of these). Lynda Measor and I came across numerous examples of this 'knife-edging' behaviour in our research on pupil transfer between middle and upper schools. We argued that this was fundamentally a matter of identity, and that all pupils aspired towards their concept of the 'normal pupil' though, of course, that might be different for different groups. For example, deviant boys did not wish to appear clever, but they also shunned being considered 'thick'.

> *Bill*: I don't want to be top all the time, but I don't want to be bottom. I just want to be in between.
> *Pete*: In the other school we were in groups for maths and English and French. I was in the middle group.

> There was a particular incident in the course of the year which made this clear. When the class was streamed for maths, Roy was placed in the bottom group — the remedial group, along with Alan and Geoffrey. This reflected his low marks and his general 'mucking

about' in the subject. Within two weeks, however, he had worked sufficiently hard to be promoted two groups to the middle group, where many of his friends were. Doubtless the fact of being separated from his friends may well have motivated Roy, but that was not the way Pete and Andy saw it. Andy started to tell the researcher about Roy being put into the low group. Pete very uncharacteristically stopped him. 'Shut it And!' he said loudly, but Andy failed to get the point. Pete again intervened, 'Just shut up will you,' and he would not allow Andy to finish. However, when Roy gained promotion, Pete thought it worth telling the researcher about it, and the language he used was interesting. 'Roy has got into our maths group now. He was too good for that other group. That was the group for the dummies.' Roy therefore had worked his way clear of the dreaded label of 'too thick'. In the same week that he gained promotion, he had a skinhead haircut, but being deviant and being 'thick' were two different things.

There were a number of other strategies employed by the deviants to maintain this knife-edge image. For one thing, you could be seen to be very good at some things, such as practical subjects. Bill, for example, was very good at woodwork. We have mentioned already the issue of 'finishing first' and the signals it involves in terms of conformity and the academic hierarchy. Yet Bill Stoop is ready to acknowledge that in woodwork he always 'finishes first, then I have to wait'. Pete was 'pretty good' at art, especially at the kind of graphic design that enabled him to employ symbols drawn from the punk subculture. Roy was exceptionally good at all sports, and was in the school teams for almost all of them.

Pete made another issue clear. It was unacceptable in his terms to be seen to be working hard and doing well. On the other hand it was equally important that one should not be thought of as incapable of doing well, if one should so choose.

Pete: I got a really bad report in maths, and I'm meant to be clever.

R: Are you?

Pete: I could be it. I really worked at it. I don't want to be bored stiff though. Kids like Phillip sit down and work all day. I just can't do that.

Incidents recorded in classroom interaction confirmed this view. In maths Bruce put up his hand to tell the teacher, 'I've finished.' The teacher responded, 'That's good.' Pete then said 'I finished before him.'

Teacher: You didn't put your hand up.

Pete: I didn't want to show off. (Measor and Woods, 1984: 134–5)

The above illustrates some 'deviant' boys' 'knife-edge' behaviour. The following, by contrast, illustrates that of some 'knife-edge' girls.

Like the boys, these girls indulged in occasional deviant acts, but at times and in places where they either would not get caught, or it didn't matter if they did. Supply teachers provided good opportunities. Diane once spent part of such a lesson shouting loudly across the room to her friends. Julie engaged in a fair amount of general 'mucking around', for example, throwing rulers across the room when someone asked if they could borrow them. They made full use of the opportunity to chat and gossip. Sally and Jenny ate bubble-gum and blew large bubbles, which came to some sticky ends, in a humanities lesson taken by a supply teacher, and called Amy's name loudly to attract her attention.

Registration was another arena for stategic deviance. One day the class was exceptionally rowdy. Christine, for example, was throwing polo mints around. Julie, a typical 'knife-edger', was not doing anything this strong, but she was, under the cover of all the other noise, shouting across the room to someone else. Yet she deliberately chose a point when she was unlikely to be detected by the teacher. To some, even this would not matter if the teacher had discipline problems anyway and was not generally respected. Thus Diane did not seem unduly perturbed when, after laughing very loudly during registration, Mrs Gates reprimanded her with 'I don't expect bad behaviour from you.' This 'teacher-certificated deviance' may have been useful to Diane and this was a safe place to get it. Mrs Gates would not take the matter further, and in any case her opinion was not respected in the school. The class already knew that Mrs Gates would not be their form tutor the following year . . .

Some areas of the curriculum lent themselves more readily to strategic deviance than others. In one language class, for example, the discipline frame was constantly being challenged. Sally used the cover given by this to make a small paper plane and send it flying around the room. Woodwork and metal work were 'safe' to ignore. Sally stated her dislike of this subject and her view that it was a waste of time. She and Jenny did no real work for the entire lesson, but sat and talked to the researcher. In a technical design lesson, which many of the girls characterized as being 'really for the boys', anyway, and in which supervision was lax in the large room with big tables and a lot of activity, Diane and Julie 'mucked about'. They took the waxed paper straws they had been given and had a sword fight with them, and then made moustaches out of them, holding them over their top lip. Nevertheless, they did not actually damage the equipment they would have to work with. These knife-edge strategists were all placed in the top group for maths. Diane and Julie went into the top science group, Sally and Jenny went into the second from top stream. Both girls frequently talked of their shared attitudes to science, emphasizing their dislike of the smells and their anxiety about the bunsen burners, yet they had clearly managed to achieve a certain competence in the subject.

Some of the knife-edge girls played around on the fringes of the deviant groups in a whole series of ways. Friendship ties were one of these. Jenny and Sally maintained their co-operative links and some friendship links with Amy and Rebecca who had been at middle school with them. Diane did the same with Jacqui, who was one of the 'ace' deviants in her class. Sometimes they were prepared to extend such links into out of school activities. For example, by the summer term, Diane was meeting other more deviant girls in the evenings. Kerry actually said 'Last night me and Diane went out for a muck about.' While maintaining weak but still useful friendship ties with 'the deviants', the 'knife-edge' girls could also decry the 'conformists' and hence dissociate themselves from any possibility of being identified with them. On occasion they might do this more directly by making fun of the conformist. For example, Sally and Jenny were talking and giggling in an art lesson, while Janet went on working very hard, totally absorbed in her drawing. They pointed at her mockingly, signalling the fact that they placed informal issues higher on the list than Janet. The fact that their values were seen to be shared helped show up their middle-range position. Another technique was simply to distance oneself publicly from extreme behaviour. Thus, Sally complained about Janet, 'In English she wanted everything her way, she wouldn't let anyone else have any ideas, she really annoys me. She is always going on about her ballet exams, especially at dinner times. Even Jane, and she's her friend, says she goes on about it too much.' Sally thus publicly announced her disapproval of these attitudes and actions, and simultaneously signalled her shared perspective with youth culture which, as we have seen, deprecated 'bossiness' and 'boastfulness' . . .

Knife-edgers, who had previously run the risk of being labelled with the conformists, themselves indicated the extent of change such strategies meant for their identities.

Julie: I used to get called a snob, and I still do sometimes, because I go to church. And 'teacher's favourite', people used to call me that at junior school, it's if you do good work, and always get chosen to do the jobs and that.

Sally: Some people called us snobs, last year, when we first came . . . because . . .

Jenny: Bridget thought we were as well, because we never said anything the first couple of weeks, but she knows now we're not.

R: Does she? what have you done to prove that?

Sally: We swear a bit, but only a little bit . . . well quite a bit.

Jenny: We don't swear at home.

R: What do you think is a snob?

Diane: Well it is people who turn their noses up at everybody else. Yes, and if they are always good and never do anything wrong. I couldn't do everything right. I have to do something wrong.

Sally: We're in between.

R: What do you mean?

Sally: We are not bad exactly, but we are not good exactly, we are in between.

The other side of the 'knife-edge' was to do well at school, and this they also managed to achieve. They were consistently awarded high marks and were eventually placed in the higher streams. They saw themselves as basically positively oriented toward school values. Diane admitted she was quite 'good' at school. She was discussing the issue of teachers using corporal punishment on girls: 'My dad wouldn't care [if the teacher hit her], but he knows no one would hit me 'cos I'm good.'

Julie: People always say I am a goodie-goodie, because I play instruments like the violin.

R: But why do they think you are a goodie-goodie?

Julie: I think it is because you do your work, and you are not getting told off and that.

Diane: I don't think it is right . . . you should get on with your work and then have a laugh, when it is the right time.

Thus by a careful mixture of strategies and a careful presentation of self, these girls managed to survive and indeed prosper within the youth culture, in a way the highly conformist could not. One important aspect of this was keeping a low profile on one's academic success, as opposed to the conformist's tendency to 'boast'.

Sally: I don't tell the people in my class anything because some of them are at a lower standard than me, and if I told them, they would think 'snob', she got 80 per cent for maths. Why should we want to know her high marks?

Diane: After the maths test I went home and told my mum that I had got 98 per cent. I did boast a bit to my mum, but I didn't keep saying it at school.

R: If you had got 98 per cent in English (mixed ability teaching), would you keep quiet about it?

Diane: I would only tell certain people like Jane and Emily but I wouldn't tell everybody.

R: Were you pleased when you got into that top maths group?

Jenny: Well it's not something you can show off to your friends, that you are in the top maths group, and they are not.
(Measor and Woods, 1984: 148–51)

The majority of pupils in the school of our research were 'knife-edgers' to some degree or other. But where are they to be found, or identified, in the schools of Hargreaves's, Lacey's or Willis's research? Of course, they may not have been there. But the point is that those approaches and methods would not have revealed them if they were. The examples show the typical interactionist concern with personal interests, choices, decisions, perspectives, identities and strategies. They also show the importance of different situations. These 'knife-edgers' might appear as totally different people to different teachers on different occasions, but all these appearances were essential parts of the composite identity.

The Accommodating Subculture

This all puts more emphasis on the individual's room for manoeuvre, and less on the influence of subcultures. Individuals are seen to indulge in strategical thinking and behaviour, weighing up trade-offs, and profits and losses, seeking to adapt situations to their interests, or where that does not work, adjusting interests and goals. It does not mean that subcultures do not exist, nor that they are not important elements in pupils' lives. But it does suggest a rather looser relationship. L. Davies (1984) found this in her year-long study of 'problem' girls in a mixed comprehensive. She felt that the concepts of 'subculture' and 'femininity' had been overworked, perhaps as a consequence of previous studies' concentration mainly on boys and on oppositional behaviour. There were common concerns among the 'wenches' (a local term that Davies chose as a counterpoint to Willis' 'lads'), but not the solidarity of some other groups (such as Willis' 'lads'). Group allegiances were weakened if they threatened a girl's status, derived from a pattern of values involving peer group, boy friends and family. Thus, by the end of the year, Donna was 'going off' Sandra because 'I can't stand going about with people who's always going off with chaps. I used to hang about with them night-time, but hers an old bag now...'. Kath similarly was growing less keen on being 'hard'. Terri was becoming sceptical about some of the wenches' places that they frequented outside school — 'used to be ever so nice, but now it's a right dump' (p. 56). She had also stopped missing lessons with Carole, and was 'settling down'. Carole and Lorraine now had steady boy friends, and saw less of Rajinder. 'Overall', Davies concludes, 'mates are still important, and provide certain rules of behaviour and group definitions and boundaries: but the wenches are increasingly looking for individual rather than collective solutions to status concerns, whether in or out of school' (p. 56). Unlike some of the boys' groups studied earlier, the wenches did not replace 'commitment to school values with profound allegiance to the norms of the counter-culture' (*ibid.*). They were indifferent rather than oppositional, but certainly not 'passive' and 'conformist' as in the gender stereotype. The wenches' individualism and 'private interests' seemed uppermost here. Davies concluded that

> The subculture may be less a place to celebrate similarities as to demonstrate differences. The task for pupils in an anonymizing institution is to remember and prove that they *are unique* (although not too unique); the subculture provides a safe foil for this display, especially in the face of the inevitable depersonalization of the large classroom. Subcultures are not a kind of superglue where pupils must instantly 'adhere' to the rules of the group, but at most a cavity foam filling with plenty of air space to manoeuvre. (Davies, 1984: 57)

Theoretical Implications

How, then, do the approaches discussed, in this chapter and chapter 2 (also interactionist) relate to those in chapters 3–5? This is no less difficult a question than the relationships between social class, 'race' and gender, but as with that, so here certain observations can be made. There are two lines of thought on this relationship. One emphasizes the differences and incompatibilities and points to the different assumptions on which they are based. Rosser and Harré, for example, in chapter 2 are making a case for viewing pupil cultures produced within the institution in a different way from any that the others suggest. According to them, the cultures are held together by a code that protects the pupils' dignity, and is honed by teacher 'offences'. The code was the same for *all* the pupils studied, both male and female, and whose backgrounds ranged across working and middle class. Now this is clearly different from 'reaction formation' or 'cultural production'. It appears to have little to do with the organization of the school, such as streaming, or for aspirations for status judged by some external criteria. The pupils had their *own* notions of rules and of deviance — they were not derived from or modelled on others' sets of rules. There are several other fundamental differences. Where, for example, does the violence and aggression so characteristic of male pupil culture come from? Is it an inversion of middle-class peace-loving values, a product of working-class culture, or is it derived from the culture of masculinity?

The interactionist approaches also emphasize individual interests and choices, and situational influences upon them. This shows the problems of assigning individual pupils to categories, such as 'conformist' or 'deviant', or to whole 'cultures', such as pro- and anti-school cultures. Interactionists also contest the extent of cultural determinism implied by the subcultural theorists. There is too, a different set of concerns among these interactionist studies arising from their different starting point of the pupils' own construction of meaning. This takes us into areas rather different from, for example, the norms of the peer group.

There are, too, fundamental differences stemming from the broad lines of theory, associated with the approaches. Willis's account is basically at odds with that of Rosser and Harré, and though it seems on the face of it to have fairly strong connections with Miller's cultural transmission theory, the Marxist tradition that Willis relates to finds little sympathy for the subcultural approach. Furlong posited his conception of interaction sets as a more valid representation of pupil cultures than that of Hargreaves, for his was based on pupil knowledge, and that of Hargreaves on a cultural norm. Similarly, Turner felt that pupil interests were a better basis for a model than approaches which focus on official goals/means, while supporters of the latter might feel he was being excessively individualist and subjectivist. Even within these broad divisions, there are differences, for example, between Willis and Bowles and Gintis.

The other line of thought, while recognizing certain incompatabilities among these various theories, feels that there are some complementary features, and consequently some cumulation of understanding of pupil cultures. The criticisms set up between and among these studies may not always be appropriate, as I argued in chapter 2 was the case concerning the debate about differentiation-polarization theory. The research studies are not all concerned with the same thing, or pitched at the same level. The individual, the group and sub-group, the institution, and society are all represented. Though we may analyze at one level, we need to take others into account for a full understanding.

There are consequently a number of pupil cultures overlapping and intersecting, to which individual pupils are variably attached. Codes of masculinity and femininity for example are basic and common to all pupils, but there are subtle differences between those from middle- and those from working-class backgrounds. Pupil cultures develop within schools, and aspects of these may be peculiar to the institution, quite separate from other cultural forms they subscribe to outside the school. Thus Rosser and Harré's 'pupil rules', which they found were common to all pupils, do not exclude the possibility that pupils also subscribe to social-class-based cultures, and that there were profound differences among them on that basis. Rosser and Harré would not necessarily have identified these, because they were not the object of study. Similarly, the fact that pupils participate in variably constituted 'interaction sets' for a multitude of different purposes, does not preclude the possibility of more firmly based groups, any more than Turner's emphasis on 'individual interests' debars more generalized adaptations. In the complexities of pupil cultures, there are many such possibilities.

Some might criticize the interactionist approaches for being too concerned with fine detail, in the here and now and within particular situations and consequently missing the broader patterns and structures both in the wider society and historically: with having faithful description and the delineation of the 'how' as the major aim, rather than the 'why'. However, these are not essential properties of interactionism, though they may be reasonable comment on some interactionist studies that have been made. Equally, interactionism can not offer a *complete* understanding of pupil cultures. It offers evidence bearing on many aspects of theories of pupil cultures that have been advanced. For example, it is a useful corrective to crude empirical claims that are sometimes made about what happens in schools. It forces us to modify any extreme notions we might hold of the monolithic behaviour, beliefs and attitudes of individuals that some subcultural studies might lead us towards. It can show how some of these theories might relate together, for it focuses on the point of intersection of social class, gender and ethnic cultures, institutional forces such as school organization and teacher culture, and individual biography. It is ideally suited to the study of small groups, and for the appraisal of mediating forces within the school. At this level it can generate new theory, such as that of Rosser and Harré, which then has to be taken into account within the full analysis of pupil cultures. It would be a mistake to regard this as offering a complete picture. Equally, it cannot be ignored in appraising other theories.

In summary, class, gender and racial differences are general and deep-seated, and will have broad effects. These will be mediated differently through different regions, school, teachers and pupils. It is these local effects the inter-actionist attempts to chart, but they should not be allowed to blur the wider forces. The institution's influence is seen in the rigid streaming of the 1950s and 1960s with the polarization that Hargreaves and Lacey described. Comprehensivization and mixed-ability teaching has obscured some of it to some degree, though not entirely. The divisions are still there, but interwoven with the fabric of school life in more subtle ways — for example, through the options system, banding and setting. This brings the variability of pupil cultures more to the fore. The answer, then, as to whether these explanations of pupil cultures are complementary or competing is, inevitably perhaps, that they are a bit of each.

Policy Implications

Three broad themes run through chapters 2–6.

(a) Pupils negotiate with teachers the basic rules of their classroom interaction. This may not always look like 'negotiation' as we know it, nor may the rules always be made evident. Both may reside deep within pupils' and teachers' understanding or subconscious.

(b) Pupils both contribute to and are influenced by cultures, of which some of the more prominent are social class, gender and race. Pupils do not analyze these in studied fashion: they live them, and interact with them. They are vitally important in formulating identities, for which the secondary school, covering the period of adolescence, is a crucial arena. There are many other cultures, of course, not exa-mined here, which might be dear or otherwise highly relevant to particular individuals — cultures based on age, on neighbourhoods, on activities, for example — which might cross-cut those we have looked at. But the three considered appear to be the most pervasive, and to lie behind another pressing issue, that of educational inequali-ties.

(c) Pupils have their own individual interests, which they will seek to promote in various ways, developing a range of strategies to cope with conflicting elements surrounding them.

Some of the most important influences operating on pupils are located outside the school and, some might argue, outside the school's control — in, for example, the social-class structure, in racism, in the gender divisions that permeate society, or in the promotion and maintenance of a particular form of political and economic structure. The school does not exist in a vacuum but, most currently believe, it does have a certain measure of autonomy from the wider system. Some external influences and constraints also appear to be mediated by school organization and processes. How a school organizes its classes, distributes its resources among subjects, establishes its principles for counselling, and how its teachers actually relate to pupils — such matters can promote or modify the effects of external factors. This raises the question, then, of what implications the analysis here has for school policy and practice. The detail of this must be left to individual schools and teachers, for they have many other factors that have to be taken into consideration — LEA policy, parental pressure, public examinations, teacher cultures, to name but a few. In general, however, putting oneself in the position of the pupils requires an examination not only of one's own practices but also of the beliefs and values upon which they are based. This cannot be done without a certain openness of mind and the cultivation of an ability to empathize with others, especially those who seem particularly oppositional. The extent to which racism, sexism and classism are imbued into some teachers' consciousness, beliefs and daily practices does not admit to easy and overnight solution. But 'taking the view of the other' has been shown to be an excellent basis for a start (*see*, for example, Arnot, 1989b).

With such an approach teachers can extend the choices before others and before themselves. An authoritarian approach will interpret pupil behaviour from its own perspective. If institutional rules are considered the only legitimate ones, contraventions of the rules will be considered deviant behaviour. The imposition of sanctions for the transgression of rules is one choice open to teachers, and in some circumstances it may be the correct one. However, in other circumstances it may be inappropriate, if the aim is to promote the conditions conducive to learning. It may encourage confrontation and rebellion. Something needs to be known, therefore, about the causes of the behaviour in question if the most productive response is to be achieved. Teachers are not unlike doctors in this respect — they must make a diagnosis in order to prescribe a remedy. Sometimes these diagnoses are straightforward, sometimes they are rather difficult; sometimes mistakes are made, perhaps because the more important symptoms are not apparent, or because similar symptoms can have vastly different causes.

Applying this analogy to pupil behaviour, the appropriate response can be worked out according to the interpretation of the cause. If, for example, it is due to 'sussing' or 'testing out', teachers might be prepared to 'negotiate', but from a positon of firmness. If pupils are 'being nasty' or 'looking cool', teachers might examine their own conduct to find out how they might have given offence. If pupils are indulging in teacher-baiting or being rebellious, teachers might look for cultural associations and help them to understand them better. Schools might also consider how school organization and processes might aggravate, or indeed be the major cause of, that kind of behaviour. Teachers might be particularly alert to retreatist modes of pupil adaptation, common amongst girls, and consider how far such behaviour is produced by the school and other factors. Similarly, if black pupils appear to be at odds with teachers with regard to both academic achievement and behaviour, teachers again need to examine both their own practices and the school for contributory causes. If some pupils show highly variable behaviour, now conformist, now deviant, this is not necessarily the product of a schizophrenic personality, but a response to a variable situation where such a pupil's interests are only partially met by the institution.

All these examples are opposed to a rationale that interprets all pupil behaviour that deviates from some official norm in terms of a deficit model, that is that pupils are defective in some way, in terms of 'not having the right attitude', 'not having the appropriate mental faculties', 'lacking the right background', 'being insufficiently mature or motivated', 'being easily misled', being 'too quiet' or 'too noisy', and so on. Such a conception of the ideal pupil is much too narrow for the range of cultures and of individuals that populate school. Transforming the site of interpretation to within those cultures and individuals might lead to discovery of storehouses of learning resource and eliminate the myth of deficit.

The Development of Pupil Strategies

In chapters 3–5, the power of cultural influences on pupils was examined. Largely, these were seen as considerable resources in pupil's attempts to cope with school. They help shape identity, but they do not determine the individual. In this chapter, the balance of the relationship between individual and culture has been examined and argued to be a fairly loose association, involving a dialectical exchange, and possibly variable over time and across situations. The one constant is the individual pursuing his or her goals and interests through a range of strategies. This implies a different model of socialization from that involving induction into certain roles or cultures, as in 'sex-role socialization'. That is too determining. It inhibits rather than promotes strategical thinking, yet plenty of this (strategical thinking) has been in evidence thoughout this book. How does the facility develop?

Fred Davis (1972: x) adopts the view of person as:

A perplexed, somewhat anguished, yet essentially well-intentioned character groping his(sic) way among alternatives, most of which are given him by the world and some more nearly of his own making. He sees none of the alternatives as ideal, although he reasons that one *must* after all be better than all the rest. The object of his quest is to decide on that alternative. Since life can offer no certainty that he has indeed chosen best, what else to do but fashion with the help of others a small 'master plot' of language, thought and action which in its playing out convinces him, most of the time, that he has chosen wisely.

This may be, as Davis says, only an image (he uses the term 'homunculus') of the real person, but images, according to Schutz (1967), are all that the social scientist is able to construct of his subjects. This particular image of person as coper, manager, dramatizer, rationalizing a way through means to ends, adjusting behaviour according to situations and contingencies, continually monitoring the process of action, checking and re-casting thoughts and intentions in line with changing possibilities and expectations, in short, as a devizer of strategies, is basic to interactionist approaches, and particularly apt for the study of largely conflictual situations like schools.

Such an image of person carries obvious implications for pupil, and indeed all human development. The process of socialization includes learning strategies to cope with the world. Highly appropriate to this concept is the notion of primary and secondary socialization (Berger and Luckmann, 1967; Musgrove, 1977). The situation of childhood is given, and one has no choice over the significant others through whom the world is mediated in the first years of life, when primary socialization occurs. It consists of acquiring perspectives, becoming accustomed to certain cultural forms and learning some basic strategical techniques — how to behave as boy or girl, how to act at table, speak to strangers, play games, relate to parents, brothers and sisters. Some of these may be seen as given properties of personality, such as patience, persistence, tolerance, when they may well be attributes learned socially, so deeply are they internalized. For the child, at this stage, before going to school, the family *is* the world, and what is mediated through the family is the only reality that is known. This reality is a basis for life, has an obdurate completeness; it is the root stock on which later secondary socialization is grafted. Thus the child internalizes these mediations, builds up a personal identity, and also learns the valuable lesson of 'taking the role of the other', that is of seeing things from others' points of view and not completely egocentrically (Mead, 1934).

Secondary socialization, according to Berger and Luckmann (1967: 158) involves 'the internalization of institutional or institution-based "sub-worlds"' . . . the acquisition of role-specific knowledge . . . role specific vocabularies . . . and tacit understandings.' Some of these sub-worlds phase into each other. For example, the first lesson the child has to learn on going to school, is how to become a pupil, in general terms, as distinct from 'a certain mother's child'. In the early years of infant school, the boundaries between school and home are softened to ease this transition. Eventually, however, other sub-roles come into play as the pupils become categorized into good or poor academically, well or badly behaved, proficient at certain subjects rather than others, and so on. There are fairly well-defined types, of which there are fairly clear expectations, and pupils, having signalled the appropriateness of their allocation to them, further learn to respond to these expectations. One's identity, thus, takes a further twist in sub-roles, but this is not so intractable as in primary socialization.

This is mainly because, as a corollary of learning to take the role of the other, the child may also learn — though perhaps with varying degrees of success — to cultivate the art of 'role-distance' (Goffman, 1961). These roles, then, that are encountered in secondary socialization, even with their various specific languages, semantic fields and legitimations, may not be internalized to the same degree as those of early childhood. They can be held at arm's length, as with the prisoners studied by Taylor and Cohen (1976) when they steadfastly refused to allow their own sense of themselves to be changed or overcome by the dehumanizing tasks they were forced to do; or they can be used in the furtherance of the self, as with Goffman's (1961) surgeon, who used joking asides while doing surgery, to show personal command over the role. That, perhaps, is not a bad recipe for education in modern industrial society, that is learning to accommodate to a variety of roles in a flexible way, with maximum command but personally adjustable commitment. In his ability to change readily according to the situation, the perplexed coper, when winning, becomes protean person (Rapoport and Rapoport, 1978).

The art of role-distancing is aided by the different character of the individual's relationships with the secondary sub-worlds. The affective ties with parents are very strong, with functionaries, they are formalized. The child

> does apprehend his(sic) school teacher as an institutional functionary
> in a way he never did his parents, and he understands the teacher's
> role as representing institutionally specific meanings — such as those
> of the nation as against the region, of the national middle-class world
> as against the lower-class ambience of his home, of the city as against
> the countryside. Hence the social interaction between teachers and
> learners can be formalized. The teachers need not be significant
> others in any sense of the word. They are institutional functionaries
> with the formal assignment of transmitting specific knowledge. The
> roles of secondary socialization carry a high degree of anonymity;
> that is, they are readily detached from their individual perform-
> ers ... the consequence is to bestow on the contents of what is
> learned in secondary socialization much less subjective inevitability
> than the contents of primary socialization possess. Therefore, the
> reality accent of knowledge internalized in secondary socialization is
> more easily bracketed ... (Berger and Luckmann, 1967: 161).

The child therefore moves from the confidence and certainty of primary socialization, where the world is one and indivisible, and within which he or she is totally immersed, to a functionary world of many parts, which is quickly learned to be of a different order — more distant, more utilitarian, more manipulable. The groundwork for the development of strategical thinking and behaviour is laid during this process.

The child learns this ability to change and to adapt according to circumstance mainly through negotiation, a key concept in interactionist thought, and basic to strategical action (Strauss, 1964; *and see* Chapter 6). Indeed, for a view that lays stress on strategies, negotiation is life. Though individuals have learned to take the role of the other, they still like to maximize their own interests. Being able to put themselves in the other's position adds sophistication to their negotiative skills, a keener sense of when to press harder, when to give way, what gratifies the opponent, what displeases, how to make the best out of a situation, how to turn loss into gain, disadvantage to advantage. All school life is of this kind, for even the most conformist pupil will fall short of the teacher's ideal, and somewhere along the line there will be a truce, agreement or compromise, that will reflect the nearest both sides can approximate to their aims, given the opposition's alternative aims and resources. Negotiation is the activity that lays the basis for the truce, and it is composed of strategies (Reynolds, 1976).

The concept of negotiation rests on certain assumptions. One is to do with power. Though generally recognized that teachers have more power than pupils in the sense that they create the demands, set the scene, and are imbued with authority, all against a background of compulsory education, the extent to which teachers can influence pupils in accordance with their intentions in any given situation is highly problematic. This is what the art of teaching is all about — getting pupils to do what you wish — and for the teacher of course, this is just as much a matter of learning and devising strategies (Pollard, 1985). It cannot be achieved, as many new teachers find to their cost, by a straightforward appeal to authority or exercise of power — this latter can be quite ethereal, especially in secondary school. It can be argued that the teacher's authority has considerably diminished in recent years, and the rights of the pupil improved, together with the rights of other underprivileged groups in society. Teachers' resources are slender in terms of the job they are expected to do, especially in the stark confines of the classroom, where they are vastly outnumbered, and, unless careful, stand to be outmanoeuvred. For many pupils do not have the same purpose, nor even the same basic reality as teachers, and the order is ever a precarious one.

Another assumption is that relationships are variable, that is to say that teacher-pupil relationships are not all of a kind, except in the general functionary sense which defines the boundaries of them. Instead, the interactionist view is that teachers and pupils are continually creating relationships, changing them, shifting bases of them, new ways of getting round them, plugging holes in one's own versions, detecting weaknesses in others. It is the greatest exercise of one's powers of ingenuity, for both teacher and pupil, and at its best can be attended by the subtlety of manoeuvre, respect for opponent, and joy in accomplishment, whether winner or loser, that accompany the best of games. At its worst, it can be humiliating in the extreme for either teacher or pupil, for here it will breach the strategical defences constructed during primary socialization, and hence the basis of one's identity. Relationships will vary according to certain conditions, such as how pupils relate to a certain teacher, subject or activity, what the particular constellation of the group happens to be, how they are feeling at the time. Of course, some negotiations and strategies will be more routinized than others. Even with established relationships between teacher and pupils, however, the forms of negotiation are still acted out, and subject to revision. For individual relationships are also changeable, especially where they rest on broad categorizations rather than intimate detailed knowledge of each other.

A third assumption is that the parties to the negotiation have different interests. The majority of pupils appeared to have conditional relationships with their teachers. But even with those that might be viewed as 'conformist' types, there are, as noted in chapter 6, great problems of definition. The concept, like any monolithic treatment of 'deviance', can be seen, fundamentally, as oppositional to interactionist concerns. For these, conformity in the generally accepted sense, does not exist. The most dutiful pupil will vary his or her behaviour to some degree in accordance with one or some of the factors discussed above. Intentions will be liable to change, both at a local everyday level, and on a longer term basis. At times they may well coincide with those of a teacher, or teachers, but there is no bland internalization of institutional goals. Thus, conformity, if and when it occurs, is only one form of negotiation. For example, teachers' demands might frequently be pitched well above what they expect pupils will do, or what they are even capable of, as a bargaining position. The sheer impossibility of such goals necessitates negotiative strategies.

As it is, most pupils' most favoured mode of adaptation appears to be some form of 'colonization', and this neatly fits the strategical conceptual mould. For if we regard primary socialization as the home base, then during secondary socialization individuals colonize other areas of activity in the outer world, get out of them what they can to further their own interests in true imperialistic fashion, though in some areas they might feel more at 'home' than in others, and on occasions shift the locus of identity to one of these sub-areas. Here is the classic conflict between self and society. How can individuals both maximize their own interests, and avoid conflict with others all engaged in the same enterprise? Negotiation is the interactionist's answer.

An instructive example from a related sphere is Becker *et al.'s* (1961) study of medical students, a group with strong commitment to a common aim — becoming doctors. But his observations revealed that the students were less concerned, in the day-to-day action of their lives, with learning how to become doctors, than with learning how to become students. They had 'impossible' demands made on them in the form of extent of knowledge they were expected to absorb, and in work assignments set. The ultimate vocational call to medicine became more distant under the pressures of having to pass examinations. They were forced to devise short-term measures to cope, quite cynically, in order to qualify, but they preserved their long-term aim of becoming good practising doctors after qualification. Becker introduces the notion of 'time perspectives' to explain this disjuncture, and argues that it is essential to see the short-term strategies as a temporary expedient to meet present contingencies against a much broader career backcloth. One might wonder, however, whether the ideal doctor *ever* emerges, any more than the ideal teacher, or barrister, or whatever. For constraints on action and variable resources, both personal and in the situation, follow one thoughout life, and the moment is often a compromise between aspirations, possibilities and strategical knowledge. In this way, the short-term and the long-term are not as discrete as Becker suggests, but firmly related. In practice they remain inseparable. Our 'perplexed coper' is perplexed for life. Though s/he finds out more answers as s/he progresses through life, and some areas of thought and activity become routinized, s/he may also discover more questions, so that bewilderment may appear to increase. The point is, therefore, that such strategies may appear temporary, but they become part of the individual's stock of experience, which provides a resource for meeting future contingencies which are bound to arise. It would be an interesting exercise to investigate how far pupils' experience of strategies generally provided a basis for coping with the problems and vicissitudes of later life. A strong connection would support the view of secondary socialization advanced in this chapter, and of the school's integral part in that sphere of experience.

Of considerable relevance to a developmental study of pupil strategies is another well-tried interactionist concept — that of 'career' (Hughes, 1956). In one sense, the 'pupil career' seems clearly and progressively constructed from infant to junior to senior, one passes examinations or goes through grades toward the ultimate symbol of completion, a certificate or reference; even with respect to one's fellows there is often a clear route from innocent freshman to seasoned veteran. There are appropriate strategies at each point along these careers, influenced by such factors as status, power and aspirations, and also different strategies between different careers. For example, Hargreaves (1967) and Lacey (1970) identified pro- and anti-school groups of pupils, Dale (1972) 'planners' and 'drifters', Willis (1977) 'lads' and 'ear 'oles', Wakeford (1969) 'conformists', 'colonists', 'rebels', 'intransigents', and 'retreatists'. Though all of these might be better regarded as modes of adaptation which pupils shade in and out of, they might also represent the major orientation of certain pupil careers, and clearly the form of strategies deployed will differ considerably among such types. But all, nonetheless, will progress, whatever their career.

The pupil's career is a series of steps or stages. Progression is through a number of status changes occurring at significant points determined in the first instance by the institution. One such career is: at eleven-plus, as it used to be, transfer from junior to secondary school, at thirteen-plus, translation from preliminary groundwork to examination-orientated schemes, at fifteen-plus, movement into the new maturity of sixth forms, and at seventeen-plus, departure into occupation. At each such stage, there is a marked change in the status and role of the pupil, the expectations required, and treatment. Having 'mastered' the previous stage, new problems, new situations arise in the next, making new demands on coping resources and ingenuities. The status change acts therefore as a stimulus to increasing strategical sophistication. During the 11–13 period, the new secondary school recruit learns to cope with the demands of the new senior school; during the 13–15 stage, new patterns are learned and are superimposed upon the former, and so on. This socialization into ways of managing, solving problems, reducing perplexity, meeting demands as efficiently and economically as possible is preparation for later life, and arguably one of the most valuable lessons the pupil learns at school.

The properties of status passages have been considered at length by Glaser and Strauss (1971) and discussed in relation to the career of the pupil by Dale

(1972) and Measor and Woods (1984). A glance at these properties reveals the perplexities that might be initiated: the passage may be desirable or undesirable, voluntary or involuntary; its features may not be clear, one's perceptions of them inaccurate, and control over it negligible; one might go through the passage alone, or with others, though awareness of this might be variable. In negotiating the passage and learning to cope with new situations, one might argue that behaviour might tend to take certain forms. For example, in a strange situation, the pupil might tend to be withdrawn, not active, a recipient rather than giver, consumer rather than creator. There is an initial reconnoitering phase, when those problematic elements of the passage are being worked out — what it constitutes, who else is involved, its duration, its relevance to one's own concerns, the space for manoeuvre, and so on; and when knowledge about how previous crossers of the passage coped, and similarities in one's own previous experience are brought to bear. Perhaps the most obvious example is beginning at a new school. The comparative 'innocence' of first year pupils is always endearing to teachers, and this 'innocence' appearance may be aided by another factor attending the onset of a status passage. While the reconnoitering is going on, there is a kind of 'playing safe' — meeting organizational requirements without fuss or contradiction, assuming, for the time being at least, that the passage is in one's own interests. To be sure, at later stages of the pupil career, this might be viewed with increasing scepticism. Pupils' increased stock of experiences will then provide them with more of a basis for a preliminary evaluation. But even then, on occasions, a status passage may offer a kind of redemption, an opportunity to round off one not entirely satisfactory episode in one's life, and to begin again. So that we may well see, in the early stages of such passages, a kind of ultra-conformity, a new and inspired investment of self.

The degree of conformity might vary according to the degree of consonance or personal fit felt by the pupil to these events. Pupils are not equal, either in their resources or in their aspirations, as they approach these passages. They differ in the degree to which they are already equipped to cope, and to which they are already familiar with certain indices of the passage, and to which the passage appears problematic to them. This may be connected to primary socialization, to social class, gender, or 'race', to certain previous experiences and forms of secondary socialization, to idiosyncratic differences, to different aspirations, or to different levels of mental or physical development. It might also vary according to the degree of role continuity or discontinuity (Benedict, 1938). For, while a status change may imply a change of role also, some are more progressively continuous than others. Thus, if on change of school, a previously top stream child, for example, continues in this position in the new situation, the passage will be less problematic than if the new alignment involved a comparative demotion to mid- or bottom stream.

Following initial reconnoitering, there might be considerable experimentation in the sort of negotiative work discussed earlier, as one searches for ways in which to secure one's interests, perhaps also to identify what those interests are. In the last resort, individuals must work out their own passage, but they receive considerable help from their fellows, both those who have gone before, and current colleagues. Some strategies become routinized, almost folklore, and these are passed on tacitly and often unconsciously as ways of doing things that have been tried and tested over time, in many different ways, such as myths (*see* Measor and Woods, 1984), stories and legends, actual knowledge from, perhaps, siblings or parents, connivance from teachers who have learned the usefulness of such strategies for *their* purposes, or trial and error in discovering the norm. Much, however, is discovered in the company of contemporaries. On occasions, one individual might take the initiative in a certain lesson, perhaps with a piece of homework, with a new teacher, trying a new leisure pursuit, a new way of doing things, of answering questions, perhaps, and getting things right, as well as exploring the boundaries of tolerance. Frequently, a group acts as a team, be it playing up the teacher, (*see* chapter 2) or finding the best way to do the work, pooling knowledge, ringing the changes, taking cues from each other, changing tack as they take turns in experimenting.

Small wonder that a great deal of pupil activity has a brittle, transient quality about it. Some may never progress to the stage where negotiations are resolved, and where strategies settle into a well-laid plan of campaign, logically related to the individual's past and future, that is sensible within the individual's own conception of career. Such resolution takes the form, in the case of the group, of cultures. Cultures provide a firmer platform for action. They recommend the boundaries within and criteria by which strategies shall be devised and deployed, as well as their nature. Again, there will be a tendency for more experimentation earlier in a pupil's career rather than later, given that some of these matters, like identification of interests, together with knowledge of system, have proceeded apace. But radical changes are not unknown at sixth form level, and indeed it is becoming increasingly recognized that adults throughout life have much greater capacity for change than was formerly believed possible (*see*, for example, Musgrove, 1977).

Two other related factors complicate appearances. One is the 'manifest-latent discrepancy'. Things are not always what they seem. Certain behaviours might be assumed for particular, transitory reason, and might differ profoundly on different occasions. To recall one example from chapter 4, Dumont and Wax (1969) have shown how some Cherokee pupils appeared ideally conformist in their classroom behaviour; but this was because 'within their homes they have learned that restraint and caution is the proper mode of relating to other' — classroom and Cherokee culture coincided on appearances on this point, but differed in meaning — they apparently *learnt* very little. The teacher did not detect the latent culture for what it was, interpreting it instead as conformity to her own. This could be a commentary on commitment and centrality. Pupils might become skilled at putting up appearances, reserving their best attentions, skills and efforts for other areas and activities.

Similarly, Becker and Geer (1977) have discussed the importance of latent identities, that is that derive from cultures having 'their origin and social support in a group other than the one in which the members are now participating.' This raises interesting questions about the relationship between primary and secondary socialization, and between areas of secondary socialization. The pupils' culture, like that of Becker and Geer's students, grows out of the problems of pupils as a group in the context of the school, and derives from their manifest identities as pupils — how to learn work, do problems, avoid failing examinations, or getting into trouble, relating to particular teachers, and so on. But just as it is possible to suggest ways in which pupil culture is strongly relevant to the future, so one can argue the potential significance of latent identities to such cultures, particularly when shared by a group. 'The girls from the Hurley estate' or 'the boys from Badcombe' may have such powerful, integrated and long-standing cultures developed that they display a collective identity that impinges powerfully on the school world. Complementary cultures, no less, blend in with those of school. Thus, latent cultures and identities may be very influential, providing a rich fund of resources for strategical action.

Other significant features of the pupil's career affecting strategical development are 'transformational episodes', catalytic moments, periods or events when the pupil undergoes significant change. They may occur during status passages, but they may occur at other times also, for there are other catalytic agents. Strauss (1969: 92), in speaking of 'transformations of identity' has insisted that it is change, and not just development:

> As he (sic) 'advances', his earlier concepts are systematically super-seded by increasingly complex ones. The earlier ones are necessary for the later; each advance depends upon the child's understanding a number of prerequisite notions. As the newer classifications are grasped, the old ones become revised or qualified, or even drop out entirely from memory.

This is remarkably similar to the conception of strategical socialization as mentioned above. Strauss provides a list of 'critical incidents' or 'turning points' that can lead to such transformations, such as the 'milestone', an event that brings home to one, or crystallizes a progression or retrogression. As Berger and Luckmann (1967) point out, 'bring home to one' is a peculiarly apt expression for this experience, for it strikes into the world of primary socialization. Another 'critical incident' is playing a new role well, discovering perhaps hidden and unsuspected capacities. Two that we might insert that are particularly relevant to pupils, are the acquisition of new knowledge, and the influence of others, whether parents, teachers or peers.

The first is a factor which seems curiously absent from sociological literature. Perhaps this is because sociologists have been more interested in the social construction of knowledge, and in the 'hidden curriculum'. The impact of knowledge on self-identity is but little studied. But we know, from our own experiences at least, the power of knowledge to transform selves. Thus there may be revelations for pupils along the way — indeed, this is what teachers are supposed to be providing — the discovery of an activity or area of knowledge that seizes the imagination, summons up new powers of applica-tion and ingenuity, that cuts through both the pupil's own possible undervaluing of self and the labelling prescriptive of others (Hargreaves *et al.*, 1975; Bird, 1980). This could lead to a re-routing of career, or a powerful impulsion to a new role level, from, for example, 'struggler' or 'drifter' to comparative 'expert'. We can speculate that, on occasions, the transforma-tional agent is not unconnected with growing acceptance of future responsibi-lities. Yet others that occur later in life do so perhaps because they are elsewhere, that is to say generated not in the sphere of public, institutional life — the world of secondary socialization — at all. Motor-cycling, stamp-collecting, hi-fi, photography, bird-watching, pigeon-fancying, fishing —

these are all examples of interests that in a sense, for some, are oppositional to school, though it may have clubs and societies in some of those pursuits, because this deep, personal interest derives from the freedom of one's own initiative, which is more commonly experienced in the private sphere of life — the area more connected with primary socialization. The 'progressive' movement in schools, which actually seems to recur quite regularly throughout history in some form or other, could be seen as an attempt to soften the school's own constraints and blockages to 'transformational episodes', and the public-private divide; while perhaps the greater success of the primary school in this respect, and in securing the pupils' motivation generally, is related to its proximity to the complete, real world of first childhood.

The second factor that might induce one of these 'transformational episodes' is an outstanding educational agent — perhaps a parent or other relative, a teacher or a friend. Most of what we learn, we learn from others, be it school learning, or learning about new situations, people and tasks, and events in life generally. An outstanding teacher can 'transform' a pupil in an educationally beneficial sense. Some do the opposite, and cool out pupils who otherwise might have made progress educationally. Transformations are not always the result of beneficial incidents, but might arise from 'stressful situations'. Strauss (1969: 106) suggests that these occur if 'motivations are inappropriate for further passages and when self-conceptions grate against arrangements for sequential movements.' Dale (1972: 82) adds two more factors — 'when no clear career-line is offered by the institution, and when an institutionally discouraged but competing value system is found.'

If pupils' behaviour and attitudes often appear unaccountable, erratic, and inconsequential, it may well be because of the extreme marginality of their position. It could be argued that the whole period of pupilhood is marginal. In Van Gennep's (1960) classic analysis of 'rites of passage', he distinguished three main phases — separation, transition and aggregation to a new condition or reincorporation. The first phase is marked by behaviour symbolizing separation from a particular point in the social structure or a set of cultural conditions. The second is distinguished by marginality or 'liminality', wherein the characteristics of the passenger are ambiguous, neither belonging to past or future status. In the third phase, the subject is re-united with the social order with the clearly defined rights and duties attaching to the state. Victor Turner (1969: 95) says the attributes of liminality are necessarily ambiguous, since this condition and these persons elude or slip through the network of classifications that normally locate states and positions in cultural space. Liminal entities are neither here nor there; they are betwixt and between the positions assigned and arranged by law, custom, convention, and ceremonial. As such, their ambiguous and indeterminate attributes are expressed by a rich variety of symbols in the many societies that ritualize social and cultural transitions. Thus, liminality is frequently likened to death, to being in the womb, to invisibility, to darkness, to bisexuality, to the wilderness, and to an eclipse of the sun or moon.

It might seem to be stretching a point to claim that pupilhood is marginal, since it is well established by law, custom, etc. However, pupils leave the primary world of early childhood at age five, and do not return to a 'primary' state until they leave school. At school, they are under tutelage, subordinate, directed. They are 'growing' or 'becoming', without actually ever getting there. The whole period is transitional, from being a mother's child to being an independent citizen. Liminality, for the pupil, has been likened to prison, being in the army, Colditz, and Stalag camp 15 (Woods, 1979). It is not surprising that strategies more associated with those institutions abound at school, from 'bunking off' to undermining the morale of one's captors and sustaining one's own.

'Stressful situations' and 'liminality' bring us back to our 'perplexed coper'. We are perplexed for life, but pupils have reasons for special perplexity. At school, they are initiated into secondary socialization, and inducted into a functionary world of utilitarianism and manipulation among roles. They are especially subject to status passages and changes and transformational episodes, over which they have little control. They are exposed to a number of new experiences and phenomena, such as individual teachers, aspects of school organization, problems of work and knowledge, class cultures, teacher and pupil cultures, peer groups, towards which they are required to make a response. Through this maze of activity and encounters pupils negotiate their way, making the most of their power and abilities in furthering their interests, often in company with their fellows, discovering and inventing strategies of infinite number and complexity. It is, arguably, the pupils' most valuable lesson.

Chapter 6

Pupils at Work

In these final chapters, I examine two prominent features of pupils' school life — work and laughter — in a little more depth. These two activities take up a large proportion of the pupil's day, sometimes in conjunction with each other, sometimes in opposition. Many would claim, for example, that pupils go to school to work. As noted in chapter 1, it is high on pupils' own list of priorities. There might be gaps in the system, but the central official activity is without doubt 'work', for all concerned. School rituals, pedagogical orientations, examinations and careers are all geared to its production. Most pupils recognize that they go to school to 'work', and dislike situations not conducive to its production.

However, in the 'Lowfield' study (Woods, 1979), there seemed to be a considerable difference between teachers' and pupils' perceptions of work. Pupils resisted socialization into the teachers' model, and were not always moved by the thought of personal gain. They were, however, deeply influenced by the status of the work and the personal qualities of the teacher. For them, work was relationships. I shall consider this aspect in the first half of this chapter.

Given the differences between perceptions, the chief characteristic of teacher-pupil interaction was negotiation, as teachers sought to maximize pupil efforts on their terms, and pupils often to modify them on theirs. 'Negotiation', therefore, is the subject of the second part.

Relating to Schoolwork

Teach us, O Lord, to labour and not to ask for any reward, save that of doing Thy will.

The Happiest Days?

Introduction

This prayer, frequently used in Assembly at the beginning of the day in many secondary schools, is highly appropriate. Pupils are not paid wages for their work and for many, the purpose behind the product is equally as mystifying as 'God's will'. Some have concluded that there is little relationship between school and 'the world of work' (Carter, 1966). Correspondence theories, on the other hand, seek to show a degree of inherent similarity between school and work (Bowles and Gintis, 1976). The emphasis here is not so much on content as relationships. At school, it is held, pupils learn the social relationships appropriate to a capitalist society. If some are mainly engaged in 'defeating the school's main perceived purpose — making you work' (Willis, 1977), this is a form of adaptation that will serve them well in later life. Above all, they come to accept things for what they are. Most of these studies focus on the teachers as perpetrators, either intentionally or, more commonly, un-intentionally (Sharp and Green, 1975).

The pupils' approach to schoolwork has been less commonly researched. In what few studies we have, all concerned with small groups in individual schools, 'school' is not an organizing principle in the structure of their lives (Birksted, 1976); pupils typify teachers mainly by their 'strictness' or 'softness' in relation to either avoiding 'trouble' or 'learning' (Furlong, 1976); or they apply an 'evaluation scheme' to teachers beginning with 'keeping order', and progressing through 'having a laugh', 'understanding pupils', 'utility of subject', etc. (Gannaway, 1976).

In my own research in a secondary school, I was interested to discover what affected pupils' attitudes to schoolwork, from their own perspectives. Though the class factor had a strong influence on outcomes (Woods, 1979), all pupils identified two main items in their view of work within the school — the school's own distinctions among forms of work, and the quality of the teacher. Unless the work 'counts', nothing can redeem it. If it does count the teacher can transform it into either something felt to be enjoyable, constructive and rewarding on the one hand, or something painful, inhibiting and onerous on the other. Within these two major constructs, other factors come into play. By and large, then, this suggests the kind of progressive evaluation model proposed by Gannaway while indicating a hierarchy of categories, and suggests that for many working-class pupils there are items within the school that profoundly influence their perception and accomplishment of work. I now present the gist of the pupils' approach to these items, drawing on my conversations with and observations of over two hundred pupils in the fourth and fifth years of a secondary modern school in both examination and non-examination classes. I use chiefly the comments of fifth-year examination pupils who were at the end of their school careers, for such 'conformist' pupils are even more under-represented in the literature. First, however, if we are seeking more general influences on conceptions of and attitudes towards, work, there are some to be found that cut across class divisions. I therefore begin with a consideration of 'the meaning of work'.

The Meaning of Work

The distinction is commonly made in society at large between pleasurable work, which involves making things, and 'labour' which one engages in to survive, and which 'leaves nothing behind it'. William Morris championed the cause of 'craft work' against the toil and curse of 'slave's work' (Briggs, 1962). The latter has been seen to be increasing, and possibly moral concern at this was behind the attempt to establish progressive styles of teaching in schools, seeking to transform what had become little more than hard labour into more creative work. As Arendt has said, 'The industrial revolution has replaced all workmanship with labour, and the result has been that the things of the modern world have become labour products whose natural fate is to be consumed, instead of work products, which are there to be used' (Arendt, 1958: 124).

This then raises questions about the centrality of work in people's lives. Some hold that it has now become a peripheral element, or at best a means to an end, and that they now seek enrichment and fulfilment in their private lives through their own interests and hobbies (Berger *et al.*, 1973; Luckmann, 1967). The metamorphosis of work in industrial society has led to a breakdown in the old meanings of work. But schools are enormously conservative institutions in some respects. Rather paradoxically their 'progressive' solution to the modern malaise, purportedly in a spirit of advancement, was conceived around old, outmoded notions of work which now lack cultural and structural support in society at large. Protestant ethic type notions of work abound in school. The categories used of pupils are usually framed in these terms — 'idle, 'lazy', 'good worker', 'industrious', 'needs to work hard', 'more effort needed'. And my study school, for one, seemed preoccupied with instilling the moral virtue of the industrious worker. Its hopes of winning must have been based on optimism at its chances of overcoming other influences, or a belief in a basically instinctive *homo faber* or *homo laborans* which they needed to awaken. However, attitudes to work are learned, and they are learned partly outside school through cultural permeation. Teachers wish to inculcate other, often contrary attitudes, which have become structurally outmoded, and to which they themselves only partially contribute in practice (Woods, 1979). What happens in school under the label of 'work' is largely an accommodation to these two oppositional tendencies. Teachers seek to bridge the gulf by various 'motivating' devices. The whole school day rings to the sound of inducements to work. But general exhortations and the cultivation of a 'workish' climate are limp forces beside the quality of the work and the quality of the teacher, as perceived by the pupil. In all this, 'work' is not easily defined. Rather, it is a 'patchwork of diverse values and purposes, displaying many contradictions and inconsistencies' (Fox, 1976: 18).

Hierarchies of Work

There is a hierarchy of work as there is a hierarchy of knowledge (Young, 1971; Hextall and Sarup, 1977). One can distinguish on one level, differences between 'O' level, CSE, and non-examination work and between different levels within the GCSE (Nuttall, 1988), as between the GCSE and other forms of assessment; and on another, within these varieties, work that is meaningful, work that is productive, work that is play, and work that is useless. One distinction was made between the examination work of the fourth and fifth years, and the 'junior' work of the first three years in the school. Frequent references were made to the size of the disjunction. Suddenly, they were treated like adults, 'It was more like a break of ten years than just the one'. They were not supposed to come late to lessons *now*, were expected to set an example to the whole school. But it was the increase in work load that hit them most, 'because in the third year we didn't do much, but in the fourth and fifth years we had to do a great deal more'. Teachers were, 'more strict' the work a 'lot harder'. They suddenly found themselves doing 'masses and masses of homework'.

The distinctions among varieties of examination groups are revealed by examination pupils commenting on their non-examination colleagues:

P. Woods: Is it as worthwhile as the programme you've been on?

Diane: I think they do more social work — learning about the community more than actual education like Maths and English an' that.

Vera: They've been going out a lot, and been doing work around the school, going out for Community Service.

P. Woods: Is it as worthwhile as the programme you've been on?

Diane: I think it's worthwhile in their own way because a lot of them aren't intelligent enough to take exams, some of them are, but not all of them . . . and they spend their time doing a worthwhile programme really. They can't learn much in Maths and English, that sort of thing, but they can learn about the community.

The divisiveness among groups of pupils and their accompanying characterizations fostered by this division of labour and knowledge is clear and all pupils recognized it, though not all believed it legitimate. CSE work apparently, was only semi-proper.

Kenny: I regret having chosen History. It's boring, I find the teaching methods a bit off-putting though I like the subject-matter. I used to at any rate before the exam course. The teacher *tells* you everything. I would have liked to have done more work, more things myself, more practical work, like. In geography too, that would help.

Shirley: I agree about the CSE History Group. We were neglected in favour of the 'O' level group, and spent much of the end of the fourth year, and all the fifth year doing a project.

Elaine: Yes, he taught the 'O' level group separately in a different part of the room, and left us to get on with it.

Shirley: We never actually got taught anything for the actual exam course, 'cos the project's only part of it, see.

Elaine: Mind you, towards the end he did give us books and tell us to get on with it ourselves — revising and reading about it.

But the people of 'iron' were the non-examination forms:

> *Steve*: It would've worried me to get into 4L because the only way to get on outside school is with exams. You've only got to look through the daily paper — three 'O' levels for this, four 'O' levels for that.
>
> *P. Woods*: What have 5L done over the past couple of years then?
>
> *Steve*: They went out on lots of trips, more than we did, and they've been doing different things round school — like doing the greenhouse up an' that.
>
> *Martin*: They just seem to do odd jobs around the school.

So the non-examination forms, 4L and 5L are not engaged in 'proper education'. The pupils are making the distinction between mental and manual labour. Actual education involves cognitive processes, but 4L are not strong on these, so they learn by 'doing'. It is clearly seen as inferior.

The most important prestigious work is that done for examinations. This is so important, that the work done by non-examination forms is often rated valueless:

> We had to keep working to do exams this year, they didn't, they haven't anything to aim at. They just keep going till they leave. They're not left with anything really, because they could've left at the end of the third year — and they've still not got anywhere now. They've just done nothing.

This applies to the examination pupils' own non-examination work like 'community service', which involved helping in hospitals, visiting old people, etc. This was adjudged 'boring' and not very 'meaningful'.

> *P. Woods*: Would you rather have taken an extra subject instead?
>
> *Des*: Well, not another subject, but perhaps visiting places of work, like 5L, where you see what they're doing, and you'd see if you want to do that when you leave school.
>
> *Steve*: Because that's to do with your future.
>
> *Des*: I think the community service was just to get us out of school so that other kids could have a lesson, just to let other people look after us for a bit so other children could have the teachers.

However, this does not mean that all their activities at school were subsumable under work. Rather, work itself had to be put into another context. Time and again, these pupils, when asked what they valued most highly in school, replied 'mixing with friends', with 'sports' a worthy second. Work was not usually enjoyable for most of them, in fact, at times, it was very painful. It was an accepted necessity, and inasmuch as it might have repercussions for the conditions and opportunities attending the delights of life, it had to be taken seriously. But as an intrinsic activity it hardly figures in their scale of priorities (though it is a priority in their assessment of teachers).

Dave: No, I'm not actually looking forward to leaving school, I think a lot of people say they are, but when it comes to the actual day, I don't think they will be. I mean my sister always said that, then on the day she was very upset.

P. Woods: Are you saying you enjoy school?

Steve: Yeah, I have.

Ken: It's been all right.

Dave: I have enjoyed it, yeah.

P. Woods: What, mostly?

Dave: Sports, mostly.

Ken: I think there'll probably be a lot more freedom than there is at work.

Dave: Another reason — you've got all your friends here, so you come to see them as well.

P. Woods: What about you, Steve?

Steve: Yeah, mainly, sports, I suppose, swimming, that's about it.

P. Woods: Have any of you enjoyed the *work*? You're all telling me about sports and mates. You might as well go to a recreation centre, but this is a school, its purpose is to teach isn't it? What about the work?

Ken: I think it's the teacher that makes the work interesting, you know. If you don't like him you don't like your work.

This brings us to the second point. What matters to *these* pupils is relationships, with their friends, with teachers. These are different 'relationships' from those posited by Bowles and Gintis, who suggest a correspondence between school and work. For these relationships are often produced against, and in spite of the official programme. Further, the initiative for them is being articulated here by the pupils, from all streams in the school, and from all social classes. If all is well here, work is accepted. If not, it presents uncommon difficulties, and other activities are elevated to first-rate importance. But relationships are not enough on their own. The importance of the status of the work means that a 'recreation centre' would not, in fact, do just as well, or better. For it would lack the material support of the 'work' on which the economic futures of these pupils is seen to depend. This is why 'community service' is irrelevant, even though 'relationships' is its rationale.

Work as relationships

Many pupils appear to hold the assumption, so long-lived within their background culture as to make it seem 'natural', that there is no or little intrinsic satisfaction in work. Work is distasteful, unwelcome, unpleasurable, painful, but perhaps necessary. Teachers provide a scheme of thought to accommodate pupils' unwillingness, yet still provide a rationale for motivation: 'all work is like this — this is how it is — your reaction is normal — your minds must learn to accept this inevitability, but also pick up ''out of the air'' as it were, the crushing need to do it'. The reward, however, is somewhat obscure at this stage. It has to be taken on trust for a long time, in the form of marks, grades and reports. This conception of work is reinforced by artificial stimulants which dominate the atmosphere of the school — on the one hand motivators, such as competition and inducement, appeals to vanity, pride, and one-upmanship, and on the other, penalties — reports, detentions, reporting to parents.

This logic, lacking essential structural support is entirely dependent on trust. Thus, the contrary paradigm on work is itself dependent on relationships. Through them, pupil need meets teacher aim. The articulation of this need shows a variety of adaptations to school, but a common concern with what they perceive as the human properties of the teacher. A powerful message coming over from all the pupils I spoke to at Lowfield was that work can be both odious and burdensome, *and* pleasant and enjoyable and that what makes the difference is not so much the content of the work as the relations with the teachers concerned. In other words, teachers can actually transform the experience. Many pupils accept the need to be 'made to work'.

'Yeah, I think they should be made to work. When you go to Tech., for example, it's your choice, so you're not made to work, but school isn't your choice, so I think you should be made to work, otherwise you wouldn't because it's not your choice.

Many seem to accept this social Darwinist view of themselves as recalcitrant, and project an adult judgement on themselves. Thus, forcing them to work is right, because it is 'for their own good', 'it helps them in the future', they are 'not old enough' to appreciate the benefits. They come to have a socialized instrumentalism, which does not always hold up in fact, and which is sometimes less clear-cut in the fifth than in the fourth year, illustrating the shifting sands of pupils' outlooks. Thus, although many talked in the same kind of instrumental terms as teachers, in work being important for future career, in actual fact many of those in the fifth year who had already secured jobs, and many who had a definite one in view said they did not require examination qualifications. Even for some girls on the commercial course there was not a good fit.

> *Barbara*: I'm going to the Tech. to do a child-care course for two years. I don't need any qualifications for that, but I've got to do Human Biology and Sociology 'O' level in the course.
>
> *Shirley*: I'm going to work in a day nursery. I don't need qualifications. I already had the job at Christmas. Mrs. Warner asked me if I wanted to go down there.

This cut a lot of material ground from under teachers' feet, and made pupils rather ambivalent. This in turn reinforced the emphasis on relations with the teacher, makes that, in fact, the basis on which 'work' stands. It all depends on how it's done:

> I think if you were made to work in a different sort of way, in a sort of friendly atmosphere . . .
> If you've got the right kind of teacher. With some teachers, like if you like working in the lesson you do work hard, but other teachers, when you can muck about like, you enjoy it, but really at the back of your mind is really you should be working, and if teachers don't seem to take no notice of you and they're not interested in you so you don't feel like working. But with other teachers like Mr Kingley and Mrs Coles, you know they make you work and you enjoy it in a

way. They make the lessons interesting, and they're interested in you, you're interested in them.

These pupils recognize a need to work and their own recalcitrance. That means an acknowledgment of need for discipline, but this other element is equally important:

> *Kathleen*: Some teachers can make the lesson interesting but that don't mean you're going to work. They've got to sort of treat you like human beings — you know, listen to what you want to say, not treat you like kids.

Work can be a weapon, bribe or reward in pupils' dealings with teachers:

> He's always so happy, isn't he? . . . friendly. He comes down . . . like most teachers expect us to come up to their level, he's prepared to come down to ours. He's more like a friend isn't he? Because you like working for him, you don't mind. A lot of teachers you don't want to work for to spite them'.

Teachers, it would seem, could learn much from the human relations school with regard to industry (Mayo, 1933; Whyte, 1961). To these pupils at least, it is not the work that is important, and any intrinsic satisfaction to be had from it is dependent on the relationship with the teachers concerned. This squares with their general emphasis on social criteria in their outlook on school.

> (The main thing I hope to get out of school is) relationships with different people, that's what I think. But I don't mix much when I'm out of school, and I've got a number of friends here, and I enjoy going around with them. That's the main reason with me.

Teachers are not blind to this of course. Talking about a four-period block of environmental studies with a non-examination group, one teacher said, 'we might not get much work out of them, but it has a social value — at least we can try to develop some relationships with them'. However, this division between work and relationship did not hold entirely. Developing relationships had implications for how he (the teacher) saw their attitude to work. The girls had complained to me about how he favoured the boys, and did not care about them. The implications are apparent in this comment he made to me about the group:

They're good lads, you know, they're earthy, but they're not villains. They're not angels, either, you know, they'll break the rules, but they're OK. The girls on the other hand are a bit wishy-washy. There's not one character amongst them. Basically they're idle. They'll all probably end up with jobs in Woolworth's.

Thus, teachers' perceptions of pupils' work and their capacities are also mediated through relationships — sometimes on a sexist or racist (chapter 4) basis.

Work in itself does not seem a natural activity to these pupils, but it might be a natural adjunct of sociation. Where this is successfully established, work is a pleasure. Where not, it is a toil. This is just as true for the most instrumentalist examination forms as for the non-examinations. The same is true for teachers. Thus work is a 'negotiated' activity.

Work is the activity that produces the desired outcome. At Lowfield, these outcomes were always fixed by teachers — examination passes, exercises, projects, games. They would then deploy various strategies to get the pupil to perform the relevant activity. An interesting one at Lowfield which neatly fitted the pupils' preoccupation with sociation, was to collude with them, against a third party as it were — the 'school', the 'headmaster', 'society at large' or 'life'. In this way, teachers remove their personal responsibility for the productivity demands being made on the pupils, they are bigger than both sides, and only through the trust built up between them can they consider it legitimate. The activity of the work is a joint, shared enterprise, subsumable under the general relationships — that is what makes it enjoyable. Elsewhere, with an authoritarian teacher, there is no such attempt at collusion. A different teaching paradigm is in play, and unless there are other factors promoting the worthiness of the work (such as personal ambition) the activity will be un-pleasant and distasteful hard labour.

Alan: We had one teacher, he used to make us line up outside (others = Idiot!) file in single file, stand at your chair behind the desk, no talking, pen, pencil, ruler and rubber on the desk. He used to come round and check them, and you couldn't talk at all, and you mustn't move your chair.

P. Woods: But how did he treat you when you were working?

Alan: Say you're doing some work, he'd come up to you, and he'd think you're not doing it right and he'd start moaning at you, and he'll come up and say 'Good God boy, what are you doing!' — some'at like that. You know he won't stop to see what you're doing. He'll tell you what you're doing wrong, but he won't help you to remedy it.

It should be noted that much of the teacher's conditions of work militate against forming the desired kind of relationships, which are premised on individual contact and appreciation. Dealing with pupils in groups of classes (Lortie, 1975), the pressure of the system as mediated through headmaster, parents and examination, the demands of professionalism and tradition point teachers toward a different model of teaching (Hargreaves, 1988).

Certainly, basic perspectives are influenced by gender, 'race' and class cultures, and clearly the school's hierarchies of work and knowledge can be linked to the class structure of society. But there is another dimension which cuts across the class factor, which we might term the 'institutional'. Inasmuch as there has been a flight from identifying the 'real' self in the institutional sphere toward the 'private' sphere (many of the working class probably never have done so), from formalized structures towards informal, from planning, control, discipline and achievement to 'permissiveness', the lowering of inhibitions, and the inner 'quest' for identity, a new emphasis is put on relationships (Bell, 1976; Turner, 1976; Berger et al., 1973). This school illustrated a huge disjunction between obsolete models of work advertised by the school embedded in an outdated Protestant ethic ideology and pupils' interpretations of work. These pupil interpretations arise generally from shifting definitions and loci of self mediated to them through mass communications, changing patterns of child-rearing, career opportunities, and so forth; and they put the emphasis, not on the intrinsic qualities of work, the virtues of industry, nor primarily on the personal benefits to be gained. Motivation for these pupils was not to come from socialization into a work ethic, nor from an appeal to instrumentalism, but from the school's own valuation of work, and above all, the relationships with the teacher. This, then, is another factor to set beside the importance of 'marketability' of subject, as discussed in chapters 3 and 4. The simple moral is to make the work count, and for teachers to be human. Fake products, however, or exhortations without structural support, are quickly spotted, and only compound the problem of 'how to get pupils to work', an issue itself embedded in antiquated pedagogy.

Negotiating the Demands of Schoolwork

I use the term 'negotiation' here as in Strauss *et al.* (1964). Strauss and his colleagues showed the importance of informal arrangements, often contrary to official policy, in the running of a hospital, but the concept is applicable to all institutional life, including schools (Delamont, 1976). These negotiations are marked by much skill, ingenuity, diplomacy effort and study on both sides — the very qualities one might look for in an idealized notion of 'work' (Anthony 1977). Through their study we might get closer to that mysterious central activity.

One way to represent the experience of the pupils I encountered is by the four categories 'hard work', 'open negotiation', 'closed negotiation', and 'work avoidance'. 'Hard work' implies full commitment. 'Work avoidance' at its extreme implies total lack of commitment and is where the real counter-cultures flourish. However, the majority of pupils are mostly to be found somewhere in between indulging in 'open' or 'closed' negotiation. Both arise from partial commitment and hence a mismatch between teacher and pupil aims. Open negotiation is where parties move some way to meet each other of their own volition, and subsequently arrive at a consensus. Closed negotiation is where the parties independently attempt to maximize their own reality in opposition to and conflict against the other, and each makes concessions begrudgingly, and only if forced. However, they do make concessions, unlike the 'work avoiders'.

From all these positions, the experience of work is somewhat different, and I shall try to describe the three categories containing work for both pupils and teachers, concluding with some speculations on the forces that lie behind a possible 'shift to the right' (i.e. towards 'work avoidance') in pupils' accomplishment of schoolwork, when teachers perpetually seek a shift to the left. I should make clear that I am talking about categories of work, rather than individual pupils, who can move among them according to subject, teacher, and time of day, though pupils often have a predominant mode.

Open Negotiation

Command of the process of negotiation is at the heart of being a successful teacher. Quite often, if the teacher overdoes concessions, the pupils will demand more and threaten to take over the lesson. It is also to be reviled as offending the norm: 'He's a bit of a queer teacher. He's not like a proper teacher. He doesn't tell you off'. If not enough concessions are made, pupils might become resentful, and potential colonizers might be turned into rebels. What the standard lesson consists of then, is a number of checks and balances, prompts and concessions, motivations, punishments, jollyings, breaks and so forth, as the teacher displays professional expertise in getting the most out of pupils, while the pupils, seeking basically the comfort of their own perspective and reality, will tend to react according to how the teacher's techniques mesh with that reality.

One of the most common gambits the teacher makes is to offer to do a great deal of the necessary burdensome work and to 'carry' the pupil along. For the pupil this is what I would term 'distanced work', because the pupil is a long way from its point of origin. The most common illustration of this is teacher talking — pupil listening. It has many variations, including the standard question and answer, board work and doing experiments. Pupils are constantly reminded of the terms of the contract:

Example 1

Teacher: I'll do the algebra for you now. There are six methods of factorization, give me one. [No hands go up, a certain lethargy.] I'll make you do the lot if you start yawning! [Several hands go up.]

Teacher: Formulae are getting longer and more complicated, and your memories are getting worse, So what do they do? Give you the formulae to take in with you! There's not enough practice learning or memorizing these days. Do you have to remember passages in English Literature? [they shake their heads.]

Example 2

Teacher: [During experiment on expansion of liquids.] I'm going to record the results now [noise increases in class]. I gather some of you would rather *write* the whole double period!

Example 3

Ricky and (To me, after teacher experiment): We've got to work now.
Lawrence: (They came back automatically, armed with a piece of paper from the front).

Example 4

Teacher: I've talked enough, now I think it's time you did some work. I'm going to give you four essay titles, choose one and make a start in these last 20 minutes. You can get half your homework done if you get your minds on it.

In this last example there is a double bargain. The teacher has 'worked' for 20 minutes of the scheduled 40-minute period, while the pupils took things easy. Now it is their turn. Furthermore, extremely valuable leisure time in the evening is offered as an extra inducement. Another element appears in this example:

Teacher: [After a few admonitions at the beginning of lesson, and one pupil getting moved up to the front.] I'm going to start with a promise, or two. In the second period we'll have a film — if you're good, and work well this first one! Then I thought next week we'd go out and do the nature trail in the forest [pupil talking]. I think you're adopting a very anti-social attitude, and that became apparent the moment you walked through the gate this morning. [Quiet, but a ripple of noise again.] Now don't let me have to nag!

Thus, not only do pupils stand to gain pleasurable experiences if they comply: if they do not, they will earn the teacher's wrath and precipitate what Furlong's (1977) pupils called 'trouble' which at all costs they sought to avoid. Individuals might get 'shown up' or verbally (even physically) assaulted. (Woods, 1979).

Teacher: If I hear another burble from your stupid little mouth, I shall push your head through the top of that desk! [With nose an inch from pupils', and eyes wide and unblinking. Ghostly quiet in room, and they go on writing.]

Thus bargaining tactics of the teacher are not always pleasant ones.

> *Sandra*: I think some of the teachers are frightening. They frighten you into working. I don't think it should be like that really. I'm frightened to walk into some lessons.

Lessons frequently proceed in this way, with pupils exploring the boundaries of tolerance, and teachers continually defining them, though in ways that accord with general and particular teacher-pupil norms and rules (*see* chapter 2). What is being bargained for is often 'control' rather than 'work'. Here the distance between the pupil and 'work' is at its greatest. That is to say that there may be no passage through the pupil of the teacher-initiated activity whatsoever, even though there might be an appearance of it.

The extreme bargain derives from situations where children do hardly any 'work' at all, and teachers have long since given up trying. But because teachers can cause 'trouble' and pupils can be extremely awkward, both trade appearances for tolerance. Much 'work' in the school day therefore is counterfeit. No productivity rates are required, there is no factory line, no next stage in the process waiting, and for non-examination forms, no examinations. The only kind of productivity rate demanded by 'supervisors' is a semblance of work and a semblance of good order. Interestingly, this is maintained when the teacher is absent. The semblance of work and good order will be preserved by the semblance of a teacher in the form of notes mediated through a proxy stand-in teacher. Notice how the bargaining is built into these notes:

> Classwork 2B/2H Thursday 7th February
> READ THE NOTES CAREFULLY AND THEN COPY THEM INTO YOUR BOOKS. ON TUESDAY I SHALL COLLECT 2Bs EXERCISE BOOKS IN AND ON THE THURSDAY OF NEXT WEEK 2Hs.

> READ AND COPY THESE NOTES
> [Two pages of notes, and a diagram follow]
> IF YOU DO NOT FINISH THIS IN CLASS IT IS YOUR HOMEWORK TO FINISH IT OFF. I WILL COLLECT YOUR BOOKS NEXT LESSON TO MAKE SURE YOU ARE DOING YOUR WORK. THOSE OF YOU WHO HAVE TAKEN NOTES ON PAPER DURING LESSONS GET THOSE COPIED IN AS WELL.

There is a negotiated ambience in established classrooms which all implicitly recognize, and teachers and pupils are continually reminding each other of the terms, if one or the other steps over the boundaries:

Teacher: Hey! Now look! We know there has to be a certain amount of noise — as long as it's a working noise.

Teacher: How many have not brought pencils? Now look! This is not on! You've been told before!

In stating the terms of the negotiation, some teachers keep constantly in mind the ideal product they would like to see, while many pupils' ideal in my study school was 'doing as little work as possible'. Again, the 'mass' nature of his work causes the teacher to take action on the basis of how the majority behave. But one or two pupils might aspire to the teacher's pole position and they serve to reinforce the point for the majority.

Teacher: I was a bit disturbed when marking these books to find only a few had finished off this work, the questionnaire on page 124. It must be finished. But in order not to hold others up, we must press on. We're staying with education, and I want to finish by break. Tomorrow I want a discussion — a sensible one — therefore do your homework properly. Question 10 on page 16, I want some thought given to that. 'Parents should pay directly to the costs of their children's education' [all write]. John, I want you to think of an argument for why parents should pay, and Steve, you second it. [But sir, I don't agree with it!]. Never mind, I want you to argue for it. Tim and Harold, I want you to oppose the motion. The rest, I want you to think along those lines. Now do this, please, that's your homework, and we can have a good debate. We can always find less pleasant things to do.

(Next day)

Teacher: Due to some people not having done their homework, we'll have to postpone our discussion, and continue, straight on . . .

This teacher lays down the parameters of his objective, and consistently reminds the class of how far short of them they fall. This may be a tactic to optimize their performance in the heavily teacher-directed classwork. However that may be, the pupils are a long way from involvement in this work and it is a good example of 'distanced work'.

Even if not productive in the same sense, and thus enabling appearances to be substituted for reality, much of this bears interesting similarities to work on the factory line. The literature abounds with parallels. Compare these extracts from research accounts:

> The whole bench dreams like this. It is a galley of automatons locked in dreams. (Fraser, 1968).
> When I'm here my mind's a blank. I make it go blank (Beynon, 1976).
> You can't expect much out of work — you just have to do it (Carter, 1966).
> The technological environment is so overwhelming that nothing the foreman can do would really make the workers like the work they do (Whyte, 1961).
> The mental demands of a majority of automobile assembly jobs are for surface attention; the work does not absorb mental faculties to any depth (Miller and Form, 1951).

Much schoolwork, similarly, seems to call for only surface mental attention. It constitutes no challenge, calls for minimum skills, is marked by repetitiveness, yet pupils must pay some attention. Perhaps this is the nearest, given the constraints under which they have to work (Ashton and Webb, 1986; Hargreaves, 1988), that teachers can get to Protestant ethic-type work with certain pupils. It succeeds, possibly because it bears many of the qualities of 'real' work in the world outside, and thus has strong cultural and structural support. Indeed, some of the studies discussed in chapter 2, especially those taking a 'cultural production' approach, would suggest that pupils collude in such a definition of work. In this sense, pupils themselves are one of the main constraints that stand in the way of teachers making work more meaningful.

There is a great deal of 'play' in pupil work. Teachers, who are interested in pupils' *learning* by whatever means, or if that is completely impossible, keeping them occupied in as pleasant a way as possible, often devise games as part of their teaching strategy. Teachers thus provide curriculum forms to compensate for the basic curriculum, the relevance of which, for many pupils, is not clear. This is one of the paths to 'good relationships'. Those teachers high on the pupils' list in this respect were adept at humanizing the basic drudgery with departures from routine, attention to individuals, skilful use of laughter, converting 'work' to 'play', and so on.

They will sell such activity to the pupils as 'play' both as a learning enterprise in itself and as a balance to more grisly business. Thus: artwork, pottery, craftwork, needlework, domestic science, science experiments in the labs — such activities could often more appropriately be classified as play. Pupils might seek to transform any dull activity into play. For example, in one physics lesson observed, pupils were set four problems of balance to work out. The class proceeded with these in a mood of happy and casual industry, chattering in groups, sorting through the problem, but with frequent and cheerful digression to the state of the football league or the current pop scene.

'You can't expect much from these' the teacher told me. 'If you wield the big stick, they rebel. At least like this we stay friends, and they do learn something.' Some pupils thus are perceived as having 'limits' in their capacity to do schoolwork. Some need extending, others need indulging. For the latter there is much play, games and laughter. If teachers can incorporate some of these elements into their programme, rather than allowing them a subterranean, illicit existence, they might achieve some learning via the back door as it were. At the very least, they will achieve a *modus vivendi* and a spirit of sociability, which is not a bad platform for work, given the 'relationships' preoccupation of the pupils.

Some teachers thus deliberately construct the learning process as a game. After all, it is not self-evident *why* one should have to learn about Roman villas, upland sheep, the area of an annulus, the Citizen's Advice Bureau, how to make a canoe, the principle of levers, similes, and so forth. Thus a rather dry social studies lesson on 'educational expenditure' was relieved by sending pupils all over the school to get essential information from the caretaker, the cook, the secretaries, and so on. A history lesson on strip farming was lightened by allocating the class character parts in a medieval village. A project on housing, was spiced by sending pupils around householders with a questionnaire. The point of the Citizen's Advice Bureau was incorporated into a strip cartoon and the pupils invited to supply the words. The pupils all entered all these activities in a friendly and lighthearted manner. They were all games, with various winning points (for example, pupils tried to outdo each other in rude repartee in the strip cartoon). They were certainly not 'work'.

Some pupils are considered incapable of much mental work at all. The fourth year 'Maths Remedial' group, for example, could only 'work' as individuals in cooperation with the teacher. There were only six of them, but as the teacher moved on round the group, the rest fell into a completely different world of conkers (one had a 120-er, only half of it left, but hard as iron), fireworks (screechers, air bombs, rockets and flares), bike-racing, trips to the toilet ('but put your cigarettes on my desk first'), and ruler-fights. The high point of this lesson, which dominated their day, was when Vince asked if anybody had a pen he could borrow. Norman whipped open his jacket to reveal a festoon of pens in a crammed, glittering line, and selecting one at random, offered it to Vince. Unfortunately, it turned out to resemble very closely the pen that had gone missing from Vince's own possession but the day before. The teacher then had to exercise the judgement of Solomon, but to no one's satisfaction. Vince wanted his pen back, and if Norman lost it, it would spoil his priceless collection. Vince was eventually moved, but they carried on from afar, with mysterious looks, signs and gestures. Both got all their sums wrong.

> *Teacher*: Oh Vince! What on earth have you done, you silly boy! You've *added* them! Where's the sign? Where is it, isn't it big enough? Really! You just can't be bothered! If I took the same attitude as you, dear oh dear! The mistakes you've made are inept. This one is totally wrong. Six plus six is twelve and three makes fifteen. How do you get twenty-one? Is that how many conkers you've got on that piece of string?

In the last remark, the teacher recognized the paradigmatic influence of the pupils' social world. Perhaps it contained a hint of a point of entry.

Hard Work

If negotiating more tolerable degrees and forms of work is the main activity, there are times when pupils do *hard* work. 'Copying notes from the board', for example, can be extremely 'hard work' for some pupils. The difficulty lies in the mental effort required in concentrating on the task, and in the act of writing. What has become easy and second nature to some, almost a natural extension of the self, to others poses the greatest problems:

He gives us loads and loads of writing.
What I don't like is when they get on about your writing.
'E makes us do a load of writin' . . . I don't mind the drawin', but writin' — huh!

This might not be perceived as hard work for the pupils by teachers, since they have devised the notes and written them on the board or dictated them. More likely are they to put into this category work that more obviously requires a stirring of the mental processes and some initiative on the pupil's part. Thus working from work cards, doing exercises — this kind of set work, which involves some form of problem-solving on their own initiative, is the ultimate in pupil hard work to many teachers. So it is, of course, for many pupils. I joined in one group activity with some 'deviant' fourth-year boys, based on a comparison of two housing estates. We had to find answers to a list of questions from the evidence presented in the form of photographs, statistics, tenants' comments, etc. I taped this discussion, and playing it back to them several days later, one remarked. 'Cor! We was workin' 'ard then! That's the 'ardest I've worked all term!' Another interesting comment one boy made on hearing the tape was, 'Listen at the noise! You don't realize when you're there, do you?' Neither work nor control always correlates with noise, the central feature of the hidden curriculum detected by Henry (1963). What made this 'hard work' for these pupils was the extent of application of mind needed to grasp the series of problems, the *creative* task of coming up with ideas in interaction with the elements presented to produce solutions, all of which made it an individualistic effort. Contrast this with the routine procedures of 'distanced' work, which can either be a drudge in calling on one's powers of attention, but nothing else (e.g. interest), or euphoric in permitting its sublimation in some other activity.

The greatest physical effort I witnessed at Lowfield was in the gym, especially circuit training, which involved press-ups, shuttle-running, sit-ups, bench jumping, and rope climbing, all performed, of course, against the clock. The staff certainly perceived this as work of the first order. It involved application, determination and the utmost investment of one's physical resources. 'Old Gary Simpson, he works, but he never seems to be on his beam ends' (P.E. teacher).

The games teacher's approach was framed in a 'workish' rhetoric. Thus, in games, pupils were often urged to 'work'. 'You must work for it' was often impressed on them. The techniques were ground out to them in forceful terms: 'Serve, Dig, Catch! Serve, Dig, Catch!' Games involved skill, which required practice, but other gym activity tests the limits of human endurance. Some pupils have an instinctive fascination for this especially after the boredom and distance of classwork, and will rally group support to push an individual on, as when they all shouted Gregory Beech up the rope for a third, very painful, time within 60 seconds at the end of his circuit training.

However, this does not constitute work for pupils. For them, it is a respite from the usual school chore, an opportunity to expend a great deal of bottled-up energy in a direction that they can comprehend. For some pupils, therefore, it comes under an *opposing* category — that of 'sport' or 'games'. It is perceived as a peripheral activity within the school's official programme, but in some pupils' lives, it is central — 'the best part of the week' — but as 'play', 'sport', 'leisure', uncontaminated by the alienating characteristics of 'work'.

Most 'work' is done by the examination classes. The rest of the school do very little 'work' in proportion to their other activities over the week. There was frequent reference to this divide. Exams meant 'work' for both teacher and pupil. 'No exams' let them both off the hook:

Dianne: They should push you now and then, 'cos up till the third or fourth year really if you didn't want to do a thing, they just let you get on with what you wanted to do. They didn't tick you off much, they used to occasionally moan at you an' that, but I don't think they did enough about it really.

Vera: I thought that was the only time we really worked hard, for exams. The rest of the time we was just told to do some work and that was it. Then when it come to the exam and they mentioned that, we was all working very hard and I found it difficult really.

Dianne: As you get nearer the end of the school, you more aim for something than during your first years an' that. So you do work harder.

Elaine: In the fourth and fifth years you're more dedicated to work, other years you muck about as well.

Much of this work, as noted earlier, is seen through the medium of relationships with the teacher concerned. But what of the activity itself? Mostly I got the impression that pupils felt they were 'shovelling away at a giant slagheap' (Taylor and Cohen, 1976: 203). This applied even to the supposedly 'creative' work of CSE projects and English essays. This is illustrated in one way by the quantification applied: 'I got a bit bored when I was doing the geography project and I couldn't decide what to do and had to do about 40 sides, and after about 10 I was fed up with it'.

The same applied to the English 'folder':

Andrew: In English, homework was one or two essays a week, and that was purely for the folder wasn't it?

John: That was about the 'ardest, building up a folder.

Shirley: I quite liked English actually. Miss Dickens, she's a nice teacher. The only trouble I had was with essays. You know, we had to do a folder for CSE, and we had to keep changing our teacher, because Mr Johns had to take us in the fourth year, and he'd come in once a week, and we had to do essays every weekend, sometimes two a weekend, and it really got us down a bit.

But mostly, for examination pupils, work consisted of attempts to commit to memory slabs of knowledge by various means of varying tedium.

Dave: The metalwork homework was to copy 10 pages out of a book, and that took three to four hours.

P. Woods: Was that usual?

Dave: Every week, for a year.

Ken: It seemed pointless, because we kept the book anyway.

Des: The idea was to make us learn it, I think, but he said 'copy it down and learn it', but I just copied it down word-for-word and didn't achieve anything from it anyway.

P. Woods: Did it have any bearing on the exam?

Des: Not all that much.

P. Woods: Did you revise your notes?

Des: There was too many of them!

Steve: Time you'd learned your tools an' everything . . . you couldn't learn it all. Not like history.

Dave: In history, we do the same thing — just copy — but we have tests, you see — so we have to learn it.

> *Daphne*: I would have been much happier taking fewer exam subjects, because there's so much forcing you to do what you don't want. Then you try to cram more in at the end, and that was too much. Especially physics, I found that very hard, and chemistry.

I found few expressions of 'enjoyment' of work. This answer was typical:

> *P. Woods*: Was there anything you really enjoyed?
> *Julie*: No. Nothing I really enjoyed.
> *Elaine*: I didn't mind English, but I wouldn't say I enjoyed it.
> *Julie*: It's just something you had to do. You had to do it, you couldn't get out of it.
> *Kate*: I don't think it's been really hard work. I mean when people go out to work, I bet they find it a lot harder than at school.

The demands of examinations appear to militate against the personal relationships so highly regarded by pupils. What seems fairly clear is that there is a misfit between demands and resources. Suddenly and dramatically between the easily negotiated calm of pre-exam work and the rather exciting prospect of remunerated, independent, responsible and meaningful employment, comes this period of peculiar pressure, for which it was difficult to find a consistent rationale.

> *Shirley*: I thought the normal homework during the year was quite interesting — maths and English I didn't mind doing them. But at the end when it gets towards exams, it gets you down a bit. they say you've *got* to learn this, you've *got* to learn that, or you won't pass your exams, and things like that.
> *Christine*: When you start going over things all over again, that's what I don't like.
> *Caroline*: Well, it was out of proportion. Physics we had hardly any homework, and we didn't learn much. In French we had a couple of hours every time, and we don't have the time to do that in one evening, we've got other subjects.
> *Beryl*: You're supposed to spend an hour for each subject, but physics, you can do that in a quarter of an hour, French would take us three hours.

This work has a mechanistic quality:

> *Debbie*: I don't like geography because it's all on the blackboard all the while, and I can't stand the teacher so . . . .
>
> *Angela*: He doesn't speak to you as . . . well, I dunno . . . 'e kind of treats you as machines really [yeah]. Its 'come in' he'll say, probably talk about something, not very often, it's usually straight out of a book or atlases, or off the board.

Also it seems to squeeze out those other (non-work) areas of school life that make it a humane institution. So that, for some, it is the total impact of the exam programme that impinges:

> *P. Woods*: What will be the thing you remember about school most of all?
>
> *Heidi*: Hard work.
>
> *P. Woods*: Hard work?
>
> *Heidi*: Yeah, no end of homework in the evening, especially in French.
>
> *Shirley*: Teachers tend to push you too much in the fourth year, they watch everything you do, and generally keep getting on to you all the while.
>
> *Caroline*: Yes, and, you know, a bit strict with you, they don't let you have no freedom whatsoever.
>
> *Barbara*: It starts the first day of the fourth year. We have homework sheets every month. If we miss one lot of homework or two lots of homework we get 'unsatisfactory' and if you get two 'unsatisfactorys' you have to see the year tutor and get told off by him, get put on report and everything. Really gets us down. That's why half of us don't do it really, to rebel against them, I think [laughs].

Not all my conversations with pupils were so dominated by a tone of 'complaint'. Many did express an enjoyment of the work, here and there, though that was more difficult to pin down and was invariably defined through the teacher.

Closed Negotiation

'Open negotiation' takes place together. It is a joint activity, based on a certain amount of goodwill towards each other, recognition of the value of cooperation, and belief in the possibility of consensus. But sometimes teachers and pupils take action independently of the other either in a spirit of less than goodwill or resignation, or in adapting to the circumstances that have been negotiated, thus engaging in the activity that I have called 'closed negotiation'. For pupils, this includes skipping homework, pooling knowledge and resources, cribbing, skiving, tricking the teacher into doing it for them, or simply 'mucking about' (*see* chapter 7). It is the most popular replacement of routine 'distanced' work, which can sometimes be a drudge, but on the other hand can often be euphoric in that, since it involves no interaction with the self, it permits its sublimation in some other activity. Again, this is not unlike the experience of some factory-line workers (Chinoy, 1970).

If teachers do not collude with them, and connive at the 'working game', as described in the previous section, pupils will sometimes take the initiative in transforming the activity of work into an activity of play. Thus there is a great deal of playing at working, and playing at listening. Intricate class and individual games, which the teacher might ultimately detect as 'a lot of fiddling with pen and rulers' abound. There is a great deal of pretending to work while doing something else, time-filling, going through the motions for appearances to 'avoid trouble'. If they slip up, through sheer negligence or forgetfulness, they might incur the teacher's wrath:

Teacher: Oh! I wish you people would come prepared for lessons!

However, since the chances of winning at this particular game of forcing pupils to work are remote, the teacher more often falls back on the old collusion, in exchange for some, if only a little, work:

Teacher: Paul! What have you done with the pencils? Who have you sold them to? Who can put him out of his misery and lend him a pencil? . . . That looks suspiciously like one of mine! Mr Lawton's is it? . . . . Anyway, when you've finished about from whom you nicked it, will you please get on.

There is a great deal of time-passing and time-filling, not as an adjunct to a larger purpose, but as an overall end in itself. This is earmarked by endless performances and rituals around the distribution, collection and finding of rulers, pencils, paper. The term, day, period is there, inevitably, and it is more necessary that it be 'got through' than it is the syllabus, especially with regard to non-examination classes. Sometimes this is an *ad hoc* adjustment to the contingency:

Notes: 10 October, periods 7, 8, fourth-year art and pottery.

Jack Lester is forced to take the fifth-year art group in the T.D. room for the second two periods, where he's on a hiding to nothing. That group sits around the table in there. Philip gets on with his — which he's been doing all term — passing the time. Kim is reading *Mad* and Possee is with his mates S.R., L.S., and J.T., who've been 'lobbed out' of pottery. Jack is meandering aimlessly around, also time-passing. Having discussed the *Planet of the Apes* and the *Six Million Dollar Man*, I say I'm going to see fourth-year art. 'I'll wander up with you', said Jack, 'for something to do'.

Where there is a middle, there is a great deal of eating round the edges:

At the end of these lessons, all had tidied up a good 20 minutes before the bell. Phil sits in his chair, watching them all suspiciously. 'A long day', he says. He looks worn out. What a slog! 'The time goes slower and slower, the longer it goes on in the afternoon', he says. 'My watch is a couple of minutes fast, I think'.

The critical nature of time, as ruler of content, is often conveyed by teacher comment to pupils, perhaps filling a space in one lesson by talking about the next subject which 'will take us up to half-term'. Or, by, inversely, talking about the compartmentalization of knowledge and how it is geared to time:

That's got 'maturity' done. Now we'll go on to 'availability'. We've only got 'curiosity' after that, then we'll call it a day.

In these examples teachers and pupils are similarly affected. In the following example different constructions of reality are more obviously in play.

Noisy lot. First few arrivals are quite jocular with Len. David asks 'What are we doing today Sir?'

Len:	Decimal division this afternoon, page 46.
Harry:	Oh these aren't too bad sir.
Len:	Right now, pay attention everybody, just like you did yesterday. [Len explains how to divide decimals.] Tell me what you do Jane. [General commotion while Len tries to explain division of decimals.] Just shut up talking when I'm talking, will you, you have the chance of talking when you're working. Listen to me now! Now pack up this chatting and turning round will you!!
Fiona:	What do you do with the decimal point, Sir?
Amanda:	Which side goes which Sir?
Derek:	What page are we on, Sir?
Len:	The idea of this introduction is to tell you how to do it, so stop asking questions! ... Now, when dividing, you move the decimal point two places to the left.
Amanda:	Right, Sir?
Len:	No, *left*!
Amanda:	That's what I meant sir, right, left, sir.
Len:	You said *right*!
Amanda:	I meant you were right, Sir!
Sheena:	I said left Sir, I *did*!

(Later)

Sheena:	Oh Sir, do we have to do these?
Len:	Yes, you do, it's very important. [He explains some more.]
Sheena:	You haven't moved the point.
Len:	You don't have to with this one.
Sheena:	Oh, it isn't 'alf' ard, Sir! [Len explains more more.]
Sheena:	Can I have another piece of paper then?
Len:	Well you shouldn't have started yet!
Sheena:	I did, I thought we 'ad to!

Len: I've been here explaining, how do you know what to do before I've explained it?

Sheena: That was before I knew!

(Later)

Amanda: Sir is that right?

Len: No, that's not right! Look, you're all working, and half of you don't know what you're doing! Why don't you put your hands up and ask?

Sheena: Init 'ard?

Len: No it's not hard, it's ever so easy, it should've been done in the second year!

Christine: Who invented the decimal point, sir?

Len: [to me]: I thought I'd give them something easy to do so I could get on and mark their books — blimey!

[The lesson continued in this vein.]

Clearly, there is not much agreed consensus in this lesson. It is a good example of 'closed negotiation'. Teacher and pupil attribute different meanings to the lesson. The teacher keeps trying to impose a formal structure in the traditional mould, and keeps resolutely to it despite its apparent failure. The pupils play with the teacher, pretending at the game of learning, contriving fun and jokes out of it where they can, and devising their own amusement where not. The teacher's complete immersion in his own paradigm was shown at the end when he confided to me 'that wasn't too bad. They worked quite well in that lesson'. Most of the pupils, however, had played their way through the two periods.

In 'negotiation', teacher and pupils usually manage to arrive at a 'core' universe of meaning which has properties recognized by all parties to it. Perspectives, to some degree at least, lock into each other at certain points. In other areas of school life, as in the example above, teacher and pupils remain firmly within their own 'sub-universe of meaning'. The physical points of contact are mentally transformed into matter appropriate to the sub-universe (Berger and Luckmann, 1966).

Conclusion: Cultural Lag and Structural Fault

Approaches to 'work' in school show a variety of perspectives. Teachers would say their aim is to accomplish learning, and that to learn, pupils have to work. Some pupils work hard, those with total commitment, very hard. The majority, however, at my study school had less straightforward attitudes to work. The teachers moved to meet these in various ways from the almost continuous urging and enticing to work that went on in assembly, lessons, speech day, headmaster's office, reports, etc., and the parading of ideal models to a variety of adaptations to pupils' own adaptations or recalcitrance. The extreme example of this, very pervasive at this school, centred on 'survival' (Woods, 1979, 1990a). Much activity, therefore, was a product of teacher striving and pupil recalcitrance — negotiating, bargaining, with teachers persuading, forcing or kidding pupils to work, doing most of it for them, chivvying them along, creating atmospheres of obligation, with pupils passing the time, playing, working the system. Some teachers and pupils spent their whole time thus engaged, and this therefore was the measure of their work.

More 'hard work' was to be found among the examination forms, but it was a strange activity, at times difficult, tortuous, and much disliked, not at all involving the ingredients of 'fulfilment' — opportunities for choice, decision, acceptance of responsibility, self-determination and growth. This 'work' was often the opposite of these, suppressing rather than encouraging them. There is a great deal of talk of work as a commodity, matched with notions of quantified capabilities (Young, 1975). Teachers compose imperatives like 'proper amounts', 'fitting into periods', 'finishing before the bell', 'what these kids can or can't do', 'the need to catch up', 'that's that subject done'. As Bernstein (1971) notes 'Children and pupils are early socialized into this concept of knowledge as private property. They are encouraged to work as isolated individuals with their arms around their work'.

An interesting yardstick on close personal meanings of work today is provided by Fox (1976). Much condensed, these are:

(a) provides an organizing principle
(b) services sociability needs
(c) sustains status and self-respect
(d) establishes personal identity
(e) provides a routine

(f)   distracts from worry

(g)   offers 'achievement'

(h)   contributes to a cause.

For many pupils, at my study school only (b) and (e) of this list would appear appropriate, with possibilities of (c), (d), and (g) in 'fringe' school activities like games, the official programme being actually counter-productive in respects (a), (c), (f), and (g). This might only appear reprehensible if we regard work as *the* central life interest. But as Bell (1976) notes, 'for the modern, cosmopolitan man (sic), culture has replaced both religion and work as a means of self-fulfilment, or as a justification . . . of life'. The organization of life in the modern industrial society has brought about a heavy investment for the individual in the private sphere (Berger *et al.*, 1973). Thus the most *meaningful* activities to many of these pupils were those which made sense within their own culture, and which pertained to the 'private' sphere — 'childcare' to the retreatist 5L girls, 'social craft', swimming, and other sports to the intransigent 4L boys. But even for many of the conformist strivers, there was a 'distance' between them and their work, so that all, to varying degrees, support the contention that 'Man, once *homo faber*, and at the centre of work, is now *animal laborans* and at the periphery of work'.

This, of course, is just as true of teachers. And if work is a kind of secondary 'going through the motions' for many teachers, with its compartmentalization, systematization, subservience to time, then it can hardly be anything different for the pupils. For when teachers try to convert the business, whether for integrating or motivational reasons, into a more 'progressive' enterprise, it ceases to be work, and becomes 'play — either a familiar kind of adaptation to the work scene, or a component more in keeping with the private sphere.

This general trend, common to all, is complicated by the social class factor. The same group perspectives I identified on a previous occasion are apparent to some extent (*see* chapter 2). When turning to future occupations, as well as subject choice, it is the human face of work that concerns those from a working-class background — personal security to be sure, and the means for the enrichment of the private area ('good money', 'in the dry'), but also the desire to be with friends, the camaraderie, the good 'relations' among all concerned. The other perspective, less evident in this chapter, contrasts in its extra-personal criteria, its careerist, professional keynote and its tendency toward total commitment and matching role with person. The first aims at securing the best possible conditions for toleration purposes and maximizing the adaptive techniques. 'Fulfilment' will be elsewhere. Society is not 'their' domain, but is run by and for others — those of the other perspective. As with regard to subject choice, so too with work and future career, family perspectives are reinforced by the school, equally paradoxically against the apparent intent of the teachers (Ashton and Field, 1976).

The majority of pupils at my school were from working-class backgrounds, and this chapter shows how the influence of modern industrialism is reinforced among examination and non-examination forms alike. Pulled apart in some ways, by for example, the hierarchies of work, which possibly channelled them along different routes into the occupational structure, most brought the same basic criteria to the experience of work. Part of the answer lies in the roots of the working-class culture from which they come. The process of adaptation to work goes back many years, and the cultural forms it has given rise to have deep roots, and are very pervasive. As Fox (1976: 24) argues, 'Generations of the working-class, subjected to this pattern of work experience, have made a 'realistic' adaptation to it by relinquishing or by never bothering to take seriously aspirations towards intrinsic satisfaction'. Like the factory, school is not an area where they can 'make something of themselves' (Ashton and Field, 1976). Carter (1966) argues that 'During this century, the working classes have been systematically de-skilled . . . and with this . . . has come a contempt for work' (not, of course, to be confused with 'jobs'). There is an 'experimental separation of the inner self from work', and it is 'the sensuous human face of work as prepared for unofficially . . . in the school, much more than its intrinsic or technical nature, which confronts the individual as the crucial dimension of his (sic) future (Willis, 1977: 102). One of the keystones of this work culture is the aim to secure the best possible conditions for toleration purposes, while personal fulfilment will be found elsewhere.

Here, then is a possible explanation for the emphasis on relationships. The cultural forms that envelop pupils in their lives outside school, among which they were reared from birth, and through which they construct meanings of life, and particularly certain generalized attitudes to work, are reinforced in school. Attempts to oppose these, however well intentioned, are restricted. Those elements that are valued within their own culture, are, however, highly esteemed.

P. Woods: Do you keep your work in a folder?
Posser: Yeah, all them sort of pouffy things.

Folders, projects, exercises, writing, reading, homework, indeed all mental work as such, are 'pouffy things', not only not for the likes of some of them, but oppositional and threatening, and therefore to be resisted. Whenever the full extent of their machismo is promised satisfaction, as in games, they will perform wholeheartedly. There is dignity to be won in the gym or on the field; enemies to be resisted in the classroom. But where the agent of that enemy force, the teacher, accords with certain strands in their culture, as in the emphasis on social relationships, and sheer indulgence in the delights of sociation, the gap will be bridged. The teacher-pupil relationship is not all conflict by any means. At times it rises to great heights of togetherness, but, at least with these pupils, it is based not on the manifest role of the school, work, but something that is often seen as an oppositional force to work, in that it has no other purpose than the immediate production of pleasure. The official programme is not just middle-class. It is childish, kid's stuff. To these pupils, there are not many connections between school and work. School is for kids, almost a separate compartment of life, a glorified crèche for adolescence. Work is for adults (Carter, 1966).

It should be said that within this broad, general trend, there are many individual differences, encouraged by a certain amount of differentiation in the occupational world. There are related differences in commitment — for example, as one goes up the occupational hierarchy, more of one's 'self' is invested in the job (Berger, 1973). There are differences among teachers in commitment, and vast differences between teachers and pupils. Among the pupils also, there are degrees of involvement. Some are thoroughly attuned to school, others totally opposed. This said, the general trend remains clearly evident (Carter, 1966: 70).

All this illustrates one of the biggest paradoxes about school, in that it is often held to be in the forefront of knowledge, in its efforts to develop skills and abilities and to open minds, yet is one of the biggest victims of cultural lag in this society. Teachers go on preaching the virtues of the Protestant ethic, with its emphasis on ambition, hard work, and deferred gratification, but the structural parameters of society no longer make these viable propositions for most people. 'Work' has undergone a metamorphosis, little any longer involving the totality of the person. It is by and large a nagging necessity, to which people have adapted over the years, developing new meanings which are filtered through to their children direct from their first-hand objective experience of work and participation in work cultures, which helps perpetuate 'the cycle of inequality' (Fox, 1976). No amount of teacher advice and persuasion can scratch the surface of this massive influence. They instinctively know this, and thus their exhortations seem to have an unreal quality. This suits their own ambivalence, for they, too, are subject to the same structural forces. Teacher's 'work' is not exempt from modernizing forces which have rendered it an intermixture of pedagogy, professionalism and survival. They are thus in the curious position of sponsoring an ideology they neither follow themselves nor is any longer appropriate for the structural situation of their charges. It persists because it is associated with the self-perpetuating practices and beliefs that have been mustered by the teacher in defence against the exigencies of the job which themselves have become standardized (Lortie, 1975; Rosenbaum, 1976). The cultivation of work ethic — that work is intrinsically satisfying and rewarding — is a useful strategy when they have to co-ordinate and control subordinate labour. When a disjunction is perceived between this view and reality, it might be concluded that it is the content of the programme that is wrong, rather than their view of it, or that pupils are defective in their powers of appreciation (Anthony, 1977: 289).

Thus pupil 'work' (schoolwork) is not a straightforward matter of application to a task in hand, but the product of a series of adjustments to the exigencies of the moment, and these adjustments are strongly influenced by background cultural factors. The teacher, in turn, responding to the demands of professionalism and the needs dictated by conditions of work (resources, space, numbers, etc.), makes the requirements of the pupil even more esoteric. Schoolwork is therefore unreal for many pupils, and they duly transform it into something more meaningful — play or sociation. In this form they can live with it, even enjoy it. But work of the old-fashioned order has lost its structural supports and its accomplishment therefore will not be a result of a pure state of application, but a product of negotiation, bartering, adapting and manoeuvring. A cynical view might hold that that is not inappropriate training for adult life in the modern world. A more optimistic line would be to set in hand ways and means of bridging the gap between intention and practice in more positive fashion. That would have to take less account of 'ideal' notions of work, and more of the cultural supports which sustain pupils and which grow out of the conditions of real work actually experienced by their families and fellows.

Chapter 7

Laughing at School

School is full of tensions, dilemmas and contradictions for both pupils and teachers (Berlak and Berlak, 1981). Many pupils both like and dislike school. They want to work and to learn, but frequently do not like the work they are asked to do, or are otherwise distant from it. Some will assume the persona of 'ideal pupil' in some lessons and with some teachers, and 'ace deviant' in others. Some enjoy school greatly, though the official programme may be hated. Most pupils, however, work out a tolerable *modus vivendi* — through negotiating, through establishing relationships with their teachers and fellows, through employing sanctions from time to time. Running through all these transactions and enterprises is the powerful device of humour and laughter, the coping agency par excellence. In other institutions it has been shown to be a powerful resource in interpersonal relations in several ways, integrating, differentiating, liberating, and at times constraining. As an instrument to protect and develop the self, as political weapon to defend against or strike at an enemy, as a social regulator to highlight norms, as a bargaining counter, or as a cement for social relations — humour has been shown to be used in all these ways (Martineau, 1972). In this chapter I consider the various uses pupils make of humour and laughter in their efforts to manage the demands of school. Its essentially coping nature resides in its creative and adaptational aspects, and its resolution of problems in a way that protects and/or furthers pupil aims. I begin, however, by trying to convey some of the youthful exuberance observed during a typical day at a comprehensive school. Analysis follows in subsequent sections.

The Experience of Humour

We are on the school bus. 'What's green and goes red at the flick of a switch?' asks Pillock, through a cloud of cigarette smoke. 'A frog in a liquidizer' he explains. What else could it be? 'What's that red bit on the fish and chip shop window, do you know?' he goes on. It turns out to be 'abortion of chips'. 'Do you get it? What's red and screams?' I'm told it goes well with 'abortion of chips'. (A 'peeled baby in a salt pot'). 'Ere', says Shaz, 'what's that green streak in yer hair?' 'Er', says Pillock, wiping his hand up his nose and on over his hair, 'I dunno sir'. Up front, a group are having a competition to see who can do the biggest 'Freddy' (a burp that comes from the deepest depths, named after a local man who cannot talk, only grunt). A gang of admiring girls and smaller boys gather round 'Scop' Spencer, the clear winner, who is giving encores. Some other girls flirt with the bus driver, others exchange notes and giggle about the previous evening's activities.

'Smelt it, dealt it!' declares Spud, as he is accused of a particularly unsociable act which nonetheless appears to be a fairly common pastime among these boys. 'Said the rhyme, did the crime!' retorts Biffo in triumph, and this apparently proves beyond the shadow of a doubt that Spud did the evil deed.

At school, it is assembly time. The hymn is announced, and Nationwide, the music teacher who has rather a loud voice, goes to strike the first chord. But there is no noise. Someone has wedged a hymnbook behind the hammers. Titters run round the hall in a chain reaction. During the hymn, the boys put on their funny voices, seeing who can shout the loudest, sing the deepest, the wobbliest. After the hymn they see which of the line in front they can cause to collapse by a sudden push with the toe behind the knee.

'Legging it' up the stairs to lessons, a group of girls are doing 'Hmmmmm's', 'Wo, wo, wo's', 'Neeee-owwm's' and machine guns. Their ties are knotted at the smallest end, so that the big end hangs down inside their skirts nearly to their knees. While waiting for the teacher they see how fast they can do the 'birdie dance' and all end up in fits. 'Action Man' when he arrives sends Tracey out for cheek, and all her mates laugh some more. She puts her tongue out at the teacher's back as she goes. Settling down, Louise giggles at the letter Kerry has just written to her boy friend. Beth is making up an 'O' level paper. 'Question 1. Draw a diagram of Yacky Yopper's mouth and label the Bakerloo line, Euston and Rugby. 2. Identify these people: a) 'Oh My God!' b) 'God Love us!' c) 'I mean it, ha ha ha ha ha!' . . .'

Here is groovy, gorgefying, sexifying, handsomeifying, etc. French teacher. There is a note circulating inviting opinions on his 'good' and 'bad' points. Under the former comes 'He is good-looking (slurp, slurp, grovel, grovel)'. 'His French is coming on well' and 'He has got nice legs'. Under the bad, he is accused of not being able to afford a razor, having feet that are too big for his body, and 'exposing his legs too much — longer trousers are the answer'. At the end of the lesson, the document is presented to him amid much flushing of cheeks, flashing eyes fanned by flickering eyelashes, and mass giggling that hangs in the air long after their departure. But who are these coming up the stairs? The giggling is suddenly obliterated by the thundering sound of a stampede. I have a vision of being trampled underfoot, and I retreat behind the desk.

In burst a crowd of 2b boys. They all have their ties knotted very loosely at the fat end, big D. M.s on their feet and split seams in the backs of their trousers (by design, not accident). They scramble for seats, punching each other, lobbing their bags into desired places in front of them, leaving a trail of rulers, pens, and books in their wake. When the teacher has established order, he asks 'Aynos' to read out his essay. Aynos begins, then hesitates. 'Sir, there are some swear words in it.' 'Leave those out then', says the teacher. So Aynos goes on, 'I decided not to take this advice . . .' and the whole form, teacher included, 'cracks up'. A little later, the teacher asks Alex why he had not done a certain test. 'Sir, I was at violin practice'. 'What a fiddle!' says the teacher, and they all crack up once more. This teacher is 'ace'. 'Where's your pen?' he demands of another. 'Dunno sir'. The teacher picks up the boy's bag and tips everything out. On the floor lie books, paper, cartridges, crayons, sweets, pencil shavings, and other miscellaneous items. Searching amongst the rubbish he suddenly shouts 'There it is!' and comes up triumphantly with a ruler to everyone's glee except Alex's. At the back of the class, Jug'ears and Dishcloth are engaged in clandestine activity beneath the desks.

At break, I witness the arrant sexism and racism of pupil humour. Fitzy has hurt his finger and can't bowl, so he is accused of 'being a woman!' I learn that black men have big fingers because they have wide nostrils. I hear about the black man who went to a fancy dress party with a piece of string hanging out of his behind — he was a conker. Bucket and Kipper are trying to talk like Lenny Henry 'Danny Brawhn, thaht was na . . ht very guhd!' 'Will you hu-ush!' Some Irishmen, I discover, made some lavatory seats, and forgot to put any holes in them. I note wryly that there is still no escape from wee-wees and poo-poos even when the thrust of the humour is elsewhere. Even when a boy arrived late for a lesson he claimed that 'he had been sat on t'toilet' (he was from Yorkshire).

Excretion from the other end of the body is also a popular topic:

Knock, Knock!
Who's there?
Spit on my shh.
Spit on my shh who?
All right, then! (Gobs on their shoes.)

Later, in science, I witness a keenly contested game of 'gobbing on the ceiling'. It consists of masticating bits of blotting paper into a suitable consistency and then projecting them at great force and with a crisp 'Phlupp!' so they actually stick on the ceiling. The champion, Boggis, has a fine technique, throwing substantial lumps with a flick of his tongue through fluted lips. The ceiling assumes a pebble-dashed effect, though as it dries, it will all fall down on some unsuspecting class later.

On the bus going home, the boys on the back seat soon have a game of 'corners' going. You lean over at a corner and everyone falls on to each other. It's 'brill'. If you have any sandwiches left over from lunch, you can lob them about the bus, and get a 'bun fight' going. Why waste them? In the middle, Pillock holds court with his day's collection of jokes. 'Have you read that book 'Bubbles in the Bath' by Ivor Windybottom?' he enquires of nobody in particular. Or 'Rusty Bedsprings' by I. P. Knightly?' ... Cazzy is telling Growmore a joke: 'The teachers asked Johnny what he did on fireworks' night. 'Stuffed a banger up the cat's bum miss'. 'Rectum, Johnny, rectum'. 'Wrecked 'im miss? It blew its fuckin' head off!' They fall about.

Identity Formation and Preservation

Much pupil humour is to do with their own personal development, with experimenting with identities, and with the social formation of the groups to which they belong. Following Freud, many have seen humour and laughter as a means of releasing excess nervous energy, especially related to unconscious sexual and aggressive urges. These are largely taboo areas, so have to be handled indirectly, and defused, through humour. It is in line with the earliest form of tendentious humour young children experience when they begin to be aware of the taboos surrounding urination and defecation (Wolfenstein, 1954). The bluntness of the 'wee-wee' and 'poo-poo' syndrome of the young child is matched by the bluntness of the sexual expression of the adolescent. During the stage before the onset of puberty, deviance and naughtiness become popular topics of humour. Misbehaviour, sexual activity, bodily functions, are all wildly humorous, without much subtlety. Redl (1966) has described this stage as the time when the nicest children begin to behave in the most awful ways. Fine (1977: 332) remarks that 'the humour to which children respond is not for the adult who is faint of heart'. Sex and violence, sexism and racism, handicap and human misery, any perceived kind of abnormality, are all there.

Some of this is to do with the quest for 'normality', however that may be defined by the culture of the preferred group. Humour is a powerful device for celebrating one's own identity and for enhancing one's status, and for whipping others into shape. Thus the young secondary schoolboy may be taunted if he shows signs of weakness, like wearing a big coat on cold days or crying when hit, with 'you're a woman!' Mealyea's (1989: 324) older (adult) students add the 'bodily functions' component to this plus a tinge of sexism, thus rendering it more vicious, with 'I reckon he'd sit down to piss'. Nothing more clearly demarcates the boundaries of the sex-role than the sharp edge of humour.

The same is true of 'race'. Racism is not a simple matter of consciousness. One of its pervasive and more insidious expressions is through humour. There is a great repertoire of jokes in pupil folklore in England about Irishmen, Scotsmen, Jews, West Indians and Asians. However, it might be argued that for many pupils, racist jokes are no different from 'deformity' jokes, and serve the same purpose though they also reinforce racism. They arise from the great desire of the adolescent to be 'like everybody else' and to be in line with a notion of an 'ideal self'. Poking fun at others increases one's own self-esteem, as well as sense of one's own self, and develops from a very early age (McGhee, 1979). 'Sick' humour, which always abounds at times of catastrophe, whether international (like the Ethiopian famine) or local (like a car accident involving a fellow pupil — though not of one's own group), is partly a release of their own aggressive instincts, and partly a celebration of new-forming selves. Moron jokes (Irishmen figure prominently here, but their own 'dibbos' are popular targets for ridicule) are an expression also of problems caused by the expansion of knowledge horizons and the acquisition of new and more complex skills. The telling of such jokes can be status-enhancing in that they show possession of 'advanced knowledge', rather like Mary Douglas' (1966) 'minor mystic'.

Clearly, adolescent development and sense of identity is defined as much through contrast as by similarity. There are a number of 'differentiation' and 'polarization' processes in operation. Pollard (1982) has suggested the potential significance of 'self' within school, recalling Mead's (1934) point about the realization of self in its relationship to others, and Cooley's (1902) notion of the 'aggressive self' which needs power (over objects, others' attentions and affections, etc.) to ensure its own development. Rock (1979: 122) has also noted that 'the contours of a self are established by opposition and contrast as well as by similarity and union'. Goffman has further observed that 'our sense of being a person can come from being drawn into a wider social unit; our sense of selfhood can arise through the little ways in which we resist the pull' (1968: 280). Thus it is *against* something that the self can emerge. Schools can be a battleground for personal identity. Hence the customary emphasis on uniform and appearance, codes of behaviour, and mortification techniques to purge the incoming tainted self.

This account is in line with infirmity and superiority theories of humour. Hobbes (1651), for example, held that the infirmities of others were a main source of laughter and humour, in the execution of which one's own sense of superiority was affirmed. This seems to be behind some of the humour that is directed against teachers. Here, personal status and identity are enmeshed with that of the group, and the process involves reinforcing and celebrating one's own, and denigrating and belittling those seen to be in opposition. A popular way of handling teachers in this respect is through the use of nicknames. Teachers are often held to provide role-models for children. They just as frequently provide 'role-butts' for them. Morgan *et al.* (1979), for example, found in their study of nicknames that most names for teachers did not reveal affection, as is sometimes alleged, but were rather nasty. They instance 'Bare bum', 'Cow pat', 'Feeble' and 'Lemonlegs'. In a comprehensive school of my research there were Spotty Legs, Womble, Action Man, Miss Piggy, Gibbon, Blubber, Gouge, Blinkers, and B.O.V.D. Collins, among others. Any imperfection, no matter how slight, is seized on with alacrity. A hair short on the head, a slight cast in the eye, a slightly portly frame together with a swarthy skin, yields 'Smack'ead', 'Popeye' and 'Niglet'. 'Noz' had a nose only slightly larger than normal (sometimes known as 'Concorde').

'Cowboy' walked with a stoop — his braces were thought to be too tight. James (1979) gives more examples in the same vein — 'Snotty Notty', 'Smelly Belly', 'Planet of the Apes' and 'Raggy Pants' — all fairly self-explanatory.

The assigning of deprecatory nicknames forms a status bridge which by displacing it in humour belittles it. It also transports the staff into a new world of the pupils' own creation. Having created the characters it is a short step to having them engage in all sorts of unlikely activity — often illicit sexual activity. At Lowfield, numerous jingles, poems and anecdotes decorated the pupils' 'quarters'. Interestingly, sexual prowess and parts seemed to conform to the staff hierarchy. Much of this is closed humour, that is to say it is used only within, from one's own culture or to oneself for the purposes of making the enemy appear ludicrous. This would include shouting out the teacher's nickname, firing missiles, and arranging booby-traps.

Pupils' use of nicknames for themselves points the contrast. Here they help to promote solidarity. They appear to have become part of a subterranean children's culture (Fine, 1977), which is a kind of unofficial and informal rites of passage. Thus there is a great deal of ritualized humour — standard jokes and situations — handed down over the years to apply to developmental concerns. Morgan *et al.* (1979) suggest that children's humorous nicknames are part of this, for they bestow time-honoured social roles upon their incumbents within the informal culture. In the apparently frivolous world of the playground, children learn about social competence. Nicknames — affectionate ones — bestow membership of a group and social recognition. James (1979) agrees that nicknames are extremely important in the pupil culture. Despite the pressures from the adult world to take them over, children through these means create their own alternative social system, with its own rules, out of bounds to adults. To be a member of a group, a child must have a nickname, usually 'short and snappy' and 'playfully affectionate', and their use helps to cement the bonds of the group. Those with no nicknames are social outcasts. Those with nasty nicknames, like some of the teachers, are members of opposing groups. Some peers might be given nasty names either to bring them into line or to mark them off; hence 'Bighead' and 'Thickhead' for excessive cleverness or stupidity, and 'Fatty Bum Bum' drawing attention to a personal feature which would not otherwise have been done but for deviating from group rules and norms.

The cultural boundaries of the group are promoted and defended with considerable vigour. They pervade the children's world, not only through word of mouth, but also by graffiti on school bags, books, and various places and buildings both inside and outside school.

The defence of the group through humour has been well illustrated by Mealyea (1989) in relation to a group of adult skilled tradespeople training to become secondary-school teachers in Australia. These men had a well-established occupational identity, which came under threat during their teacher training course. The College operated an internship model of training, involving immediate full-time classroom responsibility. They entered the course with expectations of preparing students for trade vocational work. However, six months into the course, reforms in teaching shifted the emphasis to a more general form of practical education. This meant discarding the idea that they were tradespersons. This threat to their identities, well established by many years in work, roused anger and anxiety, which they met by cementing their solidarity. Humour in various forms was a major device. It acted as tension release, a cure for frustration and boredom, and a neutralizer of the alienating effects of certain lectures. They developed their own 'in-jokes' in their own argot, which further strengthened their bonds, helped to define the boundaries of the group, and excluded the uninitiated. An important factor was 'mateship' — the spirit of men 'thrown together by some emergency in an unfriendly environment' (Horne, 1964, quoted in Mealyea, 1989: 320). This served to reinforce each other's 'trade worldview', revealed in particular by arrant sexism and racism which prevailed over lecturers' better intentions. Parrying perceived assaults with their collective strength, the group acting as 'one', and idealizing the external world as 'the real world' enabled them to preserve their sense of self against all the odds.

> Through laughter, and there was plenty of it within the cohort studied, mature-age trainees can resist the incursions of the College's attacks on their occupational self-identity and thus get through the day a lot easier than would otherwise be the case. 'Taking the piss' is the hidden curriculum of occupational transition for adults moving from industry to education. Humour served as a powerful means of catharsis for the group. (Mealyea, 1989: 331).

However, group solidarity does not always prevail over the individual. Pure superiority theory makes no distinction between those who oppose and those who support. Humour is the last bastion of the self against all comers. This formulation has been attacked (Zillmann and Cantor, 1976). Misfortunes, it is held, will only be enjoyed if they befall the right people, that is our opponents, and not if they happen to our friends. The argument derives from James' (1890) idea of the 'larger self' which includes affiliated objects, such as one's friends. If hurt befalls them, it is hurt to oneself. However, while this might apply to adults, it does not to pupils, who have been observed in some instances to rejoice equally in their fellows' misfortunes as in those of their enemies. Pollard (1979) reports on pupil celebration at their colleagues' 'getting done'. I observed similar unrestrained delight in a secondary school:

P. Woods: You always seem elated when somebody gets physically assaulted!

Stan: That's the joke! Somebody getting hit! (he dissolves into hysterics at the thought of it). (Woods, 1977: 38).

Similarly, Beynon (1985) found that for the boys of his research it was violence (mostly, but not always, to others) that provided the most and the best laughs. It was necessary for the teachers to be stern and to mete out physical punishment, otherwise '... you couldn't have a laugh watching other people getting hit. That's the best fun in school ...' and '... it wouldn't be a laugh unless the teachers hit you, would it?' The most enjoyable event in the boy's first term was 'Wyn Price getting done in by the Music Teacher'. However, unfairness and uncontrolled aggression put laughter out of court — social interaction broke down on these occasions. Again, laughter is a lubricant, mellowing the sharp edges of the aggression, perhaps allowing for some expression of aggression in oneself, but mainly, in this instance celebrating the gain to one's own identity that results from the damage done to some other's. If that other can laugh the injury off, he or she, similarly, will gain in self-esteem. By the same token, if they go to the other extreme, break down and cry, there will be great loss of face (Measor and Woods, 1984).

Much of this behaviour is constructing a protective layer around the self as well as the group, with humour as the cement. One will resist demeaning accusations that may lower self-worth, either by assuming characteristics to which they will not apply, or by countering in kind. A good illustration of the latter is the verbal exchanges of insults among black youths in America known as 'playing the dozens' (Labov, 1972, Foster, 1974). Attempts by teachers to socialize pupils along certain lines and to turn them into certain types of people will be resisted by such means. It could be argued, in fact, that the battle for identities in schools is fought with humour as weapons. Teachers, for their part, will resist attacks upon themselves by the solidarity humour of the staffroom, and by the skilful deployment of humour in classrooms based on a policy of 'divide and rule'. One example of this is the sarcasm employed in 'showing up' pupils (Woods, 1979). They do this for several reasons, prominent among them being enforcing conformity and defending their own role. Holding pupils' personal attributes or actions up to ridicule in the company of their peers is a particularly virulent and noxious form of humour. As we have seen, pupils' fellows, cruelly, are sometimes only too ready to see the joke, as long as it does not apply to them. It thus becomes part of their own means of coping.

From all this, it will be recognized that one does not cope alone simply through some psychological process. Invariably one does it either with others or against others. One seeks through humour and laughter to influence one's own and others' actions and perceptions. In this sense humour is power. A particularly scathing tongue is a considerable resource for a teacher in the immediacy of the classroom, though it can be counter-productive in the long run. Similarly, the ability to 'laugh off' a defeat or an injury is an enormous asset for a pupil. But humour also integrates and differentiates groups that in some way are aligned against each other. Despite the 'working consensus' that is more often than not achieved in most classrooms, the situation remains basically conflictual (Waller, 1932; Delamont, 1976; Jackson, 1968).

The Promotion and Defence of Pupil Rules

I described in Chapter 1 the pupils' role in the negotiation of classroom rules. Infraction of these rules, which will have been developed over a period of time through many interactions with teachers, is one of the major offences a teacher can commit. Among the sanctions pupils bring to bear is humour.

One area of agreement involves the use of humour as a coping strategy by pupils against constraints that are beyond the power of teachers or pupils to influence (resource levels, teacher–pupil ratio, system of education with regard to selection, etc.). Teachers who are 'all reight' in the terms of Dubberley's (1988b) students would recognize this, and allow them their humour, and perhaps join in. Others might either misinterpret it as subversive, or, perhaps unwittingly, spoil the basis on which it might rest. One example from the Lowfield study applied to school assemblies. Pupils not only make their own amusement during assemblies, they have their own sense of order determined by status amongst themselves. If this is disturbed by teachers there is great annoyance.

> 'Look, as far as I can remember, ever since the first year the 5L used to stand at the back didn't they Frankie? Back at the left hand side, so you work your way up the school and you get there and you got to move and then we get moved (all talk heatedly at once). Why should we suddenly get moved? All the other fifth years have been back there.'
>
> *Me*: I don't follow.
>
> 'Well, you ought to be able to find your own position, walk straight up at the back but you have to be lined up, lined in half way down, form by form . . .'

Similarly if their 'laughs' are seriously curtailed by over-zealous members of staff, they might bear them particular resentment since they are forcing them back into boredom. It is a kind of second order annoyance. They have accepted the boredom and have invented certain ways of coping with it.

An illustration of the consequences of infraction of pupil rules came during a discussion about pupil antics I'd observed during certain lessons (such as walking over desks, swinging from beams, playing tape recorders, soft and loud, and playing 'find it' with the teacher, connecting bunsen burners to water taps and directing fine jets to the ceiling, leaving the room and returning by various routes, etc. Invariably, they did these things just 'for a laugh', but occasionally to annoy a teacher.

> '. . . say if he's taken a pack of cards off someone, say, and we're just trying to get our own back to try and annoy him — we'd do everything we could think of to annoy him'.

These tactics are similar to Goffman's (1968) 'secondary adjustments' — the ways the individual stands apart from the role and the self, taken for granted by the institutions, and by which one 'makes out', 'gets by', 'plays the system' and so on. The maintenance of social order in the school depends on staff not seeing, ignoring or accepting this. They are, in fact, 'hidden norms'. Behind the apparently sterile officially ordered facade, there is operating another system developed by the pupils through time which transgresses the general rules of the institution without appearing to do so. It is 'concealed deviance' from an official point of view. But, from a pupil's point of view, time, tradition, lack of detection and spiritual and physical necessity have legitimated such activity.

There was every indication that at Lowfield, at least, pupil norms and rules were taken into account. I certainly found two groups in the school, one officially oriented, the other unofficially. The latter was not distinctively anti-school. The pupils in this group were more 'colonisers' (Goffman, 1968). Now these were in some ways encouraged in the formation of a 'culture' which in ethos is pro-school by the staff. An interesting case in illustration of this is 'the smoking game'. There was a school rule against smoking, supposedly strict, but not explicitly against the possession of cigarettes. Many in the upper school were compulsive smokers. They had to have their cigarettes, so they had to smoke secretly. A club formed behind the swimming pool, but that was highly dangerous because of the presence of oil, so the area was put out of bounds. This was strictly enforced. The club reconvened behind the potting shed, another formed on the far side of the playing fields, and these were disregarded. Clearly, it was more important to the staff that pupils should not blow themselves up than that they should not smoke. But they also realised that the smoking game was, in fact, one they could not win, and that attempts at strict enforcement would only lead to unproductive trouble. 'There goes Michael for a smoke' said one teacher to me during a lesson, 'What can you do?' — said with a humane grin rather than a tone of despair. I witnessed another teacher having an elaborate game with the boys in one class focused on the detection of cigarettes. 'Come on Dogsbody where are they? I know you've got some', and searching a boy's clothing amidst jocular protests; finding some and confiscating them in mock triumph, only to return them with an indulgent grin at the end of the lesson. Pupils played the smoking game in my presence teasing each other about the possession of cigarettes, threatening to light up in my presence and so forth.

> Give us a fag, scruff
> I don't smoke
> What are these then? (fumbling in his pockets).
> Do you want a light?

I took this to mean that I was entering into the same kind of tacit conspiracy with them as some teachers were, in recognition of their own norms and rules. Rule infraction is good substance for a laugh especially if those associated with official rule-making implicitly join in. In this sense pupils and teachers occasionally transcend the institution and find common cause in a common humanity. In this respect teachers as law enforcers are acting in a similar way to Bittner's (1967) skid-row police. They do not employ a strict interpretation of the rules, rather basing their discretion on 'a richly particularized knowledge of people and places'. They recognize that the law can be unjust. They often 'play by ear', using their own rules. We might regard this kind of teacher–pupil interaction as 'reciprocal indulgence' following Braroe's (1973) concept of reciprocal exploitation. Children are refused the privilege of playing adult roles (teachers are allowed to smoke, wear jewellery, they have freedom of movement, speech, etc.) therefore children define the self along defensible lines but in a way to permit validation of this self by teachers.

Much depends, therefore, on how teachers respond. In this respect, pupils at Lowfield seemed to see teachers in four categories:

1 Those that keep you working.
2 Those you can laugh and joke with.
3 Those you can work and have a laugh with.
4 Those that just don't bother.

The difference among them is brought out in the following conversation.

Jane: Sometimes you can hear him shouting in the other room. He won't laugh you see, they try to get him to laugh, they do these stupid things and they just want . . . If he'd laugh they'd be alright, he won't, you see.

Anne: Oh yeah, they'd do anything to try to make him laugh. He puts them in the report book and everything. They don't care.

Deirdre: Every lesson somebody is going down for it.

Jane: Yeah.

Deirdre: He put one girl in twice in one day. They do it on purpose. If he was to be more friendly with them like Mr Lennox is, 'cos he'll have a laugh with you.

Jane: You see, he won't smile and have a laugh with you like Mr Lennox will.

Deirdre: 'Cos we can have a joke with him, can't we?

Jane: Yeah, and we do work as well, but in there they play about and don't do any work.

Here the 'authoritarian' teacher intent solely on 'working' brings a counter-productive response. A more 'successful' (in his own terms) authoritarian teacher usually succeeds in displacing it towards the category 2 type teacher. As noted in Chapter 1, teachers whom you can both work and laugh with are respected. They know their job, can keep control, can teach but above all retain their human qualities in the classroom. Their perception of teacher role does not require of them any different behaviour pattern than that of human-being role. The authoritarian teacher frequently adopts a different role from choice.

> *Kathleen*: What about when we 'ad Mr Bullet? He made us stand up straight when we walked in the classroom.
> *Deirdre*: Like being in the army that was.
> *Kathleen*: He made us march out, if anyone spoke, he made us write about three essays out.
> *Sally*: There was a different side to him though 'cos me and Tracy used to go in his room at break times — he was ever so nice — didn't have to march in then, just sit on desks and chat to him, he was ever so nice.

This reminds us, as Burns (1953) noted, of the discreteness of status positions and the schizophrenic nature of our society, also reflected in the marked change in some teachers between classroom and staffroom or between on-duty and off-duty (*see also* Lacey, 1977).

Dubberley (1988) found that his fifth-year working-class pupils at 'Coalton School' classified teachers in a similar way. He stressed the importance of the culture of the local mining community. Teachers were perceived in its terms and by its values as 'hard', 'all reight', or a 'reight maunge', and so on. Two potent tests for any stranger were whether you could 'take a joke' (proving that 'you're not above yourself, that you're one of the crowd, one of us' — p. 111), and that you could 'stand up for yoursen'. The hardness of life down the pit governed relationships in the community, and any teachers not realizing that invited attack. If unable to handle that attack, they were perceived as 'soft' and treated unmercifully. It is not so much the 'hard' teachers in this community who are reviled, therefore. For them, there may be a grudging respect though they are a 'reight maunge'. But those who 'think they're hard', and are 'soft' or 'wimps' are beyond the pale and invite all that they receive.

There are teachers, therefore, you can laugh with, and those you laugh against. In some circumstances these latter might be hard, unbending teachers, in others, soft and pliable.

Negotiating through Humour

As noted earlier (Chapter 1), humour is a powerful resource in teaching. Among its various forms in this respect, Stebbins (1980) has identified what he terms 'social comic relief'. This facilitates the task of teaching and learning and obviates strain. School tasks are frequently onerous, involving long periods of concentration and intellectual exercise, which, if unrelieved, might promote fatigue or boredom. The teacher, or a pupil, might therefore inject a measure of humour at key points where attention is at risk, to provide relief and to recharge concentrative powers. Thus, 'social comic relief reduces fatigue which, if allowed to increase, threatens role performance and motivation' (*ibid.*: 86).

Humour therefore aids performance of task, preserves the teaching and learning situation, and the roles of teachers and learners. The mechanics of social comic relief may well be similar to that of the 'ripple effect' following a disciplinary measure from a teacher (Kounin, 1970). Here, though the teacher may censure one child, its effects were noted to spread, or 'ripple' among other pupils in the room. Humour, though a strongly contrasting emotion to the apprehension caused by a stern rebuke, nonetheless may spread in a similar way to affect a whole group. Denscombe (1980), in fact, describes how in an open classroom of the comprehensive school of his research, a private joke spread very quickly if laughter was heard. This tendency for humour to permeate whole groups in an instant makes it a powerful aid for teachers faced with large classes — a structural constraint.

In some instances, in fact, it can help form a cultural bond between teacher and pupils. Over time, a teacher and a class might build up an understanding coded partly in humour. After a certain episode, a simple signal may spark off its recall, with full humorous effect. This will be quite lost on the casual observer who has not been privy to the initial event, but it has become part of the culture of that particular class. Thus, Walker and Adelman (1976) give the example of a class they were observing where the pupils laughingly said 'Strawberries, Strawberries!' after the teacher had criticized one pupil's work in a certain way. The reference, apparently, was to a previous remark by the teacher that a certain boy's work was like strawberries — good as far as it goes, but it doesn't last nearly long enough (cf. the 'Horace' joke in Chapter 1).

In these examples, teachers and pupils are emphasizing through humour not only their joint definition of the situation but also their joint ability to distance themselves from it, and from the role. In the latter instance, the technique has clearly become a matter of routine. In a different study, Walker and Goodson (1977) give a teacher's view of the strategic use of humour. They argue that jokes give teachers a point of access with pupils in that they cut through the impersonal and inhibiting strictures of institutional forms and roles. This is what Mary Douglas was referring to when she described the humorist as a 'minor mystic . . . one of those people who pass beyond the bounds of reason and society and give glimpses of a truth which escapes through the mesh of structured concepts' (1966: 373). Similarly, Koestler (1964), in discussing humour as a creative art, argued that to create a joke or cartoon, an object or event had to be seen outside its normal context. 'The pattern underlying (comedy) is the perceiving of a situation or idea in two self-consistent but habitually incompatible frames of reference' (*ibid.*). The same point lies behind Goffman's notion of 'role-distance' (1961). He gives the example of a surgeon who made joking asides while performing an operation to ease the more difficult aspects for all concerned. They were not made to escape from the role, but to aid the realization of its obligations.

In this way, humour is a joint enterprise in mutual interest. Sharing a joke means making an alliance, against reality or the institution, or differences in authority or in status. A similar phenomenon has been noted in other institutions such as department stores (Bradney, 1957) and hospitals (Coser, 1958; Emerson, 1969). However, it must be said that such a state of equality between teacher and pupil rarely obtains in school. Even with Walker and Goodson's teacher, he negotiates only from strength. His joking is an expression of a desire for dominance. 'I do think you need a strong sense of being in control, and of things going well for you before you would be willing to give jokes a central place in your teaching' (Walker and Goodson, 1977: 206). He draws the contrast with another teacher, who had difficulty with pupils, not because he joked, but because '. . . he was weak and he couldn't make things stick, and he was using jokes as a way out of that' (*ibid.*: 207). When well in control, a teacher can use self-disparaging jokes.

These are greatly appreciated by pupils, for they put the teacher on the same footing as them. Where, however, the teacher's control is suspect, humour at the expense of the teacher can undermine that control altogether (Willis, 1977).

It is not surprising, therefore, to find that humour is of especial worth in so-called 'progressive' modes of teaching, or in 'open' classrooms. Ostensibly these might suggest more power-sharing between teachers and pupils in the pupil-directed learning that characterizes them. But teachers, in fact, retain control. But now the method depends on humour and friendship, rather than on authoritarian command. As Denscombe (1980: 61) noted, in his study of open classrooms,

> Friendliness, when successfully operated as a classroom strategy by teachers, allowed a subtle mode of control which shrouded the institutional disparities of power between staff and pupils and was particularly useful in the context of the open classroom where the teachers sought to minimize the appearance of authoritarian teaching styles.

Denscombe describes how, in the open-plan classroom he observed, pupils used humour to provide a 'legitimate respite from the rigours of work ... Creating a joke ... provided pupils with a means for negotiating their involvement in work' (p. 64). They had opportunities for 'chatting up' teachers in individual encounters, and a joke rapidly snowballed among a wider group. Denscombe's work again reminds us of the importance of the setting in the use of humour and how pupils, without undermining the authority of the teachers, can manipulate the situation in their favour (*see also* Mintz, 1977; Chapman, 1976).

This is one way in which pupils contribute towards what some have conceived of as a 'working consensus', whereby pupils and teachers adapt to the mutual threat they represent to each other (Hargreaves D., 1972; Pollard, 1979). They do this in various ways, which are usually identified along a conformity–nonconformity dimension. Most studies locate the majority of pupils in the middle, where negotiation has most equal input from each side. Thus Pollard, in the primary school of his research, noted extensive use of a pupil strategy of mild deception of teachers through humour. He observed a large group — over half the children — of 'jokers'. His labelling of them is significant, joking forming the most visible aspect of their interaction with teachers. They 'tended to confine their more divergent activities to "having a bit of fun" or "playing about", often with the participation of their teachers and seemingly mainly for intrinsic as opposed to subversive enjoyment' (1979: 88). It was done with the approval of the teachers and at no cost to their learning which they valued highly:

> *Child*: I like teachers who make things interesting so you can learn, you can have a laugh a bit but you still learn — that's the best (*ibid.*: 89).

At other times, they engaged in routine deviance (which falls within the working consensus and invites routine censure), for this provides 'laughs and a release from boredom and routine'. This kind of finding, where pupils testify to the benefits of 'having a laugh' as one of the prime requisites of teaching and learning, has been replicated in many studies, in several kinds of schools, and with pupils of all ages (Gannaway, 1976; Woods, 1979). Pupils also take great delight in being together, especially in the company of friends. But friendship for pupils, and much of the humour and laughter that accompanies it, has a utilitarian purpose, as well as, in some instances, emotional bonds (Davies, 1982; Measor and Woods, 1984). It protects, enhances, shores up the self, and is the basic requirement for beginning to cope.

The forms of humour discussed so far have been mainly integrational. In their various ways, they smooth the work of the school. Even pupils' 'sussing-out' (Chapter 1), though possibly uncomfortable for teachers, if represented as a search for norms and rules, can be seen in that light. Other kinds of humour, however, are more distinctly oppositional. Even so, conflict, which the situation might have otherwise warranted, is, rather paradoxically perhaps, dissipated as well as expressed by humour. It is to these forms of humour that I now turn. The argument is that because humour allows the expression of conflict in socially acceptable ways, it is acting also in these instances as a coping agency. It is meeting constraints, problems, contradictions and so forth in a personally creative way that allows for the preservation of selves and for a modicum of social order to be maintained.

Mucking About

> *PW*: What do you think about when you come through those gates in the morning?

Tracy: Well I think . . . 'ere we go again, another day for mucking about.

Gill: It's alright when you're at school really, like when you can just talk to people, have a laugh.

Tracy: It's the only place we have fun isn't it?

Sandy: It's different when we're outside, isn't it? When you're mixing with other people that are older than what you are, can't act stupid then.

PW: You act with a ladylike deportment do you?

Tracy: Eh?

Gill: Well, we have a laugh when we go out.

Sandy: I mean we don't muck about like we do at school.

Gill: No, we don't stand there throwing bottles and plimsolls about.

Sandy: We have a good laugh when we go out anyway. When we are out of school uniform, it's a lot different.

Gill: I don't know, when you go out you sort of act your age and I don't know.

Sandy: We aren't silly at home, not very often anyway. You act silly at school for a laugh.

Gill: Yeah, not all the time, but we muck about.

'Mucking about' is a kind of seemingly aimless behaviour, often labelled by teachers as 'silly' or 'childish'. Pupils do not deny this, as is clear from the above quotes. What they are doing is transforming the reality of school from something they find tedious, irrelevant and perhaps oppressive, to something more light-hearted and tolerable that they initiate and control. If it seems silly and childish, then that perhaps conveys some symbolic comment on the official programme.

Goffman (1968) has observed that joking is a way in which the individual makes a plea for disqualifying some of the expressive features of the situation as sources of definition of one's self; and to participate with a group of one's similars in this kind of activity can lend strength to the show of role distance and to one's willingness to express it. This, incidentally, illustrates the caution we must exercise in interpreting positive answers to asking children if they like school. Many of them might say yes, but only having transformed the reality of it.

In their conversations with me at Lowfield, one particular form (fifth form non-examination) talked to me about their life at school. Analyzing these recorded discussions there was a remarkable contrast between on the one hand a set of factors which could be subsumed under 'boredom' and on the other those relating to fun and laughter. The former made for dour, grim recounting while we talked within the official definition of the school. Many regretted not having been allowed to take examinations. Some had lost out by choices in the third year. The 'work' they were doing and had been doing since the beginning of the fourth year was too 'boring', too 'simple'; they were simply repeating work; or did 'useless', 'meaningless' work or 'nothing'; lessons were not 'helping for the future'; they were 'ignored', 'forgotten about', 'practised upon', 'made use of'; some teachers agreed with them, others 'didn't care', 'picked on them', 'took it out of them'.

The following examples are given to demonstrate how ingrained this boredom is within these pupils.

Example 1:

Me: Do you get anything out of school subjects?

George: No, not very helpful I don't find them, just boring.

Len: Some of them interest yer.

Harry: Everybody likes an easy time, don't they? Like our English group now, it's mad aint it? He tells you the answers before you ever do anything. Says 'Oh well, I'll write it up on the blackboard first and then I'll copy it out! Huh! rubbish!

Len: It's like Mr Brown, you don't learn nothing on that, you just copy off the board.

Harry: Blackboards and blackboards of writing, it's just meaningless. You write it down. Can you tell me what we done last week?

George: Done nothing.

Len: I wasn't here last week.

Me: What use do you make of this writing, do you ever read it again, are you ever tested on it?

Len: No.

Harry: We haven't 'ad an exam in two years, it's pointless.

Example 2:

Kim: I can do it, I just don't like it, it's too boring. The maps we are doing now are so simple really.

Christine: I've not learnt anything these past two years. The English we're doing is exactly the same as my sister's doing in the first year, and the maths work, she's doing 'arder work than what I'm doing.

Kim: What I'm doing is fractions, but 'alf of this work is only second form stuff, I just sit around doing nothing either because it's too easy or because I'm not bothered about it.

Christine: See, we're not learning anything, we've done it all before. I wish they'd give us some work, some proper work to do. It's so boring. We have two lessons with Mrs Nelson, that's interesting because she talks to us about life and things like that. Nobody plays about there because it's interesting. In chemistry the boys sit around and throw things about.

Example 3:

Sally: I'm repeating work, it's making me sick because I can remember doing it before and it was quite exciting then but now we're painting and washing up and everything else.

Susan: . . . ever so easy . . . (all talking at once in agreement).

Me: Isn't there anything you enjoy doing?

Joanne: Art, and that's about all — for a laugh.

Example 4:

John: There's nothing to do here. There's a long dinner hour, not that we mind that but us being fifth year's, we can't have a room to ourself where we can talk. If you go in the cloakroom you might be suspected of stealing if something goes wrong, but if we had us own room we could go in there and talk, but we're all outside bored stiff, there's no activity to do, it really does depress you. We ain't got nothing to do, you're just waiting for the next lesson and when it comes, you're bored stiff.

Example 5:

Me: Looking back on school, what do you think you're going to remember about it most?

Paul: Boredom, of all the lessons and that. Same thing day after day. I like primary school better, there were more things to do and I seemed to get on better there.

Example 6:

Alan: When they had speech day everyone started ripping off these bits of foam under their chairs and started throwing them about. Suddenly I noticed a line of teachers at the door taking names, everyone in the hall, you know, spaced out, sort of gestapo, spaced out, standing up for the interrogation... 'did you throw?'... 'were you in?'... some people got the cane, but it was so *boring* it weren't true, speech days. If you're sat there for a whole afternoon with nothing to do you do get bored, don't you?

Example 7:

Simon: It's not a bad school really, you know. I don't mind it you know, but... coming every day doing the same old thing one day after the other, same lessons, you know, gets a bit sickening. You can't wait until the end of the week or the end of the day, you know, when you get here.

Me: Do you find the work difficult?

Simon: No, it's not difficult, it's boring. You just sit there with a whole lot of work to do.

Me: What do you do, say in English?

Simon: Wednesdays, teacher reads to you which you nearly fall off to sleep, I do anyway. You get so bored with it you know.

Me: What else do you do?

Simon: It's hard to think. I remember once I got so bored I did fall off to sleep in English. Yeah, so bored with it.

Example 8:

From field notes 5 March 1975

Art — Periods 1 and 2, 4th form

Carol, Janice and Susan seem lost for anything to do. 'Have you any jobs sir?' The three of them shimmy idly over.

Teacher: How am I going to find jobs for you three for all of next term? (Teacher sets them arranging magazines in a file, the three exchange looks of resignation.) Teacher tells me they're not interested in art. They came to him for negative reasons. He sees some of them three times a week, twice for half days. There are four more terms to go yet.

A considerable amount of 'mucking about' was mentioned in association with expressions of boredom, itself often connected with routine, ritual, and regulations. Thus speech days, assemblies and other forms of ritual which the vast majority of pupils I spoke to described as 'boring', 'useless', 'meaningless', 'a waste of time', taxed their ingenuity in remaining sane. I witnessed many assemblies. On the surface they seemed rigid, militaristic, well-drilled affairs. Pupils filed in by form, were inspected for uniform as they passed through the door, and lined up in serried ranks. Teachers ordered them, squaring off rough corners, tidying up lines, filling up spaces. They stood amongst them at strategic points while those not on 'duty' mounted the platform. There followed, usually, a talk, a hymn, prayers then announcements. The beginning and end were monopolized by the band. For most of the pupils I spoke to in the senior school, it was twenty minutes of standing boredom. Here are some typical reactions:

> Assemblies are a waste of time. For religious people they're OK, it's a good morning's start, but there aren't many religious people in the school. You're all in there together, it's a great temptation to kick somebody's legs and make them fall down just for a laugh, just temptation to trouble.

> No, we don't listen in assembly, we just muck about. Sing to drown everyone else and that.

> Useless, rubbish.

> The boys keep tickling yer . . . All mucking about . . . boys pulling your hair and that.

> Waste of time I reckon, 'cos while you're standing there you might as well have an extra ten minutes on your lessons. All you do is sing a song and say a prayer, and that's it, you're out again. You could do that any time, couldn't you, at home?

Among the pupil assembly activities that I observed were the mutilating of hymn books, whispering messages along the row, general scuffling, teasing the nearest teacher, communicating by coughs, making faces at the teachers on the stage. The hymns seemed to be quite an exciting affair. Among the competitions I witnessed were trying to be the last one to finish a verse, getting a word in in the middle of a pause (the most amusing one I heard was a cacophony of 'harks' in the pauses between the lines in 'Hark the herald angels sing'), trying to drown the senior mistress, inventing new words for the hymn as you go along, mutilating your hymn books some more.

'One can "muck about" in classrooms by twanging rulers, shining mirrors, misappropriating school furniture and equipment, scuffling with neighbours, talking out of turn, "burping in the classroom", passing wind, throwing rubbers around, flicking "gob" around on spoons, having book fights, making motor bike noises...' (Tattum, 1982: 90). Furlong's (1977) girls' best way of having a 'laugh' was to be cheeky to teachers. 'I came in the classroom (late) and shouted "We're here again, we're here again" and she says, "Right loud mouth"...and we tell her to mind her own business' (p. 165). Willis' lads thought 'fuckin' laffing the most important thing in fuckin' everything' (1977: 29). They also delighted in teasing teachers, perhaps by 'half goading the teacher into playing his formal role more effectively: "Please sir, please sir, Joey's talking/pinching some compasses/picking his nose/killing Percival/having a wank/let your car tyres down" ' (p. 30). The pupils of Lowfield specialized in wrecking the official programme by nagging at its edges sufficiently both to score a point and escape detection (Woods, 1979). A slightly ridiculous answer, a half-mumble behind the hand, a pretence of working while surreptitiously doing something else, inventing new words and rhythms to hymns and songs, embarrassing each other by making their proper fulfilment of the role difficult — they applied to these pursuits powers of invention teachers would love to see devoted to school work.

Subversive Laughter

'Mucking about' is mainly an antidote to boredom and/or youthful high spirits impacting against deadening aspects of the school system. This, at times, shades into another form of laughter of a more political nature, aimed at countering or neutralizing the power of the teacher. This is well illustrated by McLaren (1986: 163) in his analysis of the situation in his Canadian Catholic school.

Against the 'culture of pain' of being a student, he detected a 'laughter of resistance'. The pain, not dissimilar to experiences at Lowfield, is evident in 'the bland, dreary impotency of instructional rituals and routines, the grinding, drudging familiarity, the deadening, mechanical applications of instructional rites, the unremitting banality of the subject matter, the unemotional, generalized stream of boring events, the bleak inevitability of repetition and invariance, the tedious succession of unrelated episodes, and the wearisome wait for instruction to end.'

The 'laughter of resistance' is a concerted effort, involving whole forms. At appropriate moments or at a given signal, groups of pupils will 'howl with laughter' in a way that mocks, denounces and neutralizes. This is not just cruelty or silliness, but 'a form of redefining the power structure of the class', a way for the students 'to reclaim their sense of collective identity' (p. 161). It can undermine and indeed destroy unless the teacher 'rides' with it. If the teacher goes against it, this is denying pupils their coping strategy, and invites more serious reaction, for the teacher is forcing them back into boredom or whatever problem they are countering. The problem for teachers here is not to appear 'soft', which would be just as bad, or worse. The ideal reaction is to be culturally attuned to one's students.

Subversive laughter at times takes the form of symbolic rebellion. Some people make a career of open resistance, in their terms 'playing teachers up'. Success often depends on response.

George: Jones 'e isn't worth playing up because he don't do nothing.

Alan: He don't like me, he picks on me. The other day in activities we were all sitting around the table playing dominoes and he came over and clouted me. The others were doing the same.

George: Jones just goes a bit red, it's not worth the effort of playing 'im up unless you're going to get a response. Mr Cook goes livid.

PW: Do you plan what to do in advance?

Pete: We don't often plan. We sometimes go in late, that always gets their goat. Mr Diamond gets the chin, he knows all these big words, he called George 'a churl'. We just laugh at him.

Symbolic rebellion can also take the form of destruction of school property. Thus two glasshouses which it had taken one class of non-examination boys a full term to repair and make functional were destroyed by the same boys in the space of five minutes only a few weeks after completion of the task.

Another example that occurred during my stay at Lowfield was the blazer-ripping incident. Of all the symbols of school authority and their own oppression none is more detested by the pupils generally speaking than school uniform. It is precisely because it is so closely associated with school norms and teacher authority that enforcement and conformity is pursued with vigour. After years of inspections and remonstrations about their clothing a tradition had developed among boys who were leaving that others would tear his blazer literally to shreds during the last week of term. My stay at the school encompassed the departure of one group of boys marked by blazer rippings which, in spite of the fact that they were done so near the end of the pupils' concerned school career, precipitated a teacher–pupil crisis. One boy's blazer was ripped to shreds early in the week of departure. He was seen on his way home by a member of staff and referred to the headmaster. A campaign was then launched for the detection of those responsible, which involved the whole form being detained for several periods of their free time, much vigorous interrogation and ultimately the caning of the offenders. It was a heated topic among both staff and pupils. The most quoted factor lying behind teachers' anger that I heard was connected with their *in loco parentis* role. They felt responsible for both person and property of the pupil. Thus one teacher thought the mother of the boy concerned deserved compensation for the destruction of the article. But the mother had sent a letter saying she had no objection and telling the teachers to forget the incident. However, by this time there was more at stake and the professional zeal with which the investigation was conducted is evidence to the extent to which teachers were sensitive to the symbolic assault on their authority. To the pupils, the teachers' case seemed unreasonable, unfair and altogether out of proportion to the event.

What's one blazer, it wasn't all that good anyway.

They'd been writing all over blazers, writing their names on them, it's a traditional activity at the end of yer school days.

They all get ripped on the last day anyway. You can't do much about it. Last day they all come round and cut chunks out of your hair, tie up your hair, half cut up your blazer and then messing about all the way home, sticking scarves out of the window and things like that, but they can't do much about that because you've left.

On our bus when the last lot left there was maths books all sorts of books going out of the window and that gets their hair up because all the people round about complain, bits of paper there were everywhere.

Once leavers are clear of the school they can do what they like, but this blazer ripping incident occurring at the beginning of the week in which pupils left impinged too much on school time and became, therefore, in the teachers' view not only a violation of school rules and norms and their authority but also an overstepping of the bounds of discretion most of them usually employed. Again, a situation redolent with laughter turned into heavy conflict, characterized by anger.

Some subversive laughter is a product of culture clash, especially in situations where working-class pupils come up against a middle-class school ethos. At Lowfield, on one occasion, one girl unaware of the senior mistress' presence shouted for the television set to be turned up because 'I can't 'ear the bloody thing'. This immediate confrontation of cultures from which the senior mistress felt obliged to retreat produced much laughter, as did another occasion when a girl in anger told the senior mistress 'to get stuffed'. Both these incidents show the pupils' culture impacting against the teachers' culture to the detriment of the latter. It also illustrates the important role of vulgar language, which here helps the pupils to sustain their own definition of the situation and blocks a construction of the 'official' one. Such occasions provide superb and dynamic material for laughs in the countless retelling of the incidents which will take place. The relating of them to me was yet another one of these occasions for laughter.

Authoritarian teachers, jealous of their status and sensitive to assaults on it, often try to detect or anticipate subversive laughter. However, it is not easily detectable and they may pick on a more innocent form of humour by mistake.

Wendy: Remember when we were discussing . . . (*All*: oh yeah! Much laughter).

Sharon: That was in the third year, he went off his rocker at us didn't he?

Wendy: What was it, I know we were talking about Christmas pudding and my mum said me Nan's knickers caught fire (great laughter).

Sharon: I remember, Wendy . . . it weren't very . . .

Wendy: We were both sat on the front desk chatting away . . .

Sharon: He went barmy, I told him he shouldn't be really listening (general laughter).

Here, a teacher has invaded a private area and earned a rebuke accompanied by laughter which could have done nothing for his self-esteem.

Many pupils' assessment of school is predicated on the amount of laughter they can derive from it. Remarks abound like 'we get a good laugh, generally you know in the long run', 'we'll miss the teachers because we have a lovely laugh with them, we won't get them so much', 'school isn't so bad, we can have a good old laugh here'. The importance of laughter to the pupils at Lowfield might also be inferred from the eagerness and delight which they took in recounting certain incidents to me. In this respect the discussions I had with pupils were laughs in themselves. This enthusiasm is difficult to recapture but the following transcript gets near to it. It well illustrates the manipulative power these girls had over teachers.

I was talking with a group of six girls, Kate, Tracy, and four others.

Kate: I remember Mr Gantry calling Tracy 'my pet goat'.

Tracy: Always in trouble, me and Kate.

Kate: Lazy, horrible lot, pests he used to call us. Lazy.

Tracy: You ain't 'eard 'is new saying have you? 'e says to Joanne Mackie, don't sit there looking pretty will you, so Joanne says, one thing I look a sight better than you (loud shrieks of laughter and suckings in of breath from girls).

Kate: We used to play 'im up in the third year just so's he'd give us a lecture and we wouldn't have to do no work.

Tracy: 'orrible, miserable lot, he used to say. Lazy.

Kate: Yeah, we used to laugh at 'im.

Tracy: What about when 'e made us go outside and made us march back in properly.

Kate: What about when me and you fell out and I threw your book across the classroom and 'e sent me down to Miss Judge.

Dianne: What about when Mr Bridge stood just outside the door.

Tracy: Dianne fell off a chair first and as she went to get up, she got 'old of me skirt, she was 'aving a muck about, and there was I in me petticoat, me skirt came down round my ankles and Mr Bridge came in (great screams of laughter from girls). He'd been standing outside the door.

Kate: 'e told her she'd get suspended.

Tracy: He 'ad me mum up the school, telling her what a horrible child I was.

Kate: Nobody will marry you, said Miss Judge.

Tracy: Oh yeah, Miss Judge sits there 'n nobody will want to marry you Jones', she said. I said 'well you ain't married anyway' (shrieks of laughter from girls).

Dubberley (1988b) shows how the distance between the middle-class culture of the school and the working-class culture of the mining community of 'Coalton' is reflected, emphasized and celebrated in humour. The 'lasses', perhaps because they had developed a particular creativity from their 'continued exploitation as women' were especially skilful in capitalizing on the weakness of 'soft' teachers. Mrs Galton, for example, was 'completely outmanoeuvred and outwitted', while two 'soft' men teachers were 'reduced to being like silly lads on the receiving end of the lasses' sexual power' (p. 114). They would press against them to embarrass them, and on one occasion had imprinted hand prints of talcum powder after a 'Science for Today' lesson 'on his cheeks and at t'front' of one of them.

The lads were hardly less severe on 'wimps', judged by the standards of masculinity in the pit community. Good teachers could 'have a laugh' but also 'take a laugh' and 'look after yoursen'. There was much 'banter and badinage', 'affection and regard', and 'tough love and wry humour' between these teachers and their pupils, both lads and lasses. They were culturally attuned. They were thus better able to assist the pupils in their resistance strategies against aspects of their education that were beyond their control. For example, one bottom, and difficult, group were the 'Rural Studies Group' — but known as the 'Duggie Diggers' (Duggie = 'thickee') — handled by their teacher with the 'rough good humour of a building-site ganger'.

Most teachers, however, interpreted events from firmly within their own middle-class culture, 'talking down to kids', disparaging their 'inferior' 'wit and intelligence', putting them down by ridiculing their cultural traits and holding up their own as superior, denigrating the lasses as 'tarts, slags and sluts'. Dubberley emphasizes 'the imperialistic nature of the culture of the schools' and the degree of its antagonism to working-class culture (p. 121). The lads and lasses hold their own against this with 'wit, vitality and creativity', showing that 'the potential of the human mind to operate remains the same irrespective of time and place' (p. 121). The solution, he feels, is partly a curriculum aligned to the culture of the local community, when the more educationally functional aspects of humour would predominate.

Corrigan (1979) argued that a similar kind of conflict in the school of his research was no less than guerilla warfare. School was completely irrelevant to the concerns of these pupils, who used their powerful resources of humour and laughter to cope, just as they would with the task of life in general. Their brand of 'mucking about', therefore, was a form of class cultural resistance.

> '. . . carrying on in class' represents the ability of the boys to continue their normal way of life, despite the occupying army of the teachers and the power of the school, *as well as* their ability to attack the teachers on the boys' own terms (p. 58).

Willis (1977), as discussed in Chapter 2, drew the comparison between the school culture developed by 'the lads' of his research in resistance to the impositional forces of the school and the culture of the shop floor in the factories where they expected to go to work when they left school, as their fathers did before them. For the 'lads', laughter was the ultimate panacea. It integrated them as a group, resolved so many problems, and indeed was so important that it was a condition of membership.

> *Joey*: I think fuckin' laffing is the most important thing in fuckin' everything. Nothing ever stops me laffing . . . I don't know why I want to laff, I dunno why it's so fuckin' important. It just is (. . .) I think it's just a good gift, that's all, because you can get out of any situation. If you can laff, if you can make yourself laff, I mean really convincingly, it can get you out of millions of things (. . .)You'd go fuckin' beserk if you didn't have a laff occasionally.' (Willis, 1977: 29).

Resistance to school gives the lads' humour its distinctive quality — playing with authority, devizing practical jokes that mock teachers or conformists, 'ribbing' teachers, but ambiguously or anonymously, always just outside legitimate jurisdiction, indulging in a kind of 'marauding misbehaviour, throughout the school and especially on trips, and among themselves, 'pisstaking' and 'roughing each other up' (p. 32). This, Willis argues, as noted in Chapter 2, is essentially the same as the intimidatory humour of the shop-floor, which reveals a highly developed skill in badinage and perception; and perpetrates merciless practical jokes, which again seem aligned against authority and the institution. School and place of work occupy the same structural location and present the same kind of pressures and problems on this particular kind of pupil. He copes with these problems through humour, but in a form that is only meaningful within that structural situation.

Willis' lads provide a good example of coping behaviour. The lads' humour, though apparently the scourge of the school, is contained, and not subversive though it might seem so, and indeed that may be how it is interpreted by the school authorities. Their behaviour is part of their normal adaptation to existing structures, not a challenge to them. Their distinctive humour and ebullient laughter is a time-honoured class cultural means of dealing with oppositional forces. It neutralizes them, reduces the worth of their values, discredits their way of life, and commensurately inflates one's own. Through laughter, they not only parry the opposition, but come to feel superior to them. It is the only way to live, and they feel sorry for the poor old 'ear 'oles' who grind away at their schoolwork, while the lads have a 'great time' (Willis, 1977: 14).

The interesting point again, therefore, is what it does to them, and their own sense of identity, rather than what it does to the school. Willis (1978) makes the same point about the behaviour of bike-boys and hippies in the 1960s. Both groups seemed to be in triumphant rebellion against existing structures, but basically they reproduced 'the weaknesses, brutality and limitations of their own structural locations and parent class cultures' (1978: 6). Their rebellion remained at the level of style. Thus, the bike boys 'largely accepted the values of those who locked them up. They certainly tried to outrage but their offence was basically at a surface level: it was cheek, shock, surprise, disgust, insubordination, insult — never a basic political challenge to institutional belief' (*ibid.*: 49). Similarly, Marsh *et al.* (1978) argue that, in what may appear disorder, the young construct their own rules of order. On the football terraces, as well as in school, they develop elaborate rituals which promise them status and dignity in a social system which denies them more straightforward access (*see also* Hall and Jefferson, 1976).

Yet if it is a way of dealing with constraints, and therefore inevitably reflects these constraints, it also contains elements of freedom, where, in the relative autonomy of the school, the lads are able to develop and exercise their creative powers. Here, all those 'superior' and 'transcendental' functions of humour are apparent. If the form is traditional, they are continually having to re-invent it — they are not simply aping those who have gone before. Also, there is an unceasing search for new content. That search requires skill in making often elaborate plans for new situations and new jokes, and perception and knowledge in seeking out the weaknesses of the opposition, which they learn to do with unerring and embarrassing accuracy down to the finest detail. Their mental powers are further exercised in inventing excuses for many alternative scenarios (Willis, 1977: 32). Their communicative powers among themselves and with others are stretched to the utmost, for wit and repartee rank very high among the status criteria. They are irreverent. Nothing is sacred, nothing taken for granted. And in playing the system, they do experience their triumphs. Even so, this novelty and creativity has to be seen within the larger pattern of working-class culture, though it would be a mistake to see the one as determined by the other. As Parker (1974) argues, behavioural themes like toughness and smartness are an adaptive response to situations, but they come from deliberate decision and choice, not ones that are pre-ordained in some external structure (*see also* Matza and Sykes, 1957).

Conclusion

Some school humour no doubt may be experienced in a spirit of play, with no other referents. But much of it is 'coping' behaviour, a means of adjusting the self to difficulties and problems that otherwise might result in failure of task, alienation of self, or breakdown of social order. As facilitator, it eases teaching and learning, relieving physical and intellectual strain induced by task, parrying alienation threatened by institution. It can aid the formation of a cultural bond between teacher and pupils. It is equally used as a resource by both teachers and pupils in negotiation in instances where each seeks to establish their definition of the situation. In the freedom of the extra-curricular areas of the school-day, pupils counter boredom and oppression with laughter. In the sanctity of the staffroom, teachers likewise, through humour, rescue their professional dignity and personal self-esteem. The young adolescent, experiencing new and powerful sexual drives, and encountering strongly and clearly demarcated images of identities based in part on gender lines, manages the transition to a considerable extent through humour. Some pupils, already alienated from school by virtue of their background social class culture, and similarly structurally located in school as their parents are in work, also cope, largely through humour and laughter. For them, in fact, it transforms the situation into one that they consider is of advantage to them.

Humour thus fortifies the self and manages problems at various levels. At the level of the self, it is an aid to development, to the formation of the self, and to the preservation of dignity and esteem, though one of the paths to the latter may be the humiliation of another or others. At the level of the micro-situation, humour is prominent in teacher–pupil interaction, sometimes tackling problems they face together, sometimes those produced in opposition. Humour is also a powerful resource in instances where macro forces such as social and sexual stratification or material constraint bears on groups or on the individual. It does not, of course, entirely neutralize these forces in their effects. But it helps to establish a degree of manoeuvre for the group and for the individual.

For the group, acting as a collective unit, it offers an irresistible force both in defence and offence. It forms cultural bonds among its members, and fires rapier-like wit and broadside salvoes on those who threaten them. For the individual, it offers an element of self-volition, a way of relating personal aspirations and identities to the situations and structures one finds oneself in. In different ways, therefore, for many pupils, whether they benefit greatly from the system, or just 'get by', or are 'bored stiff' by the lessons, or for the most part are completely rebellious, schooldays do often appear to be 'the happiest days'.

References

ABBOTT, B.,GILBERT, S. and LAWSON, R. (1989) 'Towards anti-racist awareness: confessions of some teacher converts' in WOODS, P. (ed.), *Working for Teacher Development*, Cambridge, Peter Francis.

ABRAHAM, J. (1989a) 'Testing Hargreaves' and Lacey's differentiation-polarisation theory in a setted comprehensive', *The British Journal of Sociology*, Vol. 40, No. 1, pp. 46–81.

ABRAHAM, J. (1989b) 'Gender differences and anti-school boys', *The Sociological Review*, **37**, 1, pp. 65–88.

ACKER, S. (ed.) (1987) *Teachers, Gender and Careers*, Lewes, Falmer Press.

ACKER, S. (1989) 'Feminist theory and the study of gender and education', *International Review of Education*, **33**, 4, pp. 419–35.

AGGLETON, P. (1987) *Rebels Without a Cause*, Lewes, Falmer Press.

ALL LONDON TEACHERS AGAINST RACISM AND FASCISM (1984) *Challenging Racism*, London, ALTARF.

ALLPORT, G. W. (1954) *The Nature of Prejudice*, Reading, MA, Addison-Wesley.

AMOS, S., CROXEN, A., GOODWIN, M., REINDORP, N. and O'SULLIVAN, K. (1989) 'Leave our school alone', *Observer*, 17 December, p. 56.

ANTHONY, P. D. (1977) *The Ideology of Work*, Tavistock, London.

ANYON, J. (1983) 'Intersections of Gender and Class: accommodation and resistance by working-class and affluent females to contradictory sex-role ideologies', in WALKER, S. and BARTON, L. (eds) *Gender, Class and Education*, Lewes, Falmer Press.

ARENDT, H.(1958) *The Human Condition*, University of Chicago Press, Chicago.

ARNOT, M. (1983) 'A cloud over co-education: an analysis of the forms of transmission of class and gender relations' in WALKER, S. and BARTON, L. (eds) *Gender, Class and Education*, Lewes, Falmer Press.

ARNOT, M. (1989a) *Feminist Issues in Education: developing a theory of class and gender relations*, Ph.D. thesis, Milton Keynes, The Open University.

ARNOT, M. (1989b) 'The challenge of equal opportunities: personal and professional development for secondary teachers', in WOODS, P. (ed.) *Working for Teacher Development*, Cambridge, Peter Francis.

ASHTON, D. N. and FIELD, D. (1976) *Young Workers*, London, Hutchinson.

ASHTON, P. T. and WEBB, R. B. (1986) *Making a Difference: teachers' sense of efficacy and student achievement*. New York, Longman.

ASKEW, S. and ROSS, C. (1988) *Boys don't Cry*, Milton Keynes, Open University Press.

ASPINWALL, K. and DRUMMOND, M. J. (1989) 'Socialized into primary teaching' in LYON, H. D. and MIGNIUOLO, F. W. (eds), *Women Teachers: issues and experiences*, Milton Keynes, Open University Press.

BALL, S. J. (1980) 'Initial encounters in the classroom and the process of establishment' in WOODS, P. (ed.) *Pupil Strategies*, London, Croom Helm.

BALL, S. (1981) *Beachside Comprehensive*, Cambridge, Cambridge University Press.

BARNES, D. (1969) *Language, the Learner and the School*, in BARNES, D., BRITTEN, J. and ROSEN, H. Harmondsworth, Penguin.

BARRS, M. and PIDGEON, S. (1986) 'Gender and reading' in *Language Matters*, ILEA, Centre for language in Primary Education.

BECKER, H. (1963) *Outsiders: studies in the sociology of deviance*, New York, Free Press.

BECKER, H. (1964) 'Personal change in adult life', *Sociometry*, **27**, 1, pp. 40–53.

BECKER, H. S. and GEER, B. (1977) 'Latent culture: a note on the theory of social roles', in COSIN, B. R., DALE, I. R., ESLAND, G. M. and SWIFT, D. E. (eds), *School and Society*, London, Routledge and Kegan Paul.

BECKER, H. S., GEER, G., HUGHES, E. D. and STRAUSS, A. L. (1961) *Boys in White*, Chicago, University of Chicago Press.

BELL, D. (1976) *The Cultural Contradictions of Capitalism*, London, Heinemann.

BENEDICT, R. (1938) 'Continuities and discontinuities in cultural conditioning'. *Psychiatry*, **1**.

BENN, C. (1989) preface to LYON, H. D. and MIGNIUOLO, F. W. (eds) *Women Teachers: issues and experiences*, Milton Keynes, Open University Press.

BENNETT, N., DESFORGES, C., COCKBURN, A. and WILKINSON, B. (1984) *The Quality of Pupil Learning Experiences*, London, Lawrence Erlbaum.

BERGER, P. L. (1973) 'Some General Observations on the Problem of Work' in BERGER, P. L. (ed.) *The Human Shape of Work*, New York, MacMillan.

BERGER, P. L., BERGER, B., and KELLNER, H. (1973) *The Homeless Mind*, Harmondsworth, Penguin.

BERGER, P. L. and LUCKMANN, T. (1966) *The Social Construction of Reality: A treatise in the sociology of knowledge*, Harmondsworth, Penguin.

BERLAK, A. and BERLAK, H. (1981) *The Dilemmas of Schooling*, London, Methuen.

BERNSTEIN, B. (1970) 'A critique of the concept of "compulsory education"' in RUBENSTEIN, D. and STONEMAN, C. (eds) *Education for Democracy*, London, Penguin.

BERNSTEIN, B. (1971) 'On the classification and framing of educational knowledge' in YOUNG, M. F. D. (ed.), *Knowledge and Control*, London, Collier-MacMillan.

BEYNON, H. (1976) 'On the line' in WEIR, M. (ed.), *Job Satisfaction: Challenge and Response in Modern Britain*, London, Fontana.

BEYNON, J. (1984) '"Sussing out" teachers: pupils as data gatherers' in HAMMERSLEY, M. and WOODS, P. (eds) *Life in School: the sociology of pupil culture*, Milton Keynes, The Open University Press.

BEYNON, J. (1985) *Initial Encounters in the Secondary School*, Lewes, Falmer Press.

BIRD, C. (1980) 'Deviant labelling in school: the pupils' perspective' in WOODS, P. (ed.) *Pupil Strategies*, London, Croom Helm.

BIRD, C., CHESSUM, R., FURLONG, J., and JOHNSON, D. (1981) *Disaffected Pupils*, Educational Studies Unit, Brunel University.

BIRKSTED, I. (1976) 'School versus pop culture? a case study of adolescent adaptation', *Research in Education*, **16**, November, pp. 13–23.

BITTNER, E. (1967) 'The police on skid row: a study of peace-keeping', *American Sociological Review*, **32**, 5, pp. 699–715.

BLENKIN, G. (1988) 'Education and development: some implications for the curriculum in the early years' in BLYTH, A. (ed.) *Informal Primary Education Today*, Lewes, Falmer Press.

BLURTON, M. (1987) *Differentiation and Division in a Comprehensive School: An Analysis of Organization. Curriculum and Teacher and Pupil Interactions and Perceptions*, Ph.D.thesis, University of Aston.

BOURDIEU, P. and PASSERON, J.C. (1977) *Reproduction in Education, Society and Culture*, London, Sage.

BOWLES, S. and GINTIS, H. (1976) *Schooling in Capitalist America*, London, Routledge and Kegan Paul.

BRADNEY, P. (1957) 'The joking relationship in industry', *Human Relations*, **10**.

BRAH, A. and MINHAS, R. (1985) 'Structural racism or cultural difference: schooling for Asian girls' in WEINER, G. (ed.) *Just a Bunch of Girls*, Milton Keynes, Open University Press.

BRAROE, N. W. (1973) 'Reciprocal exploration in an Indian-White community' in FARBER-MAN, H. A. and GOODE, E. (eds) *Social Reality*, Englewood Cliffs, New Jersey, Prentice-Hall.

BRIDGER, A. (1987) 'Processes of Gender Differentiation in a Mixed-sex Comprehensive', unpublished M.Phil. thesis, Reading, Bulmershe College of Higher Education.

BRIGGS, J. (ed.) (1962) *William Morris: Selected Writings and Designs*, Harmondsworth, Penguin.

BROADFOOT, P. (ed.) (1986) *Profiles and Records of Achievement: a review of issues and practices*, Eastbourne, Holt Educational.

BROWN, P. (1987) *Schooling Ordinary Kids: inequality unemployment and the new vocationalism*, London, Tavistock.

BROWNE, N. and FRANCE, P. (eds) (1986) *Untying the Apron Strings*, Milton Keynes, Open University Press.

BURKE, J. (1986) *'Concord Sixth Form College: a sociological case study based on history and ethnography*, D.Phil. thesis, University of Sussex.

BURNS, T. (1953) 'Friends, enemies and the polite fiction', *American Sociological Review*, **18**, pp. 654–62

BURROUGHS, D. (1987) *Teenage Belief Systems: planning for the future*, Ph.D. thesis, The Open University, Milton Keynes.

BUSWELL, C. (1984) 'Sponsoring and stereotyping in a working-class English secondary school' in ACKER, S., MEGARRY, J., NISBETT, S. and HOYLE, E. (eds) *World Yearbook of Education: women in education*, London, Kogan Page.

BYRNE, E. M. (1978) *Women and Education*, London, Tavistock.

CAMPBELL, R.J. (1989) 'HMI and aspects of public policy for the primary school curriculum', in HARGREAVES, A. and REYNOLDS, D. (eds) *Education Policies: controversies and critiques*, Lewes, Falmer Press.

CARRINGTON, B. and SHORT, G. (1989) *'Race' and the Primary School*. Slough, NFER-Nelson.

CARTER, M. (1966) *Into Work*, Harmondsworth, Penguin.

CHAPMAN, A.J. (1976) 'Social aspects of humorous laughter' in CHAPMAN, A.J. and FOOT, H. C. (eds) *Humour and Laughter: theory, research and applications*, London, Wiley.

CHINOY, E. (1970) 'Manning the machines — the assembly line worker' in BERGER, P. (ed.) *The Human Shape of Work*, London, MacMillan.

CHISHOLM, L. and HOLLAND, J. (1986) 'Girls and occupational choice: anti-sexism in action in a curriculum development project', *British Journal of Sociology of Education.* **7** (4), pp. 353–65.

CHODOROW, N. (1979) 'Feminism and difference: gender relations and difference in psycho-analytic perspective', *Socialist Review*, **9**, 4, pp. 51–70.

CLARRICOATES, K. (1981) 'The experience of patriarchal schooling', *Interchange*, **12**, 2–3, pp. 185–205.

CLARRICOATES, K. (1987) 'Child culture at school: a clash between gendered worlds' in POLLARD, A. (ed.) *Children and Their Primary Schools*, Lewes, The Falmer Press.

COHEN, A. K. (1955) *Delinquent Boys*, New York, Free Press.

COHEN, P. (1987a) *Reducing Prejudice in the Classroom and Community*, PSEC/CME Cultural Studies Project, University of London Institute of Education (mimeo).

COHEN, P. (1987b) 'Racism and popular culture: a cultural studies approach', *CME Working Paper No.9*, University of London, Institute of Education.

COHEN, S. and TAYLOR, L. (1972) *Psychological Survival*, Harmondsworth, Penguin.

CONNELL, R. W. (1987) *Gender and Power: society, the person and sexual politics*, Oxford, Polity Press.

CONNELL, R. W., ASHENDEN, D. J., KESSLER, S. and DOWSETT, G. W. (1982) *Making the Difference: schools, families and social division*, Sydney, Allen and Unwin.

COOLEY, C. H. (1902) *Human Nature and the Social Order*, New York, Charles Scribner's Sons.

CORRIGAN, P. (1979) *Schooling the Smash Street Kids*, London, MacMillan.

COSER, R. L. (1958) 'Authority and decision making in a hospital: a comparative analysis', *American Sociological Review*, **23**, pp.56–63.

COX, B. (1988) *English for Ages 5–11*, Report to the National Curriculum Council ('The Cox Report'), London, HMSO.

CROWTHER REPORT (1959) *15–18*, Central Advisory Council for Education, London HMSO.

DALE, I. R. (1972) The Culture of the School, Unit 4 of E282, *School and Society*, Milton Keynes, Open University Press.

DALE, R. R. and GRIFFITHS, S. (1966) *Downstream*, London, Routledge and Kegan Paul.

DANCE, E. H. (1960) *History the Betrayer: a study in bias*, London, Hutchinson.

DAVEY, A. G. (1983) *Learning to be prejudiced: growing up in multi-ethnic Britain*, London, Edward Arnold.

DAVEY, A. G. and MULLIN, P. N. (1982) 'Inter-ethnic friendship in British primary schools', *Educational research*, **24**, pp. 83–92.

DAVIES, B. (1980) 'Pupils' attitudes to teacher organization and discipline', unpublished paper, University of New England, Armidale.

DAVIES, B. (1982) *Life in the Classroom and Playground: the accounts of primary school children*, London, Routledge and Kegan Paul.

DAVIES, B. (1983) 'The role pupils play in the social construction of classroom order', *British Journal of Sociology of Education*, **4**, 1, pp. 55–69.

DAVIES, B. (1987) 'The accomplishment of genderedness in pre-school children' in POLLARD, A. (ed.) *Children and Their Primary Schools*, Lewes, Falmer Press.

DAVIES, B. and MUNRO, K. (1987) 'The perception of order in apparent disorder: a classroom scene observed', *Journal of Education for Teaching*, **13**, 2, pp. 117–131.

DAVIES, L. (1984) *Pupil Power: deviance and gender in school*, Lewes, Falmer Press.

DAVIS, F. (1972) *Illness, Interaction and the Self*, Belmont, California, Wadsworth.

DEEM, R. (1980) *Schooling for Women's Work*, London, Routledge and Kegan Paul.

DEEM, R. (ed.) (1984) *Co-education Reconsidered*, Milton Keynes, Open University Press.

DELAMONT, S. (1976) *Interaction in the Classroom*, London, Methuen.

DELAMONT, S. (1980) *Sex Roles and the School*, London, Methuen.

DELAMONT, S. and GALTON, M. (1986) *Inside the Secondary Classroom*, London, Routledge and Kegan Paul.

DENSCOMBE, M. (1980) 'Pupil Strategies and the Open Classroom' in WOODS, P. (ed.) *Pupil Strategies: explorations in the sociology of the school*, London, Croom Helm.

DENSCOMBE, M. (1980) "'Keeping' em quiet": the significance of noise for the practical activity of teaching' in WOODS, P. (ed.) *Teacher Strategies*, London, Croom Helm.

DENSCOMBE, M. (1983) 'Ethnic group and friendship choice in the primary school', *Educational Research*, **25**, 3, pp. 184–90.

DENSCOMBE, M. (1985) *Classroom Control: a sociological perspective*, London, Allen and Unwin.

DENSCOMBE, M., SZULE, H., PATRICK, C. and WOOD, A. (1986) 'Ethnicity and friendship: the contrast between sociometric research and fieldwork observation in primary school classrooms', *British Educational Research Journal*, **12**, 3, pp. 221–235.

DEPARTMENT OF EDUCATION AND SCIENCE (DES) (1980) *Girls and Science*, London, HMSO.

DEPARTMENT OF EDUCATION AND SCIENCE (DES) (1985) *Statistics of Education*, London, HMSO.

DOCKING, J. W. (1987) *Control and Discipline in Schools: perspectives and approaches*, (2nd edn) London, Harper and Row.

DONALDSON, M. (1978) *Children's Minds*, London, Croom Helm.

DOUGLAS, M. (1966) *Purity and Danger*, London, Routledge and Kegan Paul.

DOWNEY, M. (1977) *Interpersonal Judgements in Education*, London, Harper and Row.

DOYLE, W. (1979) 'Student management of task structures in the classroom', paper presented at the conference on *Teacher and Pupil Strategies*, St Hilda's College, Oxford.

DRIVER, G. (1979) 'Classroom stress and school achievement: West Indian adolescents and their teachers' in KHAN, V. S. (ed.) *Minority Families in Britain*, London, MacMillan.

DUBBERLEY, W. (1988a) 'Social class and the process of schooling — a case study of a comprehensive school in a mining community' in GREEN, A. and BALL, S. (eds) *Progress and Inequality in Comprehensive Education*, London, Routledge.

DUBBERLEY, W. (1988b) 'Humour as resistance', *International Journal of Qualitative Studies in Education*. **1**, 2, pp. 109–123.

DUBBS, P. J. and WHITNEY, D. D. (1980) *Cultural Contexts: making anthropology personal*, Boston, Allyn and Bacon.

DUMONT, R. V. and WAX, M. L. (1971) 'Cherokee School Society and the intercultural classroom' in COSIN, B. R. *et al* (eds) *School and Society*, London, Routledge and Kegan Paul.

EDWARDS, A. D. and WESTGATE, D.P.G. (1987) *Investigating Classroom Talk*, Lewes, Falmer Press.

EDWARDS, D. and MERCER, N. (1987) *Common Knowledge: the development of understanding in the classroom*, London, Methuen.

EGGLESTON, J., DUNN, D., and ANJALI, M. (1986) *Education for Some*, Stoke, Trentham Books.

ELLIOTT, J. and POWELL, C. (1987) 'Young women and science: do we need more science?', *British Journal of Sociology of Education*, **8**, 3, pp. 277–286.

EMERSON, J. (1969) 'Negotiating the serious import of humour', *Sociometry*, **32**, pp. 169–181.

EPSTEIN, C. F. (1973) 'Positive effects of the multiple negative: explaining the success of black professional women', *American Journal of Sociology*, **78**, 4, pp. 912–35.

EQUAL OPPORTUNITIES COMMISSION (1982) 'Gender and the secondary school curriculum', *Research Bulletin*, No.6, HMSO.

EVANS, J. and DAVIES, B. (1987) 'Fixing the mix in vocational initiatives' in WALKER, S. and BARTON, L. (eds) *Changing Policies, Changing Teachers*, Milton Keynes, Open University Press.

EVETTS, J. (1989) 'The internal labour market for primary teachers' in ACKER, S. (ed.) *Teachers, Gender and Careers*, Lewes, Falmer Press.

FIGUEROA, P. M. E. (1985) 'Racist name-calling in a British school: aspects of pupil culture', Paper presented to the *SAANZ* Conference, Brisbane, August-September.

FINCH, J. (1988) 'Ethnography and public policy' in POLLARD, A., PURVIS, J. and WALFORD, G. (eds) *Education, Training and the New Vocationalism*, Milton Keynes, Open University Press.

FINE, G. A. (1977) 'Humour in situ: the role of humour in small group culture' in CHAPMAN, A. J. and FOOT, H. C. (eds) *Humour and Laughter: theory, research and applications*, London, Wiley.

FOSTER, H. L. (1974) *Ribbin', Jivin', and Playin' the Dozens*, Cambridge, Mass, Ballinger Publishing Co.

FOSTER, P. M. (1988) *'Policy and Practice in Multicultural and Anti-Racist Education: a case study of a multi-ethnic comprehensive school'*, Unpublished Ph.D. thesis, Milton Keynes, The Open University.

FOX, A. (1976) *The Meaning of Work*, Milton Keynes, Open University Press.

FRANCIS, M. (1984) 'Anti-racist teaching: curricular practices' in ALTARF (All London Teachers Against Racism and Facism) *Challenging Racism*, London, ALTARF.

FRASER, R. (ed.) (1968) *Work: twenty personal accounts*, Harmondsworth, Penguin.

FULLER, M. (1980) 'Black girls in a London comprehensive school' in DEEM, R. (ed.) *Schooling for Women's Work*, London, Routledge and Kegan Paul.

FULLER, M. (1983) 'Qualified criticism, critical qualifications' in BARTON, L. and WALKER, S. (eds) *Race, Class and Education*, London, Croom Helm.

FULLER, M. (1984) 'Inequality: gender, race and class', Unit 27, course E205, *Conflict and Change in Education*, Milton Keynes, Open University Press.

FURLONG, A. (1986) 'Schooling and the structure of female occupational aspirations', *British Journal of Sociology of Education*, **7**, 4, pp. 367–77.

FURLONG, V. J. (1976) 'Interaction sets in the classroom: towards a study of pupil knowledge', in HAMMERSLEY, M. and WOODS, P. *The Process of Schooling*, London, Routledge and Kegan Paul.

FURLONG, V. J. (1977) 'Anancy goes to school; a case study of pupils' knowledge of their teachers', in WOODS, P. and HAMMERSLEY, M. (eds) *School Experience*, London, Croom Helm.

FURLONG, V. J. (1984) 'Black resistance in the liberal comprehensive' in DELAMONT, S. (ed.) *Reading and Interaction in the Classrooms*, London, Methuen.

FURLONG, V. J. (1985) *The Deviant Pupil: sociological perspectives*, Milton Keynes, Open University Press.

GAINE, C. (1987) *No Problem Here: a practical approach to education and race in white schools*, London, Hutchinson.

GALLIERS, D. (1987) 'A framework for anti-racist training', *British Journal of Inservice Education*, **13**, 2, pp 67–75.

GALTON, M. (1987) 'An ORACLE chronicle: a decade of classroom research' in DELAMONT, S. (ed.) *The Primary School Teacher*, Lewes, Falmer Press.

GANNAWAY, H. (1976) 'Making sense of school' in STUBBS, M. and DELAMONT, S. (eds) *Explorations in Classroom Observation*, London, Wiley.

GEER, B. (1977) 'Teaching' in COSIN, B. R., DALES, I. R., ESLAND, G. M., and SWIFT, D. F. (eds) *School and Society*, London, Routledge and Kegan Paul.

GILLBORN, D. (1990) 'Sexism and curricular "choice"', unpublished paper, QQSE Research Group, University of Sheffield.

GLASER, B. G. and STRAUSS, A. L. (1971) *Status Passage*, Chicago, Aldine.

GOFFMAN, E. (1961) *Encounters*, New York, Bobbs-Merrill.

GOFFMAN, E.(1968) *Asylums*, Harmondsworth, Penguin.

GOFFMAN, E.(1971) *The Presentation of Self in Everyday Life*, Garden City, Doubleday.

GOLDMAN, R. and J. (1982) *Children's Sexual Thinking*, London, Routledge and Kegan Paul.

GOODSON, I. (1983) *School Subjects and Curriculum Change*, London Croom Helm.

GORDON, L. (1984) 'Paul Willis — education, cultural production and social reproduction', *British Journal of Sociology of Education*, **5**, 2, pp. 105–115.

GRACE, G. (1978) *Teachers, Ideology and Control*, London, Routledge and Kegan Paul.

GRAFTON, T., MILLER, H., SMITH, M., VEGODA, M. and WHITFIELD, R. (1983) 'Gender and curriculum choice' in HAMMERSLEY, M. and HARGREAVES, A. (eds), *Curriculum Practice: some sociological case studies*, Lewes, Falmer Press.

GRUGEON, E. and WOODS, P. (1990) *Educating All: multicultural perspectives in the primary school*, London, Routledge.

GRUNDSELL, R. (1978) *Absent from School*, London, Writers and Readers.

GRUNDSELL, R.(1980) *Beyond Control: Schools and suspension*, London, Writers and Readers.

HALL, S. and JEFFERSON, T. (1976) *Resistance through Rituals*, London, Hutchinson.

HALLINAN, M. T. and WILLIAMS, R. A. (1989) 'Interracial friendship choices in secondary schools', *American Sociological Review*, **54**, February, pp. 67–78.

HAMMERSLEY, M. (1977) 'School Learning: the cultural resources required by pupils to answer a teacher's question' in WOODS, P. and HAMMERSLEY, M. (eds), *School Experience*, London, Croom Helm.

HAMMERSLEY, M.(1984) 'Marxism', Unit 3, Course E205, *Conflict and Change in Education*, Milton Keynes, Open University Press.

HAMMERSLEY, M., SCARTH, J. and WEBB, S. (1985) 'Developing and testing theory: the case of research on pupil learning and examinations', in BURGESS, R. G. (ed.) *Issues in Educational Research*, Lewes, Falmer Press.

HAMMERSLEY, M. and TURNER, G. (1980) 'Conformist pupils?' in WOODS, P. (ed.) *Pupil Strategies*, London, Croom Helm.

HARBER, C. (1989) 'Political education and democratic practice' in HARBER, C. and MEIGHAN, R. (eds) (1989) *The Democratic School: educational management and the practice of democracy*, Ticknall, Education New Publishing Cooperative Ltd.

HARBER, C. and MEIGHAN, R. (eds) (1989) *The Democratic School: educational management and the practice of democracy*, Ticknall, Education New Publishing Cooperative Ltd.

HARDING, J. (1983) *Switched Off: the science education of girls*, London, Longman.

HARGREAVES, A. (1984) 'Marxism and relative autonomy', unit 22, Course E205, *Conflict and Change in Education*, Milton Keynes, Open University Press.

HARGREAVES, A. (1986) 'Research and policy: some observations on ESRC educational research projects', *Journal of Education Policy*, **1**, 2, pp. 115–31.

HARGREAVES, A. (1988) 'Teaching Quality: a sociological analysis', *Journal of Curriculum Studies*, **20**, 3, pp. 211–31.

HARGREAVES, A. and REYNOLDS, D. (eds) (1989) *Education Polices: controversies and critiques*, Lewes, Falmer Press.

HARGREAVES, D. H. (1967) *Social Relations in a Secondary School*, London, Routledge and Kegan Paul.

HARGREAVES, D. H. (1972) *Interpersonal Relations and Education*, London, Routledge and Kegan Paul.

HARGREAVES, D. H. (1981) 'Schooling for delinquency' in BARTON, L. and WALKER, S. (eds) *Schools, Teachers and Teaching*, Lewes, Falmer Press.

HARGREAVES, D.H., HESTER, S.K, and MELLOR, F.J. (1975) *Deviance in Classrooms*, London, Routledge and Kegan Paul.

HARTLEY, R. (1959) 'Sex role pressures and the socialization of the male child', *Psychological Reports*, **5**, pp. 457–68.

HAVILAND, J. (ed.) (1988) *Take Care, Mr Baker!*, London, Fourth Estate.

HEARN, J. (1987) *The Gender of Oppression: men's masculinity and the critique of marxism*, Sussex, Wheatsheaf.

HEATH, S. (1982) 'Questioning at home and at school: a comparative study' in SPINDLER, C. (ed.) *Doing the Ethnography of Schooling*, New York, Holt, Rinehart and Winston.

HEATH, S. (1983) *Ways with Words: language, life and work in communities and classrooms*, Cambridge, Cambridge University Press.

HEBDIGE, D. (1979) *Subculture: the meaning of style*, London, Methuen.

HENRY, J. (1963) *Culture against man*, New York, Random House.

HEXTALL, I. and SARUP, M. (1977) 'School Knowledge evaluation and alienation' in YOUNG, M. F. D. and WHITTY, G. (eds) *Society State and Schooling*, Lewes, Falmer Press.

HOBBES, T. (1651) *Human Nature*, London, Anchor.

HOLLY, L. and HUME, D. (1988) 'Considering all the options', paper given at seminar on *Subject Choice*, Milton Keynes, The Open University, June.

HOLT, J. (1969) *How Children Fail*, Harmondsworth, Penguin.

HOLT, M. (1975) 'What are the real options?' *The Times Educational Supplement*, 3rd October, pp. 24–5.

HORNE, D. (1964) *The Lucky Country*, Victoria, Australia, Penguin.

HUGHES, E. C. (1956) *Men and Their Work*, Glencoe, Illinois, Free Press.

HURMAN, A. (1978) *A Charter for Choice*, Slough, NFER.

HUSTLER, D., CASSIDY, A. and CUFF, E. C. (eds) (1986) *Action Research in Classroom and Schools*, London, Allen and Unwin.

JACKSON, P. W. (1968) *Life in Classrooms*, New York, Holt, Rinehart and Winston.

JAMES, A. (1979) 'The game of the name: nicknames in the child's world', *New Society*, 14 June, pp. 632–4.

JAMES, W. (1890) *The Principles of Psychology Vol.2*, New York, Henry Holt.

JELINEK, M. and BRITTAN, E. (1975) 'Multiracial education: (1) inter-ethnic friendship patterns', *Educational Research*, **18**, pp. 44–53.

JONES, A. (1989) 'The cultural production of classroom practice', *British Journal of Sociology of Education*, **10**, 1, pp. 19–31.

JOSEPH, K. (1986) 'Without prejudice — education for an ethnically-mixed society', *Multicultural Teaching*, **4**, 3, pp. 6–8.

KELLY, A. (1976) 'Women in physics and physics education', in LEWIS, J. (ed.) *New Trends in Physics Teaching*, Vol. III, UNESCO.

KELLY, A. (ed.) (1981) *'The Missing Half: girls and science education*, Manchester, Manchester University Press.

KELLY, A. (1985) 'The construction of masculine science', *British Journal of Sociology of Education*, **6**, 2, pp .133–54.

KELLY, A. (1988a) 'Gender differences in teacher-pupil interactions: a meta-analytic review', *Research in Education*, **39**, May, pp. 1–23.

KELLY, A. (1988b) 'Ethnic differences in science choice', *British Educational Research Journal*, **14**, 2, pp. 113–126.

KELLY, A., WHYTE, J. and SMAIL, B. (1984) *Girls into Science and Technology*, final report to the EOC and the SSRC, London.

KING, R. A. (1971) 'Unequal access in education — sex and social class', *Social and Economic Administration*, **5**, 3, pp. 167–74.

KING, R. A.(1978) *All Things Bright and Beautiful*, Chichester, Wiley

KITWOOD, T. and BORRILL, C. (1980) 'The significance of schooling for an ethnic minority', *Oxford Review of Education*, **6**, 3, pp. 241–52.

KOESTLER, A. (1964) *The Act of Creation*, New York, Macmillan.

KOUNIN, J. S. (1970) *Discipline and Group Management in Classrooms*, New York, Holt, Rinehart and Winston.

LABOV, W. (1972) 'Rules for ritual insults' in SUDNOW, D. (ed.) *Studies in Social Interaction*. New York, Free Press.

LACEY, C. (1970) *Hightown Grammar*, Manchester, Manchester University Press.

LACEY, C. (1977) *The Socialization of Teachers*, London, Methuen.

LACEY, C. (1986) Review of 'Sociology and School Knowledge' by Geoff Whitty, *British Journal of Sociology of Education*, **7**, 1, pp. 87–93.

LEE, V. and J. (1987) 'Stories children tell' in POLLARD, A. (ed.) *Children and Their Primary Schools*, Lewes, The Falmer Press.

LISTER, I. (1974) *Deschooling*, Cambridge, Cambridge University Press.

LLEWELLYN, M. (1980) Studying girls at school: the implications of confusion', in DEEM, R. (ed.) *Schooling for Women's Work*, London, Routledge and Kegan Paul.

LOBBAN, G. (1987) 'Sex roles in reading schemes' in WEINER, G. and ARNOT, M. (eds) *Gender Under Scrutiny: new inquiries in education*, London, Hutchinson.

LOMAX, P. (ed.) (1989) *The Management of Change*, BERA Dialogues No.1, Clevedon, Multilingual Matters Ltd.

LORTIE D. C. (1975) *Schoolteacher*, Chicago, University of Chicago Press.

LUCKMANN, T. (1967) *The Invisible Religion*, New York, MacMillan.

LYNCH, J. (1987) 'Changing attitudes: prejudice and the schools' in CHIVERS, T. S. (ed.) *Race and Culture in Education: issues arising from the Swann Committee Report*, Windsor, NFER-Nelson.

LYNCH, J. (1989) *Multicultural Education in a Global Society*, Lewes, Falmer Press.

LYON, H. D. and MIGNIUOLO, F. W. (1989) *Women Teachers: issues and experiences*, Milton Keynes, Open University Press.

MAC AN GHAILL, M. (1987) 'Black supplementary schooling: overcoming racist inequality', Paper presented at Conference on *Ethnography and Inequality*, St. Hilda's College, Oxford, 14–16 September.

MAC AN GHAILL, M. (1988) *Young, Gifted and Black*, Milton Keynes, Open University Press.

MAC AN GHAILL, M. (1989) 'Beyond the white norm: the use of qualitative methods in the study of black youths' schooling in England', *Qualitative Studies in Education*, 2, 3, pp. 175–189.

MACDONALD, M. (1980) 'Socio-cultural reproduction and women's education' in DEEM, R. (ed.) *Schooling for Women's Work*, London, Routledge and Kegan Paul.

MCGHEE, P. E. (1979) *Humour: its origin and development*, San Francisco, Freeman.

MCKELLAR, B. (1989) 'Only the fittest of the fittest will survive: black women and education' in ACKER, S. (ed.) *Teachers, Gender and Careers*, Lewes, Falmer Press.

MACKENZIE, J. M. (1984) *Propaganda and Empire — The Manipulation of British Public Opinion*, Manchester, Manchester University Press.

MCKEOWN, T. D. (1985) *I Spy: The Perspectives of Children on Aspects of Their Everyday World and the World of Religion*, M.Ed. thesis, University of New England, Australia.

MCLAREN, P. (1986) *Schooling as a Ritual Performance*, London, Routledge and Kegan Paul.

MCROBBIE, A. (1978) 'Working class girls and the culture of femininity' in WOMENS' STUDIES GROUP, *Women Take Issue*, CCCS, Birmingham, London, Hutchinson.

MCROBBIE, A. (1980) 'Settling accounts with subcultures: a feminist critique', *Screen Education*, 34, Spring, pp. 37–50.

MCROBBIE, A. and GARBER, J. (1976) 'Girls and subcultures', in HALL, J. and JEFFERSON, T. (eds) *Resistance through Rituals*, London, Hutchinson.

MAHONEY, P. (1985) *Schools for the Boys*, London, Hutchinson.

MAHONEY, P. (1988) 'How Alice's chin really came to be pressed against her foot: sexist processes of interaction in mixed-sex classrooms', in DALE, R., FERGUSSON, R. and ROBINSON, A. (eds) *Frameworks for Teaching*, London, Hodder and Stoughton.

MARSH, P., ROSSER, E. and HARRE, R. (1978) *The Rules of Disorder*, London, Routledge and Kegan Paul.

MARTINEAU, W. H. (1972) 'A model of the social functions of humour' in GOLDSTEIN, J. H. and MCGHEE, P. E. (eds) *The Psychology of Humour*, New York, Academic Press.

MATZA, D. (1964) *Delinquency and Drift*, New York, John Wiley and Sons.

MATZA, D. (1969) *Becoming Deviant*, Englewood Cliffs, Prentice-Hall.

MATZA, D. and SYKES, G. M. (1957) 'Delinquency and subterranean values', *American Sociological Review*, 25, 5, pp. 712–9.

MAYO, E. (1933) *The Human Problems of an Industrial Civilization*, New York, MacMillan.

MEAD, G. H. (1934) *Mind, Self and Society*, Chicago, University of Chicago Press.

MEALYEA, R. (1989) 'Humour as a coping strategy', *British Journal of Sociology of Education*. 10, 3, pp. 311–33.

MEASOR, L. (1983a) 'Pupil perceptions of subject status' in GOODSON, I. F. and BALL, S. J. (eds) *Defining the Curriculum*, Lewes, Falmer Press.

MEASOR, L. (1983b) 'Gender and the sciences: pupils' gender-based conceptions of school subjects' in HAMMERSLEY, M. and HARGREAVES, A. (eds) *Curriculum Practice: Some Sociological Case Studies*, Lewes, Falmer Press.

MEASOR, L. (1989) 'Sex education and adolescent sexuality' in HOLLY, L. (ed.) *Girls and Sexuality: learning and teaching*, Milton Keynes, Open University Press.

MEASOR, L. and WOODS, P. (1984) *Changing Schools: pupil perspectives on transfer to a comprehensive*, Milton Keynes, Open University Press.

MEYENN, R. (1980) 'School girls' peer groups', in WOODS, P. (ed.) *Pupil Strategies*, London, Croom Helm.

MIDDLETON, S. (1987) 'Streaming and the politics of female sexuality: case studies in the schooling of girls' in WEINER, G. and ARNOT, M. (eds) *Gender under Scrutiny: new inquiries in education*, London, Hutchinson.

MIDDLETON, S. (1989) 'Educating feminists: a life-history study' in ACKER, S. (ed.) *Teachers, Gender and Careers*, Lewes, Falmer Press.

MILLER, D. C. and FORM, W. H. (1951) *Industrial Sociology*, New York, Harper.

MILLER, W. B. (1958) 'Lower class culture as a generating milieu of gang delinquency', *Journal of Social Issues*, **14**, 5–19.

MINTZ, L. E. (1977) 'Ethnic humour' in CHAPMAN A. J. and FOOT, H. D. (eds) *Humour and Laughter: theory research and applications*, London, Wiley.

MOON, R. and MORTIMORE, P. (1989) *The National Curriculum: straightjacket or safetynet?*, Ginger Paper Five, London, Education Reform Group.

MOORE, A. (1987) 'An English love story: some problems of converting multicultural policy into practice', Paper presented to Conference on *Ethnography and Inequality*, St Hilda's College, Oxford, September.

MORGAN, J., O'NEIL, C. and HARRE, R, (1979) *Nicknames: their origins and social consequences*, London, Routledge and Kegan Paul.

MORRISON, A. and MCINTYRE, D. (1969) *Teachers and Teaching*, Harmondsworth, Penguin.

MORTIMORE, P., SAMMONS, P., LEWIS, L. and ECOB, R. (1988) *School Matters: the junior years*, London, Open Books.

MULLARD, C. (1982) 'Multi-racial education in Britain: from assimilation to pluralism' in TIERNEY, J. (ed.) *Race, Migration and Schooling*, London, Holt.

MULLARD, C. (1984) *Anti-Racist Education: the three O's*, London, National Association for Multiracial Education.

MUSGROVE, F. (1977) *Margins of the Mind*, London, Methuen.

NASH, R. (1976) 'Pupils' expectations of their teachers', in STUBBS, M. and DELAMONT, S. (eds) *Explorations in Classroom Observation*, London, Wiley.

NATIONAL CURRICULUM COUNCIL (1989) *Mathematics: non-statutory guidance*, York.

NEWSON, J. and E., RICHARDSON, D. and SCAIFE, J. (1978) 'Perspectives in sex-role stereotyping' in CHETWYND, J. and HARTNETT, O. (eds) *The Sex-Role System*, London, Routledge and Kegan Paul.

NIAS, J. (1989) *Primary Teachers Talking: a study of teaching as work*, London, Routledge.

NORTHAM, J. (1983) 'Girls and boys in primary maths books', *Education 3–13*, **10**, 1, 11–14.

NUTTALL, D. (1988) 'The assessment of learning', Unit 13 in Course E208 *Exploring Educational Issues*, Milton Keynes, Open University Press.

OAKLEY, A. (1974) *The Sociology of Housework*, London, Martin Robertson.

ORMEROD, M. (1975) 'Subject preference and choice in co-educational and single-sex secondary schools', *British Journal of Educational Psychology*, **45**, pp. 257–67.

PARKER H. J. (1974) *View from the Boys*, Newton Abbot, David and Charles.

PAYNE, M. A. (1987) Determinants of teacher popularity and unpopularity: a West Indian perspective', *Journal of Education for Teaching*, **13**, 3, pp. 193–205.

PERRY, I. (1988) 'A black student's reflection on public and private schools', *Harvard Educational Review*, **58**, 3, pp. 332–336.

PHILLIPS, G. (1983) 'Taking political autonomy seriously: a reply to Ian Gregory', *Westminster Studies in Education*, **6**, pp. 13–20.

PHILLIPSON, M. (1971) *Sociological Aspects of Crime and Delinquency*, London, Routledge and Kegan Paul.

PHOENIX, A. (1987) 'Theories of gender and black families', in WEINER, G. and ARNOT, M. (eds) *Gender under Scrutiny: new inquiries in education*, London, Hutchinson.

PLOWDEN REPORT (1967) *Children and their Primary Schools*, Report of the Central Advisory Council for Education in England, London, HMSO.

POLLARD, A. (1979) 'Negotiating deviance and "getting done" in primary school classrooms', in BARTON, L. and MEIGHAN, R. (eds) *Schools, Pupils and Deviance*, Driffield, Nafferton Books.

POLLARD, A. (1980) 'Teacher interests and changing situations of survival threat in primary school classrooms' in WOODS, P. (ed.) *Teacher Strategies*, London, Croom Helm.

POLLARD, A. (1982) 'A model of coping strategies', *British Journal of Sociology of Education*, **3**, 1, pp. 19–37.

POLLARD, A. (1985) *The Social World of the Primary School*, London, Holt, Rinehart and Winston.

POLLARD, A. (1988) 'Reflective Teaching — The Sociological Contribution' in WOODS, P. and POLLARD, A. (eds) *Sociology and Teaching*, London, Croom Helm.

POLLARD, A. and TANN, F. (1987) *Reflective Teaching in the Primary School*, London, Cassell.

PRATT, J., BLOOMFIELD, J. and SEALE, C. (1984) *Option Choice: a question of equal opportunity*, Windsor, NFER-Nelson.

QUINE, W. G. (1974) 'Polarized cultures in comprehensive schools', *Research in Education*, **12**, pp. 9–25.

RANDALL, V. (1987) *Women and Politics*, Basingstoke, Macmillan.

RAPOPORT, R. and R. N. (eds) (1978) *Working Couples*, London, Routledge and Kegan Paul.

RATTANSI, A. (1989) 'Race', Education and Inequality', unit 24, course E208, *Exploring Educational Issues*, Milton Keynes, Open University Press.

REDL, F. (1966) *When We Deal with Children*, New York, Free Press.

REYNOLDS, D. (1976) 'The delinquent school' in HAMMERSLEY, M. and WOODS. P. (eds) *The Process of Schooling*, London, Routledge and Kegan Paul.

REYNOLDS, D. (1976) 'When teachers and pupils refuse a truce' in MUNGHAM, G. and PEARSON, G. (eds) *Working Class Youth Culture*, London, Routledge and Kegan Paul.

RICHARDSON, R. (1986) 'The hidden messages of schoolbooks', *Journal of Moral Education*, **151**, 1, pp. 26–41.

RILEY, K. (1988) 'Black girls speak for themselves', in WEINER, G. (ed.) *Just a Bunch of Girls*, Milton Keynes, Open University Press.

RISEBOROUGH, G. F. (1985) 'Pupils, teachers' careers and schooling: an empirical study' in BALL, S. J. and GOODSON, I. F. (eds) *Teachers' Lives and Careers*, Lewes, Falmer Press.

ROCK, P. (1979) *The Making of Symbolic Interaction*, London, MacMillan.

ROSENBAUM, J. E. (1976) *Making Inequality: The Hidden Curriculum of High School Tracking*, New York, Wiley.

ROSIE, A. (1988) 'An ethnographic study of a YTS course' in POLLARD, A., PURVIS J. and WALFORD, G. (eds) *Education, Training and the New Vocationalism*, Milton Keynes, Open University Press.

ROSS, A. (1984) 'Developing political concepts and skills in the primary school', *Educational Review*, **36**, 2, pp. 133–9.

ROSSER, E. and HARRÉ, R. (1976) 'The meaning of disorder' in HAMMERSLEY, M. and WOODS, P. (eds) *The Process of Schooling*, London, Routledge and Kegan Paul.

RYRIE, A., FURST, A. and LAUDER, M. (1979) *Choices and Chances*, Scottish Council for Research in Education.

SCHUTZ, A. (1967) *Collected Papers*, The Hague, Nijhoff.

SHAH, S. (1988) 'What Kind of History?', *Multicultural Teaching*, **6**, 3, pp. 28–31.

SHARP, R. and GREEN, A. (1975) *Education and Social Control*, London, Routledge and Kegan Paul.

SHARPE, S. (1976) *Just Like a Girl*, Harmondsworth, Penguin.

SHAW, J. (1976) 'Finishing school — some implications of sex-segregated education' in BARKER, D. L. and ALLEN, S. (eds) *Sexual Divisions in Society: process and change*, London, Tavistock.

SHAW, J. (1977) 'Sexual divisions in the classroom', Paper presented at Conference *Teaching Girls to be Women*, Essex (April).

SHAW, J. (1984) 'The politics of single-sex schools' in DEEM, R. (ed.) *Coeducation Reconsidered*, Milton Keynes, Open University Press.

SHORT, G. and CARRINGTON, B. (1987) 'Towards an anti-racist initiative in the all-white primary school: a case study' in POLLARD, A. (ed.) *Children and Their Primary Schools*. Lewes, Falmer Press.

SIKES, P., MEASOR, L. and WOODS, P. (1985) *Teacher Careers: crisis and continuities*, Lewes, Falmer Press.

SKELTON, C. and HANSON, J. (1989) 'Schooling the teachers: gender and initial teacher education' in ACKER, S. (ed.) *Teachers, Gender and Careers*, Lewes, Falmer Press.

SMITH, D.J. and TOMLINSON, S. (1989) *The School Effect: a study of multi-racial comprehensives*, London, Policy Studies Institute.

SMITH, L.H. and GEOFFREY, W. (1968) *The Complexities of an Urban Classroom*, New York, Holt, Rinehart and Winston.

SPENDER, D. (1982) *Invisible Women: the schooling scandal*, London, Writers and Readers Cooperative.

SPENDER, D. and SARAH, E. (eds) (1980) *Learning to Lose: sexism and education*, London, The Women's Press.

STANLEY, J. R. (1986) 'Sex and the quiet schoolgirl', *British Journal of Sociology of Education*, **7**, 3, pp. 275–286.

STANLEY, J. R. (1989) *Marks on the Memory: the pupils' experience of school*, Milton Keynes, Open University Press.

STANWORTH, M. (1983) *Gender and Schooling: a study of sexual divisions in the classroom*, London, Hutchinson.

STATHAM, J., MACKINNON, D. with CATHCART, H. (1988) *The Education Fact File*, London, Hodder and Stoughton.

STEBBINS, R. (1980) 'The role of humour in teaching' in WOODS, P. (ed.) *Teacher Strategies*, London, Croom Helm.

STEVENS, O. (1982) *Children Talking Politics: political learning in childhood*, Oxford, Martin Robertson.

STRAUSS, A. L. (1969) *Mirrors and Masks*, San Francisco, The Sociology Press.

STRAUSS, A. *et al.* (1964) *Psychiatric Ideologies and Institutions*, London, Collier-MacMillan.

SWANN REPORT (1985) *Education for All*. The Report of the Committee of Enquiry into the Education of Children from Ethnic Minority Groups, Cmnd 9543, London, HMSO.

SYKES, G. M. and MATZA, D. (1957) 'Techniques of neutralization: a theory of delinquency', *American Sociological Review*, **22**, 6, pp. 664–70.

SYKES, G. M. and MATZA, D. (1961) 'Delinquency and subterranean values', *American Sociological Review*, **26**, 5, pp.712–19.

TATTUM, D. (1982) *Disruptive Pupils in Schools and Units*, London, Wiley.

TAYLOR, B. (1989) 'Ethnocentrism in history teaching in English schools', *Multicultural Teaching*, **7**, 2, pp. 31–4.

TAYLOR, L. and COHEN, S. (1976) *Escape Attempts: the theory and practice of resistance to everyday life*, London, Allen Lane.

TAYLOR, S. (1982) 'Reproduction and contradictions in schooling: the case of commercial studies', *SAANZ* Conference Paper, Sydney, August 1982, p. 11.

THOMAS, W. I. (1928) *The Child in America*, New York, Knopf.

TOMLINSON, S. (1983) *Ethnic Minorities in British Schools*, London, Heinemann.

TOMLINSON, S. (1987) 'Curriculum option choices in multi-ethnic schools', in TROYNA, B. (ed.) *Racial Inequality in Education*, London, Tavistock.

TOMLINSON, S. (1989) 'The origins of the ethnocentric curriculum', in VERMA, G. K. (ed.) *Education for All: a landmark in pluralism*, Lewes, Falmer Press.

TOMLINSON, S. and COULSON, P. (1988) *Education for a Multi-Ethnic Society: a descriptive analysis of a sample of projects funded by Education Support Grants in mainly white areas*, Lancaster, University of Lancaster.

TROMAN, G. (1988) 'Getting it right: selection and setting in a 9–13 years middle school', *British Journal of Sociology*, **9**, 4, pp. 403–422.

TROYNA, B. S. (1978) 'Race and streaming: a case study', *Educational Review*, **30**, 1, pp.59–65.

TROYNA, B. and BALL, W. (1985) 'Styles of LEA policy intervention in multicultural/anti-racist education', *Educational Review*, **37**, 2, pp. 165–176.

TROYNA, B. and WILLIAMS, J. (1986) *Racism, Education and the State: the racialization of education policy*, Beckenham, Croom Helm.

TUCKWELL, P. (1986) 'Pleasing teacher', in BOOTH, T. and STATHAM, J. (eds) *The Nature of Special Education*, London, Croom Helm.

TURNER, G. (1983) *The Social World of the Comprehensive School*, London, Croom Helm.

TURNER, R. H. (1970) *Family Interaction*, New York, Wiley.

TURNER, R. H. (1976) 'The real self: from institution to impulse', *American Journal of Sociology*, **81**, 5, pp. 989–1016.

TURNER, S. and T. (1989) 'An international dimension to the teaching of science — opportunities in the National Curriculum', *Multicultural Teaching*, **8**, 1, pp. 34–9.

TURNER, V. W. (1969) *The Ritual Process*, London, Routledge and Kegan Paul.

VAN GENNEP, A. (1960) *The Rites of Passage*, London, Routledge and Kegan Paul.

VERMA, G. K. and BAGLEY, C. (1979) 'Measured changes in racial attitudes following the use of three different teaching methods', in VERMA, G. K. and BAGLEY, C. (eds) *Race, Education and Identity*, London, Macmillan.

WAKEFORD, J. (1969) *The Cloistered Elite: a sociological analysis of the English public boarding school*, London, Macmillan.

WALKER, R. and ADELMAN, C. (1976) 'Strawberries' in STUBBS, M. and DELAMONT, S. (eds). *Explorations in Classroom Observation*, Chichester, Wiley.

WALKER, R. and GOODSON, I. (1977) 'Humour in the classroom', in WOODS, P. and HAMMERSLEY, M. (eds) *School Experience: explorations in the sociology of education*, London, Croom Helm.

WALKERDINE, V. (1981) 'Sex, power and pedagogy', *Screen Education*, Spring, **38**, pp. 14–23.

WALKERDINE, V. (1989) *Counting Girls Out*, London, Virago.

WALLER, W. (1932) *The Sociology of Teaching*, New York, Wiley.

WAX. R. (1971) *Doing Fieldwork*, Chicago, University of Chicago Press.

WERTHMAN, C. (1963) 'Delinquents in school: a test for the legitimacy of authority', *Berkeley Journal of Sociology*, **8**, 1, pp. 39–60. Also in HAMMERSLEY, M. and WOODS, P. (1984) *Life in School: the sociology of pupil culture*, Milton Keynes, Open University Press.

WHITTY, G.J. (1974) 'Sociology and the problem of radical educational change: towards a reconceptualization of the new ''Sociology of Education'' ' in FLUDE, M. and AHIER, J. (eds) *Educability, Schools and Ideology*, London, Croom Helm.

WHITTY, G.J. (1985) *Sociology and School Knowledge: curriculum theory, research and politics*, London, Methuen.

WHYTE, J. (1988) 'Girl friendly science and the girl friendly school' in DALE, R., FERGUSSON, R. and ROBINSON, A. (eds) *Frameworks for Teaching*, London, Hodder and Stoughton.

WHYTE, W.F. (1961) *Men at Work*, Illinois, Homewood.

WILLIS, P. (1977) *Learning to Labour*, Farnborough, Saxon House.

WILLIS, P. (1978) *Profane Culture*, London, Routledge and Kegan Paul.

WILLIS, P. (1981) 'Cultural production is different from cultural reproduction is different from social reproduction is different from reproduction', *Interchange*, **12**, 2–3, pp. 48–67.

WOLFENSTEIN, M. (1954) *Children's Humour: a psychological analysis*, Glencoe, Illinois, Free Press.

WOLPE, A-M., (1977) 'Some processes in sexist education', London, WRRC Publications.

WOODS, P. (1977) 'The pupils' experience', Unit 11 of Course E202, *Schooling and Society*, Milton Keynes, Open University Press.

WOODS, P. (1979) *The Divided School*, London, Routledge and Kegan Paul.

WOODS, P. (1984) 'A sociology of disruptive incidents' in FRUDE, N. and GAULT, H. (eds) *Disruptive Behaviour in Schools*, London, Wiley.

WOODS, P. (1990a) *Teacher Skills and Strategies*, Lewes, Falmer Press.

WOODS, P. (1990b) 'Cold eyes, and warm hearts: changing perspectives on teachers' work and careers', *British Journal of Sociology of Education*, **11**, 1, pp. 101–17.

WRIGHT, C. (1986) 'School processes — an ethnographic study', in EGGLESTON, J., DUNN, D. and ANJALI, M. (eds) *Education for Some: the educational and vocational experiences of 15–18 year old members of minority ethnic groups*, Stoke on Trent, Trentham Books.

YINGER, M. (1981) 'Toward a theory of assimilation and dissimilation', *Ethnic and Racial Studies*, **4**, 3, pp. 249–264.

YOUNG, M.F.D. (ed.) (1971) *Knowledge and Control*, London, Collier-MacMillan.

YOUNG, M.F.D. (1975) 'Curriculum change: limits and possibilities', *Educational Studies*, **1**, 2, pp. 129–38.

ZILLMAN, D. and CANTOR, J.R. (1976) 'A disposition theory of humour and mirth', in CHAPMAN, A.J. and FOOT, H.C. (eds) *Humour and Laughter: theory, research and applications*, London, Wiley.

Author Index

Subject Index